Marjorie Main

ALSO BY MICHELLE VOGEL
AND FROM MCFARLAND

Olive Borden: The Life and Films of Hollywood's "Joy Girl" (2010)

Olive Thomas: The Life and Death of a Silent Film Beauty (2007)

Children of Hollywood: Accounts of Growing Up as the Sons and Daughters of Stars (2005)

Gene Tierney: A Biography (2005; paperback 2011)

Marjorie Main

The Life and Films of Hollywood's "Ma Kettle"

MICHELLE VOGEL

McFarland & Company, Inc., Publishers
Jefferson, North Carolina, and London

Acknowledgments

Matt, my adorable and supportive husband
Josh and Reeve, my adorable and supportive stepsons
Mum and Dad, for everything
Jean, for everything   Mary Jo and Lou Mari   Allan Ellenberger
Universal Studios Archives & Collections
Fairbanks Center for Motion Picture Study
Kristine Krueger   Ralph Armstrong, and his late beloved Mom, Ruth
Indiana Historical Society   Indiana State Library   Turner Classic Movies
University of Southern California for access to their
University International Studio Archive Collection
Ned Comstock — thank you for being my eyes on
the West Coast; your research skills are impeccable

The present work is a reprint of the illustrated case bound edition of Marjorie Main: The Life and Films of Hollywood's "Ma Kettle," *first published in 2006 by McFarland.*

LIBRARY OF CONGRESS CATALOGUING-IN-PUBLICATION DATA

Vogel, Michelle, 1972–
Marjorie Main : the life and films of Hollywood's "Ma Kettle" / Michelle Vogel.
p. cm.
Includes bibliographical references and index.

ISBN 978-0-7864-6443-2
softcover : 50# alkaline paper 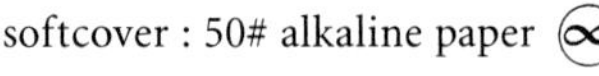

1. Main, Marjorie, 1890–1975. 2. Actors— United States— Biography. I. Title.
PN2287.M246V64 2011   792.02'8092 — dc22   2005029557

BRITISH LIBRARY CATALOGUING DATA ARE AVAILABLE

Cover photograph: Marjorie Main publicity shot

Manufactured in the United States of America

McFarland & Company, Inc., Publishers
Box 611, Jefferson, North Carolina 28640
www.mcfarlandpub.com

Contents

Preface

Marjorie Main was an American institution. As Ma Kettle, she gave life to the best loved mother of American film comedies, and maybe even American film, period. After appearing as Ma Kettle alongside her lazy husband, known simply as "Pa" (what else?) in the film adaptation of Betty MacDonald's best selling-book *The Egg and I*, audiences inundated Universal International Studios with letters demanding to see more of these lovable hillbilly folk on the big screen.

A whopping $3.5 million in box office sales for *The Egg and I* (1947), and an Academy Award nomination for Best Supporting Actress for Marjorie Main (she lost to Celeste Holm for *Gentleman's Agreement*), made Ma and Pa Kettle overnight sensations. The studio knew it had struck gold with the lovable odd couple, so with dollar signs in executives' eyes they decided to make one new Kettle film each year. That one decision proved to be the best investment in the studio's turbulent history.

The eventual nine films in the series were all low budget, and garnered big results—so big, in fact, that the Kettles went down in history as having saved Universal International Studios from bankruptcy. The films cost between $200,000 and $400,000 each, but with a consistent box office take of close to $4 million per film, the studios (Marjorie was on loan-out, and MGM were charging Universal for her services) were laughing all the way to the bank. Ma and Pa Kettle were the most successful box office attractions churned out by Universal International ... ever.

With more than 80 films to her credit, Marjorie Main was one of the most popular and one of the most overworked character actresses of her day. In most of her films she played the slum mother, the witty housekeeper, the meddling landlady, the widow, even the nosy neighbor, and all to perfection. Yet, when Marjorie Main is mentioned today, most people will remember her lovingly as Ma Kettle.

Was she typecast? Maybe. But she didn't mind. Long after she'd hung up Ma's well-worn house dress, Marjorie would often regale listeners with stories of her Hollywood life. Not surprisingly, her fondest memories were from down on the farm, struggling to survive with lackadaisical Pa, 15 wild children, a couple of wayward Indians, prying neighbors, and a variety of farm animals that lived both inside and outside their jerry-built house. It was a less than ideal situation, but the Kettles always found humor in it. They were the happiest, most contented family around. They struggled like the rest of us ordinary folk, and it was that endearing quality that made them so popular with the post-war audiences of the day.

In an *Indianapolis Star* interview (March 12, 1978), Marjorie summed up how she felt about Ma Kettle: "I always thought of Ma Kettle as a real person. She was someone that I could imagine driving out into the country to see. Ma Kettle was a grand person."

Aside from my own love of the Ma and Pa Kettle film series, I was amazed to learn that a biography on Marjorie Main had never been written. A woman who gave much of her life to her acting deserves that tribute, and now *Marjorie Main: The Life and Films of Hollywood's "Ma Kettle"* finally tells her story.

This biography covers her days as a farm girl in rural Indiana, through to her countless stage productions, her transition to Hollywood, and on to her many years of portraying Ma Kettle. Her unconventional marriage to a noted psychologist and lecturer, Dr. Stanley LeFevre Krebs, a man almost three decades older, is examined in detail. The first-time publication of letters that Dr. Krebs wrote home to his wife while on his lecture circuits gives the reader a full understanding of Marjorie's introverted private life, a mystery for many years.

After being widowed in 1935 at age 45, Marjorie never remarried, preferring to live the rest of her life alone. The rest of her life proved to be another 40 years, with the epitome of her acting success coming to her *after* the death of Dr. Krebs.

Marjorie Main died from lung cancer on April 10, 1975. She was 85. She had no children and no close living relatives at the time of her death.

Career-wise, the extensive filmography and film facts section of this book examines each and every one of her 85 films in detail. In conclusion, *Marjorie Main: The Life and Films of Hollywood's "Ma Kettle"* is the definitive reference on her somewhat eccentric life and unforgettable career.

ONE

Mary Tomlinson

She played a cook, a maid, a landlady, a widow, a town gossip and a mother; however, Marjorie Main is best remembered as the gruff hillbilly matriarch with the lazy husband and the rowdy brood of 15 children in the popular Ma and Pa Kettle film series.

With each film costing under $400,000 to produce, and shot entirely on the Universal Studios back lot in just 30 days, it was a relatively risk free project, and the public couldn't get enough of the dysfunctional Kettle family.

Marjorie in an early autographed publicity pose.

Before long the studio made plans to put Ma and Pa Kettle into a new situation, year after year. It became a production line. Universal released nine films between 1949 and 1957, at a total production cost of 4 million dollars. The entire nine-film series earned the studio a whopping $35 million return. Miraculously, it was these simple yet charming films that single-handedly pulled Universal from the brink of bankruptcy. "The Kettles" literally saved the studio.

Looking at Marjorie and Ma side by side, there were only two major differences between the woman and the character she portrayed: the children and the dirt! Marjorie, although married for many years until her husband's death, had no children, whereas Ma had an army of 15! And unlike Ma Kettle's couldn't-care-less attitude toward cleanliness, Marjorie had a lifelong phobia of germs. In hindsight, she was so neurotic about hygiene that it's a wonder she could play such a slovenly character at all.

A woman of few words, her childless marriage was her only regret. Later in life, in *The Slapstick Queens* by James Robert Parish (1973), Marjorie reminisced about what it may have been like to be a mother offscreen: "I wish I'd had some children. They would be good company for me and give me a little something more to do around the house. As you know, I had plenty of kids as Ma Kettle."

One of the earliest portrait shots of Marjorie. Although appearing a little neater in this picture, her familiar "owl's nest" hairdo was a style she kept her entire life, on and off screen.

Marjorie Main was a true character, in every sense of the word. She played the average woman. She was no great beauty. She was the said-it-as-she-saw-it type. It was those three basic traits that gave her a permanent place in the hearts of the filmgoing public. Among the bevy of 1940s and post-war movie beauties, Marjorie Main was *reality*.

Despite a distinguished acting career on stage and in minor film roles, it wasn't until her 50th birthday, after she was offered a long term film contract by MGM that Marjorie Main became a bona fide star. Middle age was a time in life when most pretty young starlets retreated to their mansions and lived the rest of their lives on the fond memories of a once glamorous profession. Advancing age (especially for an actress) can be a cruel and superficial end to a highly successful career, but for Marjorie Main middle age was only the beginning.

On February 24, 1890, close to Acton, Indiana, with the help and expert care of her maternal grandfather, Dr. Samuel McGaughey, Mary Tomlinson arrived into the world. She had a brother, Samuel; and the *Indianapolis Star* (April 11, 1975) reported that she had an elder sister who died at the age of 12, shortly after the family moved to Elkhart. Her father, Reverend Samuel Joseph Tomlinson, a Christian minister in Shelby County, ensured that his daughter Mary had a stringent upbringing in what was a predominantly rural farming community. Mary's mother Jennie (also known as Mary) Tomlinson (nee McGaughey) was a devoted wife and homemaker. Like most women of the times, she quietly went along with her husband's idea of how children should be raised.

When the mood struck him, the conservative Reverend Tomlinson would break away from his religious studies and entertain the family by reading aloud from his prized collection of Charles Dickens books. It was these rare but welcome performances that would inspire a young Mary to become an actress.

Marjorie in an early Broadway publicity pose.

The family's maid helped fuel Mary's acting bug by sneaking her along (without her father's knowledge) to Negro jubilee shows. Together they would soak up the dramatic skits and sing-alongs, getting back home in just enough time before Mary was missed. Those evenings after the jubilees Mary would reenact everything she saw that day. Her parents would watch her performances, completely puzzled as to where she got her creativity from. Little did her parents know how and where she'd spent her afternoon, and neither Mary nor the maid ever told. The Tomlinsons concluded that their daughter had an "active imagination" and left it at that.

When Mary won first prize in an elementary school reading, the *Indianapolis Star* (September 6, 1952) explained how her proud parents waited patiently for her to greet them back stage. Mary eventually turned up, some 20 minutes after the winners were announced.

"Where were you, Mary?" her mother asked.

"Oh that," said a frustrated Mary, "I was just trying to swap this watch for the second place $10 prize."

Marjorie was proud of her rural upbringing, and despite her Hollywood success, she consistently maintained a steadfast loyalty to her roots. According to the *Indianapolis Star* (July 23, 1948), on a trip back to Indiana, Marjorie told a home town crowd, "I was born on a farm not 20 miles from Indianapolis [Acton], and no matter how far I roam, it's always home to me." Not surprisingly, she received more cheers with that one line than she ever got in a movie theater.

An intensely private person, it is somewhat difficult to find firsthand accounts of what Marjorie Main was like off-screen. However, Ralph Armstrong shared some candid stories that his late mother Ruth Medsker would tell him of her days of working on the farm with a young Mary Tomlinson near Fairland, Indiana.

Ralph's mother Ruth and her sister (also a Mary) would often help Mary (Marjorie) with her various farm chores after school. They remembered her love of climbing trees and sitting up there in the branches for hours talking to herself. All the local kids thought she was nuts, but in reality she was memorizing her lines for some make believe performance that she was going to put on for whoever would take a moment to stop and listen.

Despite Ruth's steadfast insistence that she just wasn't interested, Mary would constantly try to teach her the art of acting. "Well, I'm going to be an actress someday," Mary would confidently tell Ruth and the other kids. Unfortunately, that revelation didn't help Mary in the slightest, as they still thought she was nuts.

One particular evening, Ruth recalled stopping by Mary's house, probably to discuss a school matter, something ordinary. When she arrived she was confronted by Mary all dressed up in a frilly dress and long beads, very much like a flapper of the early 1920s. However, this was the early 1900s, so it was an ensemble yet to be seen. As if the outfit wasn't enough, Mary was also singing loudly and dancing wildly right there in the living room.

Ruth was dumbfounded. She once again walked home shaking her head, thinking poor Mary had lost her mind. Ruth wondered what would become of this weird farm girl with the boundless energy and the endless enthusiasm for a dream that a girl in Indiana wouldn't normally consider, not for a minute. Yep, Ruth was convinced, there was just no rational explanation for her behavior. Mary was definitely the weird kid.

Ruth remembered Mary getting into all sorts of trouble at school for sneaking onto the stage when the teachers weren't paying attention. She would climb up to the stage and imitate someone (usually a teacher) or dance, even sing a song. She was drawn to performing, but she would always get caught, and she didn't stop getting caught until she was finally allowed to join the drama class for real.

As a young girl, Ruth had no inkling that Mary's girlhood dream was indeed a future reality. After all, rural Indiana was a long way from the bright lights of Hollywood. It wasn't until Ruth was an adult, watching Mary (Marjorie) onscreen where she belonged, that it all finally came together. Now it made sense.

Even in later years, as popular as she was, Marjorie would always make the time to travel back to Fairland School to meet the students. She would shake their hands and answer their questions about a magical land called Hollywood. The historic Fairland School, built in 1898, was torn down in the mid–1980s.

As private as Marjorie was in life, there were brief moments when she would recall stories about her childhood in Elkhart, Indiana. An *Indianapolis Star* (April 11, 1975) article reported that she and her first boyfriend, a little boy named Merrill Moore, the son of a physician friend of the family, would go wading together in the river.

Another of her childhood memories concerned the day she volunteered to take care of a neighbor's baby—without permission. After borrowing a pair of her older sister's shoes and a dress of her mother's, Mary wheeled the baby carriage containing the infant to a nearby park she recalled as being about three miles from home. There was consternation in two households until she returned with the baby several hours later.

Much later in life, while on a flight from New York to Chicago, Marjorie happened to mention the incident to the stewardess, who relayed the story to the pilot. The plane suddenly banked over and started to descend from the 17,000-foot altitude at which it was flying.

The stewardess told Marjorie, "We're going low over Elkhart; see if you can find your park." Marjorie looked through the tiny airplane windows but was unable to spot the park in which she played make-believe-mommy in all those years before.

At her eighth grade graduation ceremony, Mary recited "The Light from Over the Range." Years later, Marjorie still remembered the reading well. How couldn't she? It was the day her unmistakable gravelly voice appeared, out of nowhere! She described that very day: "My voice suddenly stepped up several gears. The effect was startling, even to me.... The audience grew tenser, mouths opened. I had them and the voice had me! It screeched on and on, with virtually no effort on my part. I couldn't have let the darn thing back down to a normal tone, that would have made my recitation suddenly ridiculous. So, I let 'er go right on to the end, with all I had, and sat down to thunderous applause. I had discovered what they called here in Hollywood, 'socko.'" (Parish, 1979)

A studio publicity pose.

Over the years her unique voice has been described as strident, galvanized, raucous, gritty, stentorian, gravelly, cindery, gruff and raspy. None of those words could be taken as a compliment; but her voice matched her look, and the entire package made her unique.

Her strict home life prevented her from attending any professional theater performances; however, her persistence and love for the arts finally saw Mary's father agree to her attending the Hamilton School of Dramatic Expression in Lexington, Kentucky. By 1909, a nineteen-year-old Mary had successfully completed her three-year course, and she quickly secured a position as a dramatics instructor at Bourbon College in Paris, Kentucky.

The successful applicant was chosen from a photograph submitted to the school administrator. "There were three applicants and my picture won," Marjorie said in a Universal International (UI) production report (January 12, 1949). Joking about her less-than-glamorous appearance, she concluded, "If that doesn't show there's such a thing as fate, then what could? You've seen my picture, of course."

After demanding an increase in salary, a feministic approach in those days, Mary was fired. She only lasted one year at Bourbon College, and although she liked it there she took her dismissal in her stride. Mary continued to study dramatic art in Chicago and New York. Her first official "paid" acting performance was in *The Taming of the Shrew.* Mary played Katherine, and she was paid $8 a week for her services.

Her next job was with a repertory theater company on the Chautauqua circuit. Mary recited Shakespeare and Dickens, in which the latter her father had given her a head start as a child. Knowing his daughter was reading such classics, and to a paying audience, helped soften Reverend Tomlinson's views of Mary's chosen profession. Her $18 weekly salary was raised to $25 after the first year, and as a bonus she was allowed to perform in short plays from time to time.

An early autographed photograph of Marjorie, signed, "Cordially, Marjorie Main."

Eventually she joined a stock company in Fargo, North Dakota. Within five months she was happily appearing on the vaudeville stage. To avoid any family embarrassment, Mary Tomlinson changed her name to Marjorie Main. In a UI production report (March 16, 1950) she explained why: "I didn't want to use my family's name on the stage because I knew they disapproved. The name I chose was my idea of a name easy to remember."

In a UI interview (September 20, 1954) she credited her late husband, Dr. Stanley LeFevre Krebs, for thinking up "Marjorie" as a first name; but she concocted "Main" as her new last name herself, explaining, "There's main entrance, main event, main street, main everything. Why not Marjorie Main? Besides, it's a name that's easy to remember." The public had no trouble remembering Marjorie's name. That face, that voice, those mannerisms. How could you miss her? She was unforgettable.

TWO

From Farm to Fame

The years of drama study had paid off, and before long Marjorie was starring on stage with the likes of John Barrymore and W.C. Fields. The humorous skit between Marjorie and Fields titled "The Family Ford" was an instant hit and played at the Palace Theater for many weeks to a packed house.

It was around this time that Marjorie met Dr. Stanley LeFevre Krebs, a widowed lecturer and psychologist with a grown daughter. Their whirlwind romance quickly led them to the altar, and they were married on November 2, 1921. Marjorie was 31. At 57, her new husband was twenty-six years her senior and Marjorie became the textbook wife. She temporarily gave up her own work to travel with her husband, tending to his every need, booking his speaking engagements and answering his correspondence as they toured the country together. Despite the sacrifice of her own career, Marjorie always maintained that her time on the road with "Doctor" (as she would affectionately call him) was the happiest of her life. "I learned a great deal about people from my husband. An understanding of people is essential to any actor worth his salt" (Parish, 1979).

As soon as the lecture tours ended they would return to New York, where Dr. Krebs would rest up from his months on the road. Marjorie would take the opportunity to look for work in the theater. By the late 1920s, and with Dr. Krebs' schedule winding down, Marjorie and her husband set roots in New York on a permanent basis. This arrangement allowed Marjorie to go back to the stage full time. Her first "comeback performance" was her appearance at Daly's 63rd Street Theater as Mae West's queen mother in *The Wicked Age,* a burlesque romp which opened on November 4, 1927. It lasted 19 performances.

Marjorie started 1928 with a new role in a play called *Salvation.* It opened at the Empire Theater on January 31, 1928. However, when a road company was formed for the Broadway hit *Burlesque* in 1929, Marjorie joined the group and toured with the likes of Barbara Stanwyck and Hal Skelly. She was once again on the road, only this time it was for her own career, and without her husband.

On December 5, 1931, Marjorie Main made the leap from stage to screen. Moviegoing audiences saw her for the very first time, albeit briefly, in her debut role in *A House Divided* (1931). She can only be seen momentarily as the town gossip — but it was the stepping stone to a future in film that she'd long be remembered for.

Marjorie returned to Broadway as a servant in the Oscar and Hammerstein musical *Music in the Air,* debuting on Broadway on November 8, 1932. It ran for over a year; however, it wasn't long before Marjorie returned to film in two small New York Productions, *Take a Chance* (1933) and *Crimes Without Passion* (1933). Again, Marjorie appeared only briefly in the crowd scenes.

Next, Fox Studios offered her the role of the servant in the film adaptation of *Music in the Air* (1934), the same part that she played in the stage version. Gloria Swanson was the lead player; but even with the film being heavily promoted as "Swanson's Big Comeback," it flopped. Much of Marjorie's performance was cut altogether. Marjorie took it in her stride, but the failure weighed heavily on Swanson. She retreated to her home and withdrew from public life.

In fact, it took seven years before Swanson considered herself emotionally strong enough to make another attempt at a screen comeback. That comeback film was *Father Takes a Wife* (1941). It lost $104,000 at the box office, and again Swanson went into seclusion. This time it was nine years before she returned to the screen, but oh what a return it was. It's ironic that Swanson's real-life comeback performance was as an aging actress intent on making a comeback of her own. For Gloria Swanson, Billy Wilder's classic *Sunset Boulevard* (1950) accomplished just that.

By mid–1935, Marjorie was back in New York and working locally to be with her now-ailing husband. She returned to the Broadway stage, appearing in the 1935 production of *Jackson White.* Marjorie's beloved husband passed away at St. Luke's Hospital on September 27, 1935. At 71 years of age he had lost his battle with cancer. Years later, Marjorie remembered her grief: "His death was the low point of my life. I was broken hearted and I desperately needed work as much to occupy my mind as to make a living" (Parish, 1973).

It's interesting to note that toward the end of her life Marjorie became less than enthusiastic about her marriage to Dr. Krebs. What's more, in a book titled *Hollywood Lesbians*, by Boze Hadleigh, she even hinted at her own bisexual tendencies. The bizarre life that Marjorie and Dr. Krebs shared together is worthy of a chapter of its own, and will be examined closely in Chapter Ten.

At the time of her husband's death, Marjorie at least gave the impression of the grieving widow. Her delicate emotional state helped her achieve one of her best stage performances as the mother of gangster Joseph Downing in *Dead End.* She played the role every night for a staggering 460 out of a total 687 performances.

Marjorie was now a hot commodity, and the stage production of *The Women* was the next big hit to benefit from her talent. Opening night was the day after Christmas, 1936, at the Ethel Barrymore Theater. Marjorie played Lucy, the less than tactful innkeeper. Her co-stars were Ilka Chase, Margalo Gillmore and Betty Lawford. Marjorie, Phyllis Povah and Mary Cecil would be the only three stage actresses to revive their roles in the future film version.

In the meantime, Samuel Goldwyn had decided that he wanted to produce the film version of *Dead End.* First, he had his spies find out how much David O. Selznick had offered for the play. When he found out it was worth $150,000 to his rival, Goldwyn went higher. He wanted it, and was not about to lose it, especially to Selznick. The film rights to *Dead End* were eventually bought by Goldwyn for a whopping $165,000. It was the largest price paid up until that time for a hit play.

After seeing *Dead End* on Broadway, Goldwyn insisted that Marjorie revive her stage role as the gangster mother in his film version. She agreed, and her stellar performance was a contributing factor to the film version of *Dead End* (1937) becoming an instant hit.

Humphrey Bogart took on the role of the no-good gangster, Baby Face Martin. Marjorie recreated the role of the slum mother, earning rave reviews. The scene in which Marjorie yells, "Ya dirty, yellow dog," before slapping her no-good son was rehearsed again and again. Bogart later joked that by the time rehearsals were over, his cheek was as dead as the title.

Not willing to let his director William Wyler take the production to New York, Goldwyn extended his *Dead End* budget by $300,000 to have a set built to mirror the slum streets of New York right there in sunny California. Academy Award–winning set designer Richard Day recreated the seedy slums, including realistic Sutton Place terraces, wooden docks, and even an East River pier with real polluted water for the Dead End Kids to jump into during the searing August heat. Except for three days of interior sequences, the entire film was shot on the makeshift streets of "New York City."

Despite Goldwyn spending a bucket-load of money on this attention to detail, he wanted *his* slums to look nice. It didn't matter that the script called for the set to look dark, dirty, and corrupt; it didn't matter that the characters inhabiting them were young gangsters in tattered clothing from the wrong side of the tracks. Goldwyn was in the picture business, and his slum was going to be the nicest, cleanest slum imaginable.

In *Goldwyn*, by Arthur Marx, Wyler remembers the movie mogul continually dropping in on the New York street set. He would survey the filth as if it were offensive to his sense of aesthetics, and shout in his high-pitched voice, "Why is everything so dirty here?"

"Because it's supposed to be a slum area, Sam," Wyler would reply.

"Well, this slum cost a lot of money. It should look better than an ordinary slum," Goldwyn stated.

Goldwyn would stroll onto the set and mutter to himself as he picked up the garbage. Now, this wasn't any ol' garbage, it was prop garbage that had been strategically placed to give the slums the "authentic" look they needed. "There won't be any dirty slums, not in my pictures!" he grumbled as he gathered the papers and walked off the set.

So that's how it went. Every morning the set would be dressed with garbage, and every morning Samuel Goldwyn would come by to clean it up. In the end, William Wyler just gave up the fight. He'd gather in a corner with Richard Day and prop man Irving Sindler until Goldwyn had finished cleaning up the set, *his* set. As soon as he left they'd redress it all over again!

In spite of Goldwyn's daily intrusion, *Dead End* was nominated for four Academy Awards, including Best Picture of 1937. Still, few independent studio productions ever win Oscars, even if they deserve it, and *Dead End* was no exception. Warners' *Life of Emile Zola* (1937) won Best Picture for that year. But *Dead End* was a hit with audiences and critics alike. More importantly, the film made Goldwyn a healthy profit. And considering the staggering amount of money invested, making a profit was no easy task.

Daily Variety (July 30, 1937) wrote: "'Dead End' is about gangsters, little and big, and how they are cradled in an environment; about harlots and harridans; about folk too rich and too poor; about warped and frustrated ambitions; about pathetic futilities, and about a few shining things looming from the darks of the tenements of wealth and poverty at the end of a street abutting the East River."

Ironically, Warners ended up making a total of six "Dead End Kid" movies. Monogram Studios picked up the pieces when Warners was all but done with them, and, after renaming them "The East Side Kids," a total of 21 films were made at Monogram. During this same period, four of the gang (Billy Halop, Huntz Hall, Gabriel Dell and Bernard Punsley) were loaned out to Universal for a dozen "Little Tough Guy" movies.

Finally, the popular "Bowery Boys" series evolved from the group. Starring Leo Gorcey and Huntz Hall, a whopping 48 films were made, well into the 1950s. From the humble beginnings of *Dead End* (1937) to the last "Bowery Boys" production titled *In the Money* (1958), some 89 film versions about delinquent kids in New York City were filmed over a 21 year period. *Dead End* (1937) was the first of many films starring Marjorie Main and the Dead End Kids. She played the down-and-out, rough-around-the-edges mother of a no-good kid to perfection.

Never content with not working, 1937 was a big year for Marjorie. She appeared as Mrs. Martin, the mother of Barbara Stanwyck's character, in the classic *Stella Dallas* (1937). Samuel Goldwyn proved to be his stubborn "know-it-all" self when it came to casting the classic weepy. Director King Vidor insisted that Stanwyck be the only one to play the lead role, but Goldwyn fought him all the way, insisting that lesser stars such as Ruth Chatterton and Gladys George were far more suitable. After days of pleading, Goldwyn gave in to Vidor's choice, but only if she'd submit herself to a screen test. At this point in Stanwyck's career, asking her to perform a screen test was not only ludicrous, it was downright insulting. Goldwyn shrewdly knew she'd reject his proposition, and she did. Her initial decision was turned around by her good friend and fellow actor Joel McCrea. In his book *Hollywood,* Garson Kanin recalls the tense conversations that followed.

"Listen, Barbara," McCrea pleaded, "You'll win an award for this picture, just do the test." She reluctantly agreed to the screen test, only to have Goldwyn tell her that he "didn't think she was capable of doing it." He continued with a list of reasons why he thought she'd be wrong for the role, such as "you're too young" and "you have no experience with children."

Director Vidor took an entire day with Stanwyck filming the emotional birthday scene in which Stella and her daughter Laurel wait for the girl's friends to show up, not realizing the guests have all been told to boycott the party. Vidor remembered, "Stanwyck's test was undeniable. She put everyone else to shame." But Goldwyn continued to dig in his heels. He still had no leading lady, but he refused to be convinced that Stanwyck had what it took to make the film a classic. It took a personal meeting with Joel McCrea to get him to reluctantly agree to hire her.

In the months to come, Goldwyn heard many "I told you so's" over *Stella Dallas* (1937). Not only did audiences and critics give the film and Stanwyck's performance rave reviews, she also received a Best Actress Oscar Nomination for her efforts. More importantly, the film grossed $2 million, a profit of $500,000 for the studio and a nice monetary return for stubborn Sam. Nevertheless, right to the very end he still refused to admit that Stanwyck made the film the hit that it was.

In *Starring Miss Barbara Stanwyck,* by Ella Smith, King Vidor recalls his own estimate of what Barbara Stanwyck brought to the role of Stella Dallas. "I do remember very well that I admired Miss Stanwyck's humanness and ability and the way she came over as a very down-to-earth person. And on screen in anything she has ever done that has been her greatest asset to me, that she makes everything entirely believable — makes you

Marjorie plays Mrs. Martin opposite Barbara Stanwyck in *Stella Dallas* (1937).

think it is really happening when she does it. And this to me is the test for all acting and directing — if someone watching in the audience can entirely forget that he's looking at a movie."

In *Movie Digest* (January 1972), Barbara Stanwyck gave her own opinion of the role: "The theme of Stella Dallas — a mother's love and self-sacrifice — when properly handled in any medium is never maudlin, never dated. I still receive letters from fans seeing the film for the first time, either on television or at one of the various film festivals, and their

Marjorie as Mrs. Martin, pictured with co-star Edmund Elton, as Mr. "Pop" Martin, in the award-winning *Stella Dallas* (1937).

comments make me doubly proud of the fact that I was fortunate enough to play this once-in-a-lifetime role."

Marjorie was equally praised for her role in *Stella Dallas*, particularly by *The Hollywood Reporter* (July 30, 1937): "Miss Main is an artist and her contribution to the picture is out of all proportion to the length of her part."

The Man Who Cried Wolf (1937) was next for Marjorie. Lawrence Fontaine (Lewis Stone) is an actor suspected of publicity mania when he continually confesses to murders he didn't commit. There is a method to his madness, however. He is setting himself up for an alibi when he finally kills the wealthy broker who had broken up his home years before. *Hollywood Reporter* (undated, 1937) said, "Robert Gleckler is outstanding as the police captain who refuses to believe Stone's confessions and testifies against him when he is held for examination as a mental case. Jameson Thomas as the murder victim, Marjorie Main as his villainous sister, and Billy Wayne also help to make this film worthwhile."

The Wrong Road and *The Shadow* rounded out 1937 for Marjorie. Both were equally forgettable. The latter was a hokey whodunit starring Rita Hayworth in her first film role with her new name. She was previously credited as Margarita Carmen Cansino, an all-too-ethnic birth name that studio bosses were quick to eliminate.

Marjorie had tallied an astounding 13 film roles in 1937. With most of those roles being minor parts, she managed to pop up in one film or another, making her a well-known face to the film-going public. On January 1, 1938, she starred as the impoverished mother in another of the "Dead End Kids" productions, *Boy of the Streets,* playing the long suffering mother of a son gone bad (Jackie Cooper). Again, she received rave reviews for her performance.

The little known productions *City Girl* (1938) and *King of the Newsboys* (1938) both offered small roles to Marjorie as a wife to a more prominent character. Her next part was a sizable one in an MGM production starring their golden boy, Clark Gable. *Test Pilot* (1938) also starred such big names as Spencer Tracy and Myrna Loy. Marjorie plays a busybody landlady meddling (as only she could) in the developing romance between Gable and Loy. In *Prison Farm* (1938) Marjorie plays Matron Brand, and in *Romancing the Light* (1938) she plays the cranky old aunt of Jean Parker's character.

In *Little Tough Guy* (1938) she plays the acid-tongued wife hell bent on destroying her husband (played by Edward Pawley). Standout performances by the six kids, Billy Halop, Huntz Hall, Gabriel Dell, Bernard Punsley, Hally Chester and David Gorcey, are capital, further developing the same characters they played in previous films. *Daily Variety* (July 7, 1938) said, "Surprising amount of comedy is evoked alongside the darker phases of the tale, with the 'Dead End Kids' whipping up much of the hilarity with pantomime as well as witty chatter and slum street commentary. Thrills and tension build to a sharply dramatic scene where Halop and his pal, Huntz Hall, are run to bay by the cops and die in a hail of bullets."

Under the Big Top (1938), a low-budget Monogram picture, was a nice change of pace for Marjorie. In it, she played Sara, the tough owner of the Post Circus, a traveling show that falls upon hard times.

In *Too Hot to Handle* (1938) she was back in the big leagues at MGM, with Clark Gable, Myrna Loy and Walter Pidgeon. Playing a secretary to William Connolly's character, she once again gave a standout performance. Her next three films were forgettable: *Girl's School* (1938), *There Goes My Heart* (1938) and *Three Comrades* (1938). In the latter she was seen only briefly as an old woman.

Although not every role that Marjorie took in 1938 was a memorable one, she had poked her face into enough productions that the public now came to the theater almost expecting to see her. By the following year her agent received an increased amount of calls in response to public demand. Letters arrived at the studios daily from fans wanting to see more of this raspy, gravel-voiced character.

Lucky Night featured her first role of 1939. Robert Taylor, a penniless, glib alcoholic, and Myrna Loy, a spoiled rich daughter of a steel tycoon, awaken in a ritzy hotel room badly hung over and amazed to learn that they are married. Sadly, this laugh-out-loud story with two A-list stars just doesn't get off the ground. Marjorie plays the real estate agent whose job it is to find the lovebirds a rental property.

In her following two films, *They Shall Have Music* and *Angels Wash Their Faces* (both 1939), Marjorie was back in the familiar slum mother role of "Dead End Kids" proportions. She fitted the role well, and she certainly looked the part. It was the very reason she was typecast as the low-income mother character over and over again.

In 1939 Marjorie once again revived a previous stage role on film, this time in the MGM adaptation of *The Women* (1939). Alongside a full cast of prominent Hollywood actresses, including Joan Crawford, Rosalind Russell, Joan Fontaine, Paulette Goddard, and Norma Shearer, Marjorie plays a Reno Innkeeper. With a tell-it-like-it-is attitude, she attends to the needs of the rich women awaiting their quickie Nevada divorces.

Next Marjorie again teamed up with Myrna Loy in *Another Thin Man* (1939), also starring William Powell. Loy and Powell revive their roles as Nick and Nora Charles, married super-sleuths and now new parents to baby Nick Jr. When three dead bodies turn up, Nick, Nora and the baby set out to solve the mystery, with acid tongued wit and good humor, as only they could. Marjorie lit up the screen playing the nosy boarding house owner.

A low-budget RKO film entitled *Two Thoroughbreds* (1939) saw Marjorie playing the role of Aunt Hildegard to a young orphan boy who falls in love with a prize horse.

Marjorie's last film of the decade had more than a few problems. *I Take This Woman* (1940) was filmed at the tail end of 1939, but, due to its extensive production problems, wasn't released until 1940. Despite the massive production cost of reshooting an almost completed film, it wasn't uncommon for Louis B. Mayer to scrap a production at mid-way point and order a reshoot, with a different script, different characters, etc. Such was the case with *I Take This Woman*. Few of the original *I Take This Woman* actors made the cut, with Mayer insisting that they were all "terrible," and the film was immediately recast. Luckily for Marjorie, Mayer liked what he saw in the first version of the film, and insisted she stay on for take two. Yet, despite the revamp, the secondary version met a lukewarm reception, and the massive production cost incurred by the reshoot was never recovered.

The low-budget Paramount film *Women Without Names* (1940) had Marjorie playing the role of a tough prison matron. *New York Daily News* critic Kate Cameron commented on her "stand out role" in a minor part.

Marjorie's next role was in Republic's big western film for 1940, *Dark Command* (1940). Starring in an ensemble cast alongside Walter Pidgeon, John Wayne, Claire Trevor, Roy Rogers and Gabby Hayes, Marjorie played the usual mother role; however, her compelling deathbed scene made the part a little meatier than the usual one-dimensional mother character she'd played many times before. *Variety* (April 5, 1940) said, "Marjorie Main etches a memorable character as Cantrell's [Pidgeon] mother, loathing him finally as a beast and ready to kill him with her own hands."

Playing a cook in her next picture, Marjorie stood out as the voice (and oh what a voice) of reason in Hal Roach's comedy *Turnabout* (1940). Carole Landis and John Hubbard portray a newly married couple who have an argument and then suddenly take over each other's bodies. It was Marjorie's character that glued the film together. Hal Roach was so impressed with Marjorie's performance that he got to work on drawing up a long-term contract in preparation to sign her permanently to his studio.

With another positive review under her belt, Marjorie took the part of the gardener's wife in George Cukor's *Susan and God* (1940). Once again, Marjorie was praised by critics for giving a standout performance amongst a competent cast — and a competent cast it was, with Joan Crawford and Fredric March giving their own stellar performances.

The Captain Is a Lady (1940) was a throwaway MGM film starring Charles Coburn as a retired sea captain who sneaks his way into a ladies-only retirement home in order to live out his last days with his beloved wife, played by Beulah Bondi. Marjorie's turn as the housekeeper, Sara May Willett, is impeccable. Her performance makes a major impact in an otherwise minor film.

Although she didn't know it at the time, Marjorie's studio-hopping lifestyle was coming to an end. Her next co-star, Wallace Beery, desperately needed a new female lead to replace his deceased partner in film, Marie Dressler. She had succumbed to cancer on

July 28, 1934, and the studio was having a tough time finding an actress who could hold her own against the brashness of Beery's characters. But when Marjorie Main starred alongside Beery in the western themed *Wyoming* (1940), their search was over.

A new partnership, this time between Beery and Marjorie, would eventually evolve into a series of films together. Marjorie had succeeded in stepping into Marie Dressler's shoes, and the public accepted her with open arms. Unfortunately for Marjorie, Beery was not the perfect partner in return. It seemed he had problems with women, both on and off the screen.

Beery started his career at Chicago's Essanay Studios. He gained notoriety as "Sweedie" in a series of shorts in which he plays a Swedish maid, in drag. An 18-year-old Gloria Swanson appeared as an extra in *Sweedie Goes to College* (1915), and the pretty young starlet caught Beery's roving eye. Gloria thought nothing of Beery at the time. A few months later, after he had left Essanay to travel to California (his departure was rumored to have been prompted by a brewing scandal involving a young woman on the set), Gloria received a postcard from Beery encouraging her to make the trip to California. "There was plenty of work," he said.

On his advice, Gloria and her mother made the trip west, and, with Beery's insistence, Mack Sennett agreed to cast her opposite Beery in *A Dash of Courage* (1916). Gloria noticed a change in Beery. The once-brash womanizer was now courting her like a gentleman. By 1916 they were married. The honeymoon was over before it started. On their wedding night Beery got drunk in a hotel bar and raped Gloria when he returned to their room. A few weeks later, after Gloria confronted him about the fate of their marriage, Beery convinced her that things would change. They did. Things got worse.

The newlyweds were living with Beery's parents, two people who were icy toward, and unaccepting of, their new daughter-in law. A month into their marriage Gloria experienced a brief moment of happiness. She was pregnant. It was a happiness that was short-lived.

One morning after awakening with severe cramps, Gloria called to her husband to get her something for the pain. Gloria needed emergency medical attention; but instead of calling a doctor, Beery conversed with his mother and returned to the bedroom with a bottle of medication. He convinced Gloria that it would make her feel better. She took it without question. Her condition worsened and she passed out. When she awoke there was a nurse in the bedroom, and the news was not good. She had lost the baby.

Suspicious of her husband's actions on the morning in question, Gloria later discovered that her husband had obtained the medicine that he said would help her from a nearby drugstore. It was a type of poison. In two whirlwind months their marriage was over. They were divorced in 1919. Gloria attempted marriage another five times. All except her last marriage to playwright William Dufty (which lasted until her death on April 4, 1983), ended in divorce. She had three children — two biological daughters, Gloria and Michelle, and one adopted son, Joseph. Her third husband, French aristocrat Marquis Henri de La Falaise, fathered a child with her, but Gloria chose to abort the pregnancy. It was a decision she regretted for the rest of her life.

Beery eventually remarried. Rita Gilman was his second wife. They had one child, a daughter named Carol Ann. They divorced in 1930. At the time of his death, Beery was involved in a paternity suit with actress Gloria Schumm. She claimed he was the father of her 13-month-old son. Right to the very end, Wallace Beery had problems with women. Marjorie was no exception.

MGM were convinced they needed to do something about keeping Marjorie on the payroll. Permanently. On October 8, 1940, Marjorie Main signed a seven-year contract with the most successful movie studio in the world—MGM. As usual, Louis B. Mayer saw what he wanted and went after it with gusto. Hal Roach realized Marjorie's talent several months before Mayer, but he was too slow in drawing up her contract. It proved a costly mistake.

THREE

Opposites Attract ... or Not!

A *New York Daily News* review of *Wyoming* (1940) by Wanda Hale said, "Marjorie Main is the first picture stealer and the greatest picture saver in Hollywood." It was her most outstanding review to date, but Wallace Beery wanted a woman to push around, not a scene stealer.

Well, it was too bad. Marjorie Main was a scene stealer from way back; she couldn't help it. Even without lines, that face and those expressions just had a way of making people sit up and take notice. Beery had his work cut out for him. His new partner could match him word for word, stride for stride, scene for scene, and he didn't like it.

Wallace Beery and Marjorie Main were complete opposites. Beery was a hard drinking, swearing bully of a man; whereas Marjorie (despite her outward appearance) was a teetotaling, mild mannered country girl. Beery learned the lines he felt necessary to the script; the rest he improvised. Marjorie, on the other hand, learned her lines and her co-stars' lines to the letter.

Beery's ad-libbing not only upset Marjorie's timing, his unpredictable demeanor, both on and off camera, upset her — period. Marjorie's world was changing fast. Her stormy partnership with Beery, the long-term interest of MGM, and nationwide critical and public acclaim made 1940 the turning point in her career — in more ways than one.

Wyoming (1940) was a western set in a post–Civil War era town where Marjorie plays the village blacksmith who makes it her business to snare the crooked outlaw played by Wallace Beery. This time her ballsy persona was matched by her gruff and tough male equal, Wallace Beery. Somehow this less-than-romantic, unconventional pair melted the hearts of audiences everywhere. It was this perfect onscreen chemistry ("onscreen" being the operational term, since Marjorie was less than impressed with Beery's behavior off-screen) that finally convinced Louis B. Mayer to offer Marjorie a permanent position on the prestigious MGM payroll.

However, before signing her to the seven year contract, Mayer had one minor grievance to pitch to his new star. He loved her as an actress, but he hated her name. In true MGM fashion Mayer set the wheels in motion to create a manufactured name for his new star. After hours and hours of discussion it was mutually decided that Marjorie had established quite a career, quite a fan base, with her own made-up name of Marjorie Main.

Marjorie and Wallace Beery strike up a tune in a scene from *Wyoming* (1940).

It was brought to his attention that she'd already made 39 pictures with that name, so he conceded that he'd just have to get used to it, and he did.

Marjorie's freelance, gypsy-like career of jumping from one studio to another was over. For the first time in her career she was an exclusive player at arguably the biggest movie studio in the world—MGM. With 5,000 people under contract, Metro Goldwyn Mayer was the grandest of the Hollywood studios.

Despite the security of a seven-year contract for the actor, it was the studio that had all the advantages. The studio had the option to terminate the contract every six months for any reason. Then there was the fine print—the morality clauses, marriage clauses, bedtime clauses, etc. Essentially the actors were "owned" by the studio. If the actor was good enough, if they made the studio money, their occasional indiscretions would secretly be hushed up. If the actor was considered too much trouble and not worth the money or the time, he or she would be simply let go.

The so-called "golden age" was a time when studios pinned a chart to the wall noting their actresses' menstrual periods. Clark Gable's false teeth and Gary Cooper's less than perfect hearing were closely guarded secrets. Two of Hollywood's most famous blondes, Jean Harlow and Carole Lombard, went as far as bleaching their pubic hair in order to "prove" they were naturally fair. How often they were asked to prove it is anyone's guess, but if they needed to they could—and probably did. Both Lombard and Harlow were far from shy.

Marjorie's new contract ensured professional stability and meatier roles. It was that newfound security that made 1941 an exciting year for her. *Wild Man of Borneo* (1941) was first up, with Marjorie taking on the all-too-familiar role of a loud-mouthed cook, Irma, in Billie Burke's upper-class New York boarding house. Frank Morgan rounded out the cast of character actors. All thrown together they proved to be a pleasant, if not formidable, force completely capable of holding their own without the usual star power to support them.

The Trial of Mary Dugan (1941) gave Marjorie the opportunity to play a landlady yet again, but this time with a twist. In one particular courtroom scene she throws herself down on the floor while the court is in session to demonstrate the exact position in which she found the murder victim. Marjorie often referred to this particular role as her favorite from her 85 films.

Next, *A Woman's Face* (1941) saw Marjorie reunited with the so-called woman's director George Cukor and MGM's queen of the moment, Joan Crawford. This was perhaps Marjorie's most challenging, non-stereotypical role to date. Barely recognizable, she appeared onscreen with a thick European accent, heavy black clothes and glasses, and with her trademark unruly hair slicked back tightly in a tame manner that nobody thought possible. Yes, she was still a housekeeper, but this was a far cry from the familiar housekeeper type that she had played to audiences so many times before.

Still, that character transformation wasn't permanent, and MGM once again decided it was time to bring back the popular Marjorie and Wallace Beery combination. After all, that was the reason she was secured with that seven-year contract in the first place.

Barnacle Bill (1941) was their second film together. The familiar formula has Beery playing a down-and-out type (this time the bankrupt owner of a fishing vessel) and Marjorie playing the daughter of a fish store owner, who resume their interrupted romance after Beery's eight year absence. Of course, nothing goes as it should, at least not at first. Ultimately, Beery cleans up his act and is reformed into a half-decent catch by the end credits. Leo Carillo, prevented from bestowing his customary exuberance upon the role of Pico, Beery's stooge, still manages to make his part noteworthy, despite the material he was given to work with. *Barnacle Bill* followed a simple yet tried-and-true path to box-office success.

As usual, there was little expense poured into Marjorie's costuming. She once again insisted on choosing her own wardrobe, and, just like in her previous films, her collective wardrobe choices tallied less than the price of one of Louis B. Mayer's lunch meetings. The few costume changes consisted of two simple cotton house dresses, one pair of denim jeans, a few check shirts and a sturdy pair of boots. That was it. "If it's wrong, it's right," was how Marjorie described her Ma Kettle ensembles in a UI production report (May 17, 1950). It seemed her wardrobe choices for *Barnacle Bill* (1941) followed the same theory.

Marjorie's wardrobe was a far cry from the lavish sequined costumes that MGM was so used to churning out for their star players. It wasn't unusual for Marjorie to walk onto the lot, do her scenes, and go home in the same outfit. There was no need to wipe off her makeup because she wore no makeup. There was no Hollywood hype surrounding Marjorie Main; she lived simply in a modest apartment just off Hollywood Boulevard. It was mostly filled with her husband's textbooks and his years of medical research, items that would allow her to feel closer to him. She threw nothing away.

A late bloomer in film, she was equally late in hitting the road. Marjorie received her first driver's license at age 51. She even bought two cars. Regardless, she still preferred to take the bus to work because she enjoyed the interaction with regular people. Not surprisingly, it was those regular people that she played so well onscreen. She believed this daily normalcy helped her with her character development. These "regular people" were the characters that Marjorie made a career out of playing, and these daily bus trips to the studio taught her everything she needed to know. She observed how they walked, how they talked, how they looked in the mornings and how they looked in the evenings after a long, hard day at work. Marjorie was an observer of life, a people watcher. It was her astute observations that gave so much depth to her characters, a rare quality that few of her peers achieved.

A loner for most of her life (especially after her husband's death), Marjorie chose to eat most of her meals, alone, at a small diner close to her home. Afterward, and only if the evening was pleasant, she would sit on her porch, alone, and watch the parade of people pass her by. All were oblivious to their simplistic performance in entertaining a woman who gave most of her life to performing for them.

In an *Indianapolis Star* interview (November 7, 1948), Marjorie told of one particular evening, right after a movie preview, when she was hungry but just didn't feel like mingling with the crowds of people at the premiere party. She preferred to go to the local drugstore, alone, where she proceeded to order a serving of hot cakes. When her order arrived with eight hot cakes on a plate, Marjorie said, "Oh, that's too many. I couldn't possibly eat 'em all." So she took the saucer from underneath her coffee cup, slid half the cakes onto it and offered them to the awestruck stranger seated on the adjoining stool.

"Thanks, but I have no fork," he stammered.

"Well, don't let that bother you, honey," Marjorie bellowed. "Here, use my coffee spoon."

That was Marjorie, the Queen of Cafeteria Society. One of her peculiar habits when dining in these modest surroundings was to put on a pair of long white gloves before eating. Besides genuinely liking the gloves, she felt it a sanitary yet classy way to eat her meal.

After her popularity increased, Marjorie moved to a bungalow closer to MGM, in the quiet suburb of Cheviot Hills. Her more convenient living arrangements gave her the opportunity to alternate her preferred bus trips with riding a bike to work. Her modest form of living was a true testament to who Marjorie was, and, more importantly, the woman she remained long after her popularity as a noted performer was recognized and rewarded. In fact, she was so unpretentious that she refused to get an unlisted telephone number, preferring to be listed in the directory just like everyone else.

The only domestic help she ever had around the house, even in her old age, was from her gardener. Even then, "As often as not, she was out working with him," a friend told the *Indianapolis News* (April 11, 1975). Marjorie's only concern about this situation was that people might think her "cheap" for not having servants and housekeepers, but in reality it had nothing to do with the money. "I don't think I could stand to have someone 'do' for me," she emphatically told the *Indianapolis Star* (March 12, 1978). "I've taken care of myself so long, I've got my own ways set. I think it's best to live alone and I like it."

Locals were used to seeing Marjorie ride by on her bike, stray strands of her graying hair escaping from her upswept style as she peddled her way to the local store. Despite

A candid shot on the set of *Barnacle Bill* (1941).

her less than perfect figure, she would think nothing of wearing a pair of shorts and a halter top in the warmer months. Marjorie's increasing bank account made no difference to her quest for a bargain, either. She once explained the reasoning behind her homely wardrobe choices, especially when shopping for food: "Why wear a mink coat to buy a pork chop? A barrier is immediately raised. And so is the price!" (UI production report, August 18, 1956).

Despite being under contract at the most successful movie studio in the world, it was certainly a bittersweet time in her career. Marjorie was far from happy with her position of "gal pal" for the somewhat difficult Wallace Beery, and being touted as his "new partner." She was stuck with him, however, at least until ticket sales showed a decline in the public's fascination with the pair — and for now the public couldn't get enough.

The equally crusty Leo Carillo was often cast as Beery's buddy, and in real life he was his closest friend. Marjorie was the rose among two very sharp thorns. In a UI production report (May 25, 1955) she spoke of the extra compensation she felt she deserved for working with the pair: "I should have got one salary for the actin' and the other for the workin' with those two, I deserved it every time I came out alive."

A *New York Times* (July 25, 1941) review of their second film together, *Barnacle Bill* (1941), observed, "Wallace Beery has found the perfect foil in Marjorie Main, all right. And, perhaps more than either he or his Metro bosses bargained for, a competitor who comes close to stealing some of his best scenes in the film."

The main gripe that Marjorie had with Beery was his refusal to rehearse his lines with her; as a result, she was never sure of what he was going to say. A notorious ad-libber, Beery's unconventional acting approach unnerved Marjorie to the extent that she reluctantly turned to his friend, Leo Carrillo, for advice on how she should handle the situation. "Just look at him and listen to him, and when he stops talking, say your line," Carrillo advised (Parish, 1973).

It worked like a charm. It certainly wasn't the ideal way to interact with a co-star, but Beery was hard headed and there was simply no talking to him. Carrillo's advice was all Marjorie could do to get through her scenes and keep the timing on track. Luckily, the on-set tension wasn't conveyed through the camera lens, and the unlikely twosome had yet another hit on their hands with *Barnacle Bill.*

Marjorie's next film on her first loan out to Paramount gave her a much needed break from the stress of Beery and his less-than-sympathetic ways. *The Shepherd of the Hills* (1941) was her first color film, and it gave her the opportunity to play the part of a blind grandmother, the matriarch of a family of hicks, who, of course, somewhat predictably regains her sight by film's end.

Her next MGM film again featured an all-star cast. *Honky Tonk* (1941) teamed Clark Gable, Lana Turner and Frank Morgan together, with Marjorie playing the religious boarding house owner who sets out to raise money to build the town a church. Again it was a minor role, but a role that Marjorie made her own.

Her final 1941 release was another pairing with Wallace Beery. Not the best way to round out the year for her, but she was under contract, and when you're signed to the studio, any studio, you do as you're told. *The Bugle Sounds* (1941) wasn't as strong in ticket sales as their previous outings, but, to Marjorie's dismay, the film redeemed itself enough to galvanize the studio into planning future films for the bickering twosome.

The Noël Coward–adapted *We Were Dancing* (1942) was a comedy surrounding the high class marriage and subsequent divorce of Norma Shearer and Melvyn Douglas. Marjorie plays a divorce judge who drags every piece of private information out of the couple with utter enjoyment at seeing their public embarrassment. "I'm supposed to sort of fall in love with Douglas, a pleasant change, I'd say, after Beery," she told the *Indianapolis News* (December 23, 1941).

Her next film, *The Affairs of Martha* (1942) had her playing the less than demure cook of a society family in Rocky Bay, Long Island. With a much needed two picture break

A rare candid snapshot of Marjorie and Wallace Beery behind the scenes on *The Bugle Sounds* (1941).

away from the feisty Wallace Beery, it was once again time for Marjorie to churn out another film with him.

Jackass Mail (1942) told the story of Tiny Tucker, played by Marjorie, the owner of a gambling saloon who takes the opportunity to lead the chorus girls in any song and dance number that she can. When she's not at the saloon she's the town's postmistress, and this is where Wallace Beery comes into the picture. Playing the mail robber who unsuccessfully tries to hold up her mail line, he concocts a scheme to marry Tiny in order to get her business legally. With lines like, "Git goin' before I blast the daylights outta ya!" Tiny enjoys every moment of abuse as she tries her hardest to reform her new beau into a solid upstanding citizen. *Variety* (June 17, 1942) said, "Beery and Miss Main of course give their all in the fiercely contested courtship."

Tish (1942) proved to be turning point number two, yet it was a letdown at the same time. In a positive step forward, Marjorie received billing *above* the title, sharing the honor with co-stars Aline MacMahon and ZaSu Pitts. The plot seemed particularly promising, with Marjorie and her co-stars cast as three meddling old ladies who made it their business to meddle in everyone else's business. But the critics panned the film. The majority of reviews were poor, and, as a result, so were box-office receipts.

A formal scene from ***Jackass Mail*** (1942).

Marjorie's final release for the year was nothing of note either. *Tennessee Johnson* (1943) was the propaganda-induced tale of President Andrew Johnson, played by Van Heflin. Marjorie had a minor part as a pioneer woman, Mrs. Fisher.

The year 1943 was relatively slow for Marjorie, who appeared in only two films, neither one of them for her contractual studio, MGM. Twentieth Century–Fox cast her as Mrs. Strabel, mother of Gene Tierney's character, in the Hollywood classic *Heaven Can Wait* (1943). For the first time in her career, Marjorie's wardrobe consisted of sequined dresses and a fine array of jewelry. She had officially crossed over to the right side of the tracks! As plain as she was off-screen, and in most of her roles prior to *Heaven Can Wait,* Marjorie appeared to be the quintessential rich woman who carried herself with the surefire confidence that money brings to a person. Still, Marjorie was happiest in her old comfy clothes, both on-and off-screen.

When it came time to attend a college reunion dance given by her sorority, Delta Delta Delta, Marjorie didn't have a stitch of clothing that would come anywhere near being labeled an evening gown. She went straight to the MGM costume department and asked for permission to choose something suitable for her night out. Of course they agreed to accommodate her, and Marjorie looked the part in the dress she chose, yet she couldn't understand why the dress made so much noise when she walked. It wasn't until she returned home and got undressed that she noticed she'd forgotten to take the weights out of the hem! These removable weights would hold the dress in shape as it hung amongst the thousands of costumes waiting to be used for a film.

Without a doubt, 1943 was a year of formality for Marjorie, both socially and professionally. Her second and last film of the year was for United Artists, and in it she was required to wear a selection of evening gowns again. *Johnny Come Lately* (1943) was a film connected to James Cagney's production company, and it starred Cagney and Grace George, making her screen debut. Marjorie plays Gashouse Mary McGovern, the owner of a dance hall who once again steals the show when she leads a posse of local townswomen to the jail in order to free Cagney's character. *Variety* (August 26, 1943) said, "Fascinating are the scenes in Gashouse Mary's place — she has always run a decent house — when the tramp reporter comes to her to enlist aid in unseating the grafting politician. Very decorous are the girls waiting the summons to their appointed chores. Treatment of these scenes is at once candidly daring and inoffensive."

It was around this time that Damon Runyon, a syndicated columnist, described Marjorie Main in the most accurate of ways. He said, "It is difficult to reconcile the name Marjorie with Marjorie Main's appearance, and her manner. She has a dead pan, square shoulders, a stocky build, a voice like a file, and an unhurried aspect ... she has a stride like a section boss. She has bright, squinty eyes. She generally starts off looking as if she never smiled in her life, then suddenly she smiles from her eyes out" (Parish, 1979).

By 1944, Marjorie Main once again took up with her home camp of MGM and Wallace Beery. In *Rationing* (1944) Marjorie plays Iris Tuttle, the postmistress and ration board official of the aptly named Tuttletown. With the plot implication that both Marjorie and Beery once dated, they're thrown together in tough times years later when Beery assists her on the rationing board. Coupled with the fact that her daughter and his son are in love and wish to marry before he heads off to war, it's the same ol' vehicle that enables the twosome to holler and fight for most of the film.

Rationing (1944) gave Marjorie the first opportunity to utilize a clause she had insisted upon putting in her MGM contract — that she not be required to "drink alco-

Marjorie and Wallace Beery hitch a ride in *Rationing* (1944).

holic beverages" in any of her films. For medicinal purposes only, Marjorie agreed to a scene in which her character takes a nip of liquor to alleviate the pain of a toothache. In *The Funsters,* by James Robert Parish and William T. Leonard, Marjorie confessed, "It was such a delightful bit of business."

In real life, Marjorie was openly vocal against the drinking of alcohol, or that's what she lead the public to believe. She maintained that it was a moral passed down to her by her grandmother, who was a founding member of the Woman's Christian Temperance

Union, known as the W.C.T.U. The organization was formed in 1874 by a group of women who firmly believed that the consumption of alcohol was the root of all family and societal problems. They believed that abstinence from hard liquor was the only way to achieve a wholesome world. The organization is still active today.

An MGM publicity still for ***Rationing*** (1944).

Coincidentally, Marjorie once had a close friend who was in danger of losing everything he had because of his drinking problem. She figured she may be able to better help her friend if she really understood his addiction, so she secretly visited an Alcoholics Anonymous meeting without his knowledge. In an *Indianapolis Star* interview (September 18, 1949) Marjorie said that on the way to the meeting she was caught in a heavy rainstorm without an umbrella and was soaked to the bone.

Despite her discomfort, she sat through the meeting until all the nonalcoholics were asked to leave the room. As she was about to leave, the guard at the door took one look at Marjorie and said, "Sit down, ma'am. Don't tell me you're no alcoholic!" He didn't recognize who she was; she just looked like a waterlogged drunk who'd changed her mind about getting sober. Instead of telling him who she was, Marjorie just played along. "I told him that I'd just gotten on the wagon. Finally he let me out," she giggled.

Work-wise, in a small-budget MGM throwaway, Marjorie starred as Muddy, the crooked but lovable mother of two train-robbing sons, played by Paul Langton and Henry Morgan. The film was *Gentle Annie* (1944). In a slight spin on the usual happy ending, Marjorie is shot and killed by the town Sheriff, as is her son (played by Langton). In the meantime, Muddy's other son is rounded up, sent to trial and thrown in jail. Justice is served.

Meet Me in St. Louis (1944) came next, a musical masterpiece starring Judy Garland in a lovable family story surrounding the World's Fair of 1903. Marjorie appeared as Katie, the maid. In *Forties Film Talk,* by Doug McClelland, Lucille Bremer, who plays Rose Smith in the film, remembered back to Marjorie's peculiar on-set habits. "I didn't have much dialogue with Marjorie, who plays the family cook, but it was obvious she was quite a character," she said. "The first day on the set, I sneezed a couple of times, and although she was famous for playing the slovenly Ma Kettle, she was a fanatic about germs. She became hysterical. 'Who is that sneezing?' she kept crying out. 'Who is that person sneezing?' When she'd talk on the phone, she'd wear a little white surgical mask."

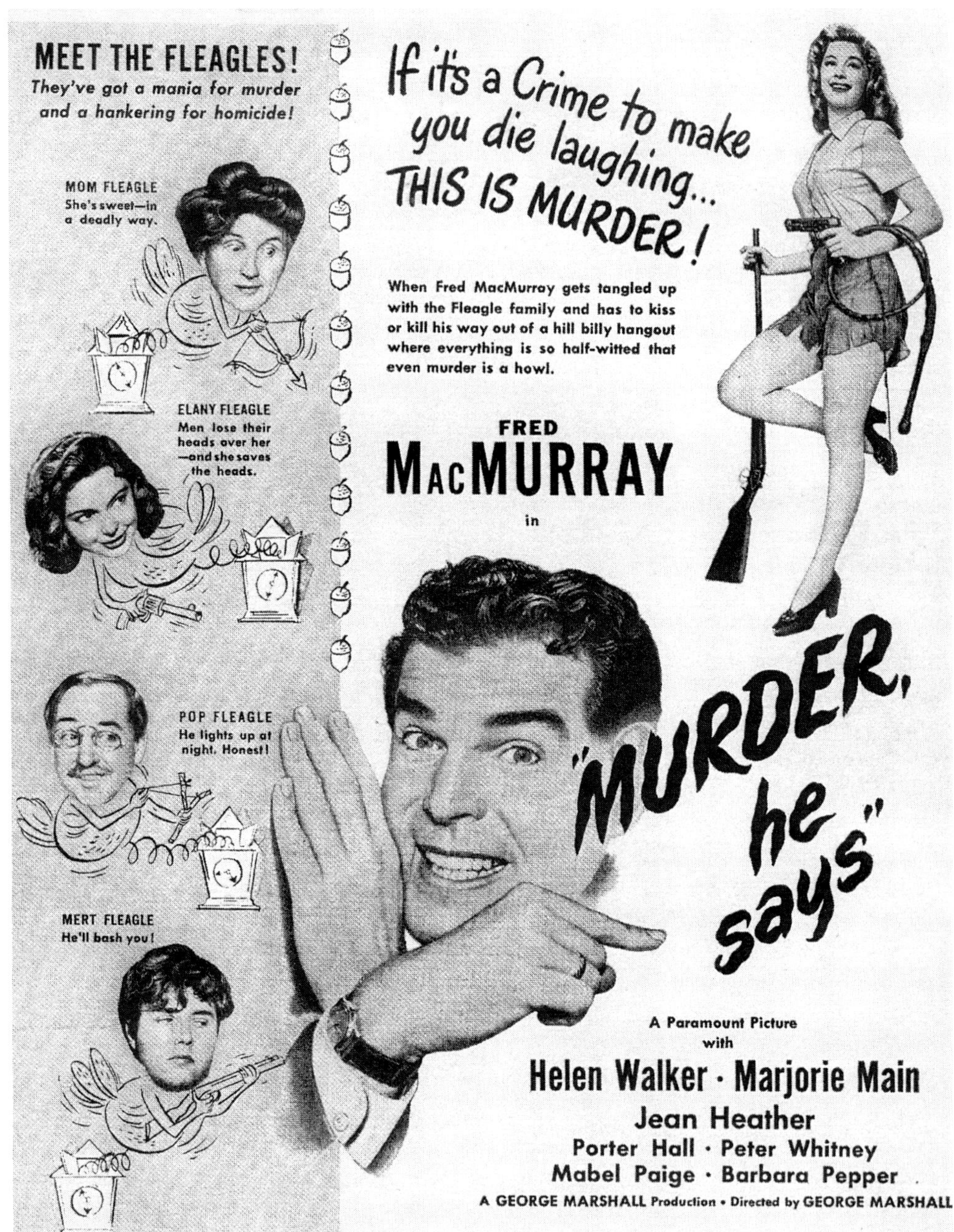

A promotional ad for *Murder, He Says* (1945).

Next up was *Murder, He Says* (1945), a Paramount comedy starring Fred MacMurray, whose job it is to investigate the disappearance of a fellow pollster. When his investigations take him into the seemingly deserted woodland area of Kallikaw City, he meets the insane Fleagle family. Marjorie plays Mamie Johnson, the mother of the half-wit clan with murderous intentions who kills flies with a bull whip and shouts orders to her husband (who builds coffins in the cellar). In this rarely seen comedy classic, Marjorie pulls

Left to right: **Jean Heather, Peter Whitney, Marjorie Main, Porter Hall, and Mabel Paige are the dysfunctional Fleagle family in the black comedy** ***Murder, He Says*** **(1945).**

out all the stops as the hillbilly matriarch, serving her pre–Ma Kettle apprenticeship with comedic ease. Once again, Marjorie received rave reviews from critics and the public turned out in droves to see this rather black comedy of *Arsenic and Old Lace* (1944) proportions.

By the end of 1945, away from the camera Marjorie was bestowed the highest honor by the 96th Infantry Division. Stationed in the Pacific region, they held a competition to decide the most popular contender for "Occupation Girl"—in other words, the girl who best represents the division. In a time where Betty Grable and Rita Hayworth were the popular pinups with soldiers everywhere, Marjorie was an unlikely candidate; yet she won the competition, and her photograph was plastered all over the base with the slogan, "a rough girl for a rough division." (Marjorie received 6,055 votes, nearly half of all cast. Joan Leslie came in second with 5,171, and Yvonne DeCarlo came in third, with 2,426 votes.)

The sergeant of the regiment, Sgt. C. R. Hutcheson, wrote a letter to Marjorie telling her of her win. In it he said, "With a shotgun in one hand and a horsewhip in the other, you are truly the epitome of all that the 96th Division has accomplished." He even vowed to name a street in honor of "their girl" just as soon as they occupied a town. Marjorie loved the letter, and when the Division arrived back in San Francisco in January of 1946, Marjorie surprised them all with a personal appearance on another ship docked at their

Marjorie all dressed up in a scene from *The Harvey Girls* (1946).

arrival point. She even got dressed up (no evening gown this time); Marjorie dressed exactly as the boys described her in their letter — in a cowgirl outfit with a pistol in one hand and a whip in the other!

Career-wise, Marjorie once again teamed up with Judy Garland in *The Harvey Girls* (1946). She plays Sonora Cassidy, the woman in charge of the waitresses along the ever-growing Santa Fe train route in the late 1800s. The rendition "On the Atchison, Topeka and the Santa Fe" is a memorable musical moment, and Marjorie even gets to join in on the singing.

Marjorie played Abbey Banks, the domineering grandmother of the orphaned Margaret O'Brien in *Bad Bascomb* (1946). There was no escaping Wallace Beery as a co-star here, and with Marjorie playing second fiddle to the young O'Brien in the credits, it was a double blow for her.

In an interview for Allan R. Ellenberger's biography on Margaret O'Brien, the former child actress further confirms Marjorie's obsession with cleanliness, both on and off the set. "While we were on location for *Bad Bascomb*, we'd go into town and play the slot machines. Then at night, Marjorie would come in with toilet paper wrapped around her arms to keep the germs and the bugs away." Her bizarre behavior didn't end there.

Margaret O'Brien continues: "When it came time to eat, Marjorie always had a place set at the table for her dead husband [Dr. Krebs] in the log cabin [where she was staying on location], she'd even talk to him during dinner!"

Howard Barnes of *Films in Review* praised Marjorie's next role, coming in the star-studded *Undercurrent* (1946). He said, "Miss Main gets humor out of sequences that are sorely in need of them." Starring alongside Robert Taylor, Robert Mitchum and Katharine Hepburn, Marjorie plays Lucy, the maid who witnesses and meddles in the love triangle involving the three lead players.

The Show Off (1946) was a comedy venture starring Red Skelton as a big-mouthed loser who marries Marjorie's screen daughter against her wishes. It was another formula comedy that looked perfect on paper yet didn't quite carry across to the silver screen. The critics gave *The Show Off* lukewarm reviews, and the public listened. It was officially a flop of the first order. Despite the failure, Marjorie still had widespread public appeal.

It was 1946, and with an impressive 61 films under her belt she was already a veteran of the industry. Now at the peak of her earning curve with MGM, earning a flat $1,000 per week for her services, she was still a far cry from the $15,000 weekly salary that her consistent partner, Wallace Beery, pulled in. His contract stated that he must work at least thirteen weeks within a twelve month period to receive that amount. MGM allowed him to spend his down time elsewhere (something that Louis B. Mayer gladly agreed to—anything to get the often vulgar actor off the lot).

Marjorie's seven-year contract with MGM was now completed. She had been a lucrative player for the studio and they certainly weren't willing to let her go elsewhere now. Her second seven-year contract was swiftly drawn up, and by 1947 Marjorie Main was again secured as an MGM star.

Ironically, just as her initial contract created a new screen team of Marjorie and Wallace Beery, her second contract was the beginning of a whole new partnership, one that she would treasure, and one that the public would lovingly remember—forever.

Ready or not, it was time to meet Ma and Pa Kettle...

FOUR

Which Came First... the Kettles or the Egg?

From the time of its release in 1945, *The Egg and I*, Betty MacDonald's humorous autobiographical account of life on a chicken farm, was a nationwide and worldwide best seller. With numerous printings year after year, it has been labeled an American classic, and rightly so.

Its first printing was in December of 1945; by January of 1947 *The Egg and I* was already into its 24th printing. The tag line on the cover of a pocket book edition dated January 1949 says, "One of the five most popular books of all time, 'The Egg and I' has sold over 1,300,000 copies at the original $2.75 price." As a result, Betty MacDonald, struggling chicken farmer, became an instant millionaire.

The Egg and I tells the story of Betty and Bob MacDonald's "adventurous" life on a run-down chicken farm. It doesn't take long for the couple to realize that raising chickens in rural America, or anywhere for that matter, wasn't such a bright idea after all.

In *Hillbillyland,* a book dedicated to hillbilly-type characters throughout film history, author J.W. Williamson says, "Betty MacDonald seems to have been a very supercilious person; she said nasty things about other people and meant them."

In fairness, maybe the poor woman just needed more sleep. The 4 a.m. outta bed and the 11 p.m. into bed routine was a seven-day-a-week job. There was no running water, no electricity, no day off, and, to top it all off, their modest house was falling down around them. Then, of course, there were still those blasted chickens to tend to.

If Betty didn't laugh at her situation she'd surely cry, and, ironically, it was those daily struggles that made for a best-selling book. *The Egg and I* single-handedly made Betty an international literary success. Those "blasted chickens" paid off, eventually...

Betty's candor and dry wit is prevalent throughout *The Egg and I,* and it was her ability to see the humor in a hopeless situation that made the book so funny. One would expect that a woman thrust into the chicken business would have to at least see the cuteness of a newborn baby chick, but not Betty. In her book *The Egg and I* Betty MacDonald describes her feelings in an aptly named chapter entitled "I Learn to Hate Even Baby Chickens."

"Even baby chickens," she scoffed. "Their sole idea in life is to jam themselves under

The most unlikely lovebirds ever to grace the silver screen — Ma and Pa Kettle.

the brooder and get killed; stuff their little boneheads so far into their drinking fountains they drown, drink cold water and die ... and peck out each other's eyes."

Betty's natural writing ability is evident, but she never intended to be a writer. In her mind she was the wife of a chicken farmer and a mother of two young daughters, Anne and Joan. She just happened to record her daily events (it's a wonder she found the time) in a diary, and it was *that* diary that eventually became *The Egg and I*.

Betty's nosy sister, Mary Bard, just happened to glance at her sister's diary one day while visiting and couldn't put it down. Of course, she was never supposed to pick it up in the first place. But Mary wasn't the shy type; and besides, if it wasn't for her inquisitive personality, Betty would never have been published at all.

Shortly after that visit Betty received word from her sister that she had arranged for a publisher to come to the farm the very next day. The publisher was promised that Betty would present their company with an outline for her new book, a comedy about life on a chicken farm. Betty shrieked in horror as she read her sister's letter. Mary had casually mentioned to a publishing scout at a party she was attending that her sister was writing a book. Mary explained the concept and it sparked his interest. He wanted to see an outline — immediately.

Pa in his sleep shirt and Ma in her sugar sack apron, familiar attire for Ma and Pa Kettle.

Betty hastily worked out an outline against her will, doing it solely to avoid embarrassing her big-mouthed sister. Well, the publisher loved it, and Betty was suddenly a new writer, reworking her diary into *The Egg and I.* She dedicated the book with her trademark sarcastic wit: "To my sister, Mary, who has always believed that I can do anything she puts her mind to."

The MacDonalds' modest ranch at the foot of the rugged Olympic Mountains in the Pacific Northwest was plagued with problems. Yet it was the couple's inexperience in handling each situation, and the amusing way Betty explains the most basic daily events, that motivates the reader to turn page after page with ease.

Despite her success, Betty's life was a tough one. She eventually divorced Bob and remarried. The chicken farm was sold; she spent eight months in a sanitarium to treat an attack of tuberculosis; and eventually she settled on Vashon Island, a brief ferry ride off the coast of Seattle, Washington. Ironically, in each house she owned she always had chickens.

Still seeing the humor in life, and to the public's delight, Betty continued to write about her own life experiences. Her other book, *The Plague and I,* was the story of her battle with TB; *Anybody Can Do Anything* was about her growing up amidst the Depression; and *Onions in the Stew* recounted her life on Vashon Island. Each book became a best seller in its own right.

Not content with writing for adults, her impromptu stories to her own children and their friends inspired her to try her hand at writing children's books too. Far from being a one-book wonder, Betty's "Mrs. Piggle Wiggle" book series is still in print today. More importantly, it's as popular with children today as it was when first published. *Mrs. Piggle Wiggle, Mrs. Piggle Wiggle's Magic, Hello Mrs. Piggle Wiggle, Mrs. Piggle Wiggle's Farm,* and, lastly, *Nancy and Plum* are all best-selling children's classics.

By 1956, after 15 years on Vashon Island, Betty and her second husband Donald moved to Carmel Valley, California. Betty upgraded herself from chickens to cows, and they settled on a cattle ranch. Sadly, it was just two years later that Betty lost her fight with cancer. She was just 49.

The majestic farm on Vashon Island is still standing today, over forty years after Betty MacDonald's death. It's now used as a bed and breakfast inn where, for a little over $100 a night, anyone can stay in the room where Betty MacDonald wrote her books. People flock to the inn from all over the world, eager to connect with Betty and witness the beauty of the Island that inspired her to write her best-selling books. A library is set up within the main house dedicated to Betty and her writing career, and, upon request, the owners of the inn will allow guests to look through the vast collection of memorabilia during their stay.

Without a doubt the highlight of *The Egg and I* is Betty's growing relationship with her hillbilly neighbors, "the Kettles." Throughout her book Betty spoke of her less-than-conventional neighbors often: "I enjoyed the Kettles. They shocked, amused, irritated and comforted me. They were never dull and they were always there."

The Kettles' take-it-as-it-is, be-it-as-it-may lifestyle didn't affect their farming in the least. Pa Kettle wasn't cut out to be a farmer, yet his neglect — both of land and animals— didn't affect the production quality and abundance of their stock; in fact, everything on Kettle soil seemed to thrive with a minimum of care.

Betty was constantly amazed when she set foot on the Kettle farm. When all other farmers were slaves to their land, Pa Kettle would sit and watch his land and animals work for him — he didn't have to lift a finger. Come to think of it, even if he had to work, he wouldn't. He was the laziest of the lazy.

Betty described the Kettle farm in her book: "The Kettle farm consisted of two hundred acres of rich black soil, of which about twenty, including the acre or so rooted by pigs and scratched by chickens, were under cultivation. Their orchard, which was never pruned or sprayed, bore old-fashioned crunchy dark red apples, greengage pears, Italian prunes, russet and Bartlett pears, walnuts, chestnuts, pie cherries, Royal Anne's and Bings. Their thirty-five Holstein cows were never milked on time but always gave milk, apparently from force of habit, their Chester White sows were similarly abused but they bore huge litters which 'Paw' (pronounced with a drawl) sold for $5.00 each piglet as soon as they were weaned." It was as if the Kettles had some magical ring of luck encircling their property line, either that, or they were simply not of this world.

In the case of Ma and Pa Kettle, opposites really did attract. Pa was the skinny, lazy, slow drawling dreamer. Much of Pa's day would be spent smoking his pipe and rocking in his chair, daydreaming about getting around to doing some work. If something was in need of repair he'd casually say, "One of these days, I'll have to fix that, Ma, one of these days." Whats more, if Pa could con someone else into doing the work for him, that was even better!

His derby hat, which he rarely took off, even when in his underwear, hid his bowl inspired haircut that Ma would give to all the male Kettles. His knack for "borrowing" from his neighbors was his way of getting anything he could for free, and meant never having to give it back. He wasn't mean, just smart! Anything he had he'd gladly lend in return, only problem was Pa never had much worth lending and whatever he had was someone else's anyway.

Grrrrrrr ... whatever you say, Marjorie!

In *The Egg and I* Betty explains, "The flour, chicken feed, eggs, bacon, coffee, butter, cheese, sugar, salt, hay and kerosene which the Kettles 'borrowed' from us, placed end to end, would have reached Kansas City. What they'd already borrowed from the rest of the farmers in the mountains would have reached Kansas City to New York and back to the coast."

Still, Betty was fully aware of Pa's shrewd behavior. He knew he could rely on the good nature of the surrounding community; and with the nearest supply store more than seventeen miles away, no one could ever refuse his requests. In the end, everyone just wrote Pa off as a tax deduction. His manners were impeccable. "Much obliged," he'd drawl as he happily took home his "borrowed" goods. It's often stated that Pa Kettle never worked a day in his life, yet in reality, "borrowing" was his job and he was mighty good at it, too.

If he cared to listen to some music he wouldn't get up to turn on the radio; no, that required too much work. He'd simply bang his chair down on the floor and on it would go. Miraculously, the radio always started with the same song, a fast-paced number that he'd usually change to a softer, more relaxing tune by giving his chair another whack on the floor. It worked every time.

And then there was Ma, with a laundry list of her own idiosyncrasies. Her fly-away hair hadn't been cut in years; she didn't see a need to cut it if you could just as easily tie it up. A loose bun would contain most of it, and any stray strand that dare come loose would be brushed aside with the swipe of her hand. After spending a day in the kitchen cooking for her brood, she'd stand on her lopsided porch, hands on hips, and holler for her clan of 15 children to "Come an' git it!"

She was the hard working leader of the family, stocky, boorish and always on the

Title card for ***The Egg and I*** (1947).

move. Her dowdy house dress was used as a napkin and towel, with any dirt, dust or food instantly wiped from her hands to her ample bosom and stomach. The stains on her dress would be a mark and reminder of how hard she'd worked that day, something to be proud of. It wasn't beyond her to reach under that dress and adjust whatever she needed to adjust, or scratch whatever she needed to scratch, either. The real Ma's motto was, "I itch, so I scratch, so what!" (MacDonald, 1945).

Not surprisingly, the success of *The Egg and I* in book form piqued the interest of several major movie studios. In the end, Universal Studios won the battle for the screen rights, paying Betty MacDonald $100,000 for the exclusive use of her best-selling story. Fred MacMurray and Claudette Colbert portray newlywed city folk coming to terms with life on a chicken farm, and all that it has to offer ... and not offer...

Betty MacDonald's brash description of the "real Kettles" was tempered for their onscreen counterparts. Some of Ma's questionable character traits, and particularly her use of inappropriate language, was cut altogether. After all, these were to be goodhearted family films, so there was to be no cursing — that was a given. The strongest words used in the film version were "gol-dang buzzard" and "dastard!"

As previously mentioned, the "real" Ma Kettle scratched; but the censors were strict, and allowing Marjorie to continue that habit on film would be crossing the taboo line.

But Marjorie was all for it, and she explained her reasoning to the *Indianapolis Star* (April 20, 1947): "It's a hot summer day in the mountains. Ma has been slaving all day in a steaming kitchen to provide food for her hungry brood. She isn't sweating, she's perspiring, and dogs and chickens have the run of the house. Naturally she would scratch. I asked the director to at least let me try it and it became a casual, natural action which couldn't possibly give offense to anyone. And the scratch stayed in the picture."

It was extraordinary to think of this mismatched pair being affectionate enough to have conceived 15 children. Not only that, but the "real 'Paw' Kettle" delivered each and every baby himself. Perhaps Pa's laziness was warranted — he was just plain exhausted from his studly endeavors.

Another feature from the book which disappeared for censorship reasons was the doorless outhouse. In a UI production report (January 14, 1946), Claudette Colbert was outspoken in her criticism of the censorial elimination, saying, "It's the silliest thing I ever heard of. One third of the nation has outdoor sanitary conveniences. How can anyone's morals be jeopardized by an architectural actuality familiar to every man, woman and child?!"

Aside from the elimination of the doorless outhouse and the real Ma Kettle's colorful language, the script adhered relatively closely to Betty MacDonald's tale of life on a chicken farm. Of course, no chicken farm is complete without chickens, and, not surprisingly, *The Egg and I* (1947) had lots of 'em!

A UI production report (January 16, 1946) stated that 5000 white leghorn hens were employed for atmosphere, which resulted in close to 2000 dozen eggs. Those which met with the Department of Agriculture's Grade AA specifications were packaged in promotional cartons (promotion for the film was commonly referred to as "Eggsploitation") and sold at the Farmer's Market by studio starlets acting as salesgirls. The money raised was donated to the Braille Institute of America.

In addition to the stock standard background hens, there were a handful of specially trained hens which were taught to faithfully follow Percy wherever he goes in the story. Five hens were trained by David Twiford, who stated in a UI production report (January 14, 1946) that "A hen is just about the stupidest thing in creation and can absorb just so much training."

According to Twiford, an overworked hen is prone to suffer from a complete nervous breakdown, which became routine before the picture was finished. As fast as one hen collapsed from the strain, a replacement went in. The ailing hen received the same treatment for a breakdown as a human — plenty of rest and quiet, a light diet, no excitement and no worrying about business. Two days' rest to a hen is equivalent to a year for a human, so all five hens finished the picture as good as new.

Aside from Percy's pet hen, the picture's other trained animal performer of the picture was "Sport," the "world's most cowardly dog." In the film, "Sport" is owned by Betty and Bob; however, real life owner and trainer Henry East rescued "Banjo" (his real name), a six-year-old English Setter, from a pound the year before production began. According to East, Banjo didn't know a single trick up until six weeks before he was due to hit the Universal International lot, which goes against that old adage, "you can't teach an old dog new tricks!"

The county fair sequence of the picture was staged on the studio back lot and on sound stages, and required the complete creation of livestock, poultry, swine, preserve and quilting exhibits. Many of the prize Herefords in the show arena belonged to

Marjorie in one of her classic "I have an idea" poses.

Hollywood personalities, such as Joel McCrea, Victor McLaglen, Jack Haley, Walter Brennan, Bing Crosby and Bob Burns.

A UI production report (January 14, 1946) states, "This is the story of 'Betty and Bob,' starry-eyed honeymooners who try to wrest a living from mountain wilderness by poultry ranching and learn the hard way that humble, domesticated fowl called chicken is one of nature's most unpredictable and cantankerous creations. The book, in which the glories of the simple life are hilariously debunked, sold over 1 million copies, was condensed in *Reader's Digest*, was the top item in the nation's lending libraries for more than a year, giving it a readership guesstimated by orthodox formula of some 25,000,000 persons."

The set constructed by the studio to represent the farm that inspired Betty MacDonald to write her best-selling story was a classic example of movie magic. Said to be the largest intramural, landscaped interior ever built, it occupied more than 40,000 square feet of space on the studio's largest sound stage, and required some 11,000 man hours of labor for construction of the dozen buildings, which were finished in both exterior and interior detail.

The farmhouse, built as closely as possible to Betty MacDonald's description and photographs, underwent the same metamorphosis in the picture that it did in her book. Some 15,000 square feet of artificial cobwebs were spun through the rooms of the house to initially give the farm that run-down look. It was the biggest web-spinning job at the studio since *The Phantom of the Opera* (1925) and was the first time the new acrylic plastic compound, which has replaced latex, was used. The old latex webs had the fault of excess verisimilitude, and became fouled up with deluded spiders. The new substance was insect repellent, and not one visiting arachnid took up residence while the picture was under way.

After the lapse of one on-screen year, the house is seen as it would look if a couple of ambitious renovators like Betty and Bob MacDonald had put a lot of elbow grease into making it habitable. It's painted outside, refurbished inside, and the shabby furniture is rebuilt and repaired. Home sweet home!

For the climax of the picture, the back lot replica of the ranch, with the exception

It takes a whole pig to feed 15 hungry children — just another day in the life of Ma Kettle.

of the main house, was burned in a spectacular forest fire. The fire was started by the special effects crew at sundown and raged until sunrise on a cold winter night, during which Claudette Colbert and Fred MacMurray both suffered frostbite while playing a scene ringed in by towering flames leaping more than 150 feet into the sky. An airline pilot reported seeing the flames at Ventura, some 50 miles away, which was 10 miles farther than the claim made by Selznick for the burning of Atlanta in *Gone with the Wind* (1939). Not surprisingly, the Los Angeles, Burbank and Glendale fire departments received over 100 calls from concerned citizens kept awake by the glow in the skies.

Willis Cook, the special effects man in charge of the blaze, came up with some staggering statistics, revealing that in a 12-hour period the following went up in smoke, literally: three acres of pine forest; 90,000 pounds of Flame (a bottled gas with a base of jellied petroleum); 475 bales of excelsior; 25,000 cubic feet of assorted kindling wood and scrap lumber; 500 gallons of gasoline; and 300 magnesium flares.

Five cameras, four of which were operated by remote control, recorded the spectacle. The fire burned away all the outbuildings on the ranch, which took three months to build and were in full operation for the six weeks of shooting. A barn, pigsty, and five chicken houses, which had been loaded with excelsior and saturated with gasoline, disappeared in a matter of minutes.

The studio's investment paid off. Audiences flocked to see *The Egg and I*, and with overall ticket sales reaching over $5 million in the United States and Canada alone, it wasn't long before "The Kettles" became a franchise of their own.

Marjorie did a slew of promotional work for the film. She attended previews, gave interviews and made public appearances all across the country. Her biggest and most enjoyable publicity stunt was traveling back to her beloved home state of Indiana to sell tickets to the first showing one Saturday afternoon. Marjorie thought nothing of going right on into the sales booth to sell tickets to the show. She played a minor part in a film with two star performers, Fred MacMurray and Claudette Colbert, but Marjorie was confident that Ma and Pa Kettle were just as important in making the film a success. Selling tickets was her connection with the people, the public, and that's what she loved most of all.

Lippincott Publishers, in connection with Universal International, thought up a whacky promotional idea to tie the book and the upcoming movie together. Jim Moran, a "professional screwball," was given the task of sitting on an ostrich egg until it hatched, while reading a copy of *The Egg and I*. Though it's unknown if he managed to hatch the egg, Moran's egg-sitting certainly generated a lot of publicity, and people everywhere were talking about the crazy stunt. As a result, book sales surged and the movie was a box-office success.

Years later, when noted film historian Boze Hadleigh (1994) asked Marjorie how she liked working with Claudette Colbert, Marjorie answered, "She was very grand."

Hadleigh questioned her about her response: "Very grand?" he asked.

"She thought so," Marjorie added dryly. Her recollections of Fred MacMurray weren't much better, as she remembered him "lacking warmth."

Despite Marjorie's characterization of Claudette Colbert, the role of Betty MacDonald was far from glamorous. The peak of Claudette's "deglamorization" came with a stint in the pig pen with "Cleopatra," a 300-pound black Tamarack sow. Though the studio used hot water in making the mud for the pigsty, it was still a messy and smelly business.

The mud was sprinkled with powdered fish meal to keep "Cleopatra" interested, and the smell, according to Claudette, did in no way resemble Chanel No. 5! Despite the foul odor and other discomforts, Claudette insisted on staying in the mud between takes. In a UI production report (January 16, 1946), she said, "If I get out, I get cold, so it's best if I just stay in here until they finish the sequence." She reported that after five steam baths, her husband, Dr. Joel Pressman, finally allowed her to enter their living room that evening.

In addition to spending the better part of an afternoon in Cleopatra's mud bath, Claudette was required to chop wood, shingle roofs, haul water from a well, plow, trim trees, and feed and water chickens, cows, goats, sheep, a dog and a horse. By the time filming had finished, Claudette had suffered a bruised shin, a wrenched shoulder, a stubbed toe, a burnt arm and scattered bruises on various parts of her body.

Not surprisingly, some of those bruises came from the ten tumbles she took from a barn roof. The script called for her to fall from the roof into a watering trough. Claudette performed the first and last parts of the fall herself. From the edge of the roof, where she hung precariously, she dropped onto a pile of mattresses, piled five deep. Six rehearsals and four camera takes later it was deemed perfect by director Chester Erskine.

For the last part of the fall, Claudette rolled off a platform into a trough, with her arms and legs in the air. This required only one take. The middle part of the fall was performed by a professional.

Fred MacMurray fared a little better in the injury department; though ironically, his most serious injury was caused by the hand of Claudette! In the scene where Betty (Claudette Colbert) discovers her husband Bob (Fred MacMurray) flirting with their pretty neighbor Harriett (Louise Allbritton), the script calls for Betty (Claudette Colbert) to take off her shoe and hurl it at her husband.

Claudette underestimated her aim, and her sharp heel punctured a small artery on Fred's scalp. He didn't realize he had been nicked until blood ran down his jowls and onto his white shirt. While he was swiftly attended to at the studio hospital, a sponge rubber heel was hurriedly substituted for the real thing.

In her book, Betty MacDonald gave life to her oven, which she aptly named "Stove." The iron tyrant of the kitchen seemed to have a mind of its own, and (aside from cartoons) this was the first time an inanimate object had been given a distinct personality. A UI production report (January 15, 1946) stated that special effects technicians ingeniously animated "Stove" to perform according to specifications lifted from the book.

Betty MacDonald wrote of "Stove" spitting soot, snarling, clanking, and puffing at her when she tried to win his friendship and cooperation. "Stove," with his insatiable appetite for wood and water, became an evil character whose perverse personality was a blend of irritant and menace. In the movie version, "Stove" was brought to life and performed all his tricks through controls salvaged from the cocking and recoil mechanisms of .50 caliber airplane machine guns.

Marjorie was nominated for an Academy Award (surprisingly, the only time in her career) for "Best Supporting Actress" in *The Egg and I;* however she lost to Celeste Holm for her role in *Gentleman's Agreement* (1947).

The success of *The Egg and I* film created a television spin-off of the same name. The series ran from 1951 to 1952. Despite its lack of success, it goes into the record books as the first ever television comedy series to hit American living rooms. Pat Kirkland played Betty MacDonald, Bob Craven played Bob MacDonald, and Doris Rich and Frank Tweddell played the parts of Ma and Pa Kettle.

Never content with being idle, and without much choice now that MGM was profiting from her recent success in *The Egg and I,* Marjorie was again loaned out to Universal, this time teaming up with Abbott and Costello for *The Wistful Widow of Wagon Gap* (1947).

Marjorie plays Widow Hawkins, a woman left husbandless thanks to clumsy Lou Costello accidentally killing him. Since the local law states, "He who kills a husband becomes the guardian of his wife and children," Lou becomes the reluctant guardian to Mrs. Hawkins and her brood of seven out-of-control children. Working on her farm during the day and at the town saloon at night, Lou does his best to pay off his debt to society, along with the debts that Mr. Hawkins left behind.

Incidentally, this plot line was actually based on a once-valid Montana law. Back in the 1880s any man who killed another man was solely responsible for the welfare and support of the victim's family. Since broods of children were common in those days, this penalty for murder was an effective way to keep the crime rate to a minimum. Murder was just too darned expensive!

The year 1947 was good for Marjorie. *The Egg and I* was Universal International's highest grossing film of the decade. What's more, it came in at eighth place on 1947's overall

Marjorie looks perfectly capable of taking care of herself in this photograph; however, when Lou Costello accidentally shoots and kills her husband in *The Wistful Widow of Wagon Gap* (1947), he's made to take care of her and her wild brood until she remarries.

list of top money earners. The studio's next best feature was *The Wistful Widow of Wagon Gap,* ranking at a respectable fifty-three on the overall list of top films for that year. Is it any surprise that both productions starred Marjorie?

Just as her hectic work schedule seemed to be winding down, Universal International was busy penning the first exclusive Ma and Pa Kettle film. Before long, Marjorie and Percy Kilbride would revamp their roles as the hillbillies with hearts of gold. But for now they'd reappear together in the comedic romp *Feudin' Fussin' and A-Fightin'* (1948).

Penny Edwards looks on as Marjorie kidnaps Donald O'Connor, intent on forcing the speedy medicine salesman into representing their town in the annual foot race in *Feudin', Fussin', and A-Fightin'* (1948).

Marjorie plays Maribel Matthews, mayor of the town of Rimrock. Percy plays her political assistant, and Donald O'Connor plays the bumbling salesman Wilbur McMurty. This musical comedy marks the first time we see Donald O'Connor dance up a wall, a credit often given to him for *Singin' in the Rain* (1952), released four years after this film.

Universal International had now arranged to pay Betty MacDonald an extra $10,000 per film for the exclusive use her characters Ma and Pa Kettle. The studio was now free and clear to place Ma and Pa Kettle into any situation they pleased, which in turn placed huge sums of money into the studio's pockets.

In an April 20, 1947, interview with the *Indianapolis Star*, Marjorie explained how she transformed herself into Ma Kettle: "I read the script [*The Egg and I*] as well as the book [*The Egg and I*] a dozen times. I designed Ma's clothes and bought the materials for them myself in cheap Los Angeles department stores. I picked up hats from the studio's wardrobe department and altered them to fit Ma's appearance. I figured out the owl nest hairdo, calling on my girlhood memories of hundreds of overworked farm wives back home in Indiana. And then the script gave me a grand entrance."

But despite her enthusiasm, Marjorie was still stuck in her seven-year contract with

MGM. None of the profits from the Kettle film series would be seen by her, and there were no bonuses as a thank you for her efforts. She continued to receive her stock standard weekly salary, and, in return, she modestly saved an entire studio empire from extinction.

FIVE

The Men Behind the Magic

March 15, 1915, was an historic day in film history. It was the day that forty-eight-year-old German immigrant Carl Laemmle (later known affectionately as "Uncle Carl") opened the gates to Universal City. Those gates were the entrance to the world's first fully self-contained lot for making motion pictures. Some 90 years have passed since that monumental day, and despite numerous rocky patches and a few company mergers along the way, Universal Studios is still with us. What's more, it's bigger, better and stronger than it ever was.

Back in those early days of silent filmmaking, Universal Pictures (as it was called then) was best known for their action-packed westerns, their side-splitting comedies and their edge-of-your-seat horror films. They were not particularly fond of, nor good at, making dramas. But some two decades down the road from their inaugural year, it was that very genre that would almost close their doors—for good.

Laemmle was by all accounts a passive, generous man not nearly as highly strung as most studio bosses of the time. He dearly wanted to share his love of filmmaking with the public, so he hatched a scheme whereby for 25 cents a ticket could be bought to gain access to the studio lot. For the first time ever the public could witness the art of moviemaking firsthand.

This novel tour lasted for almost 15 years; however, by the late 1920s the onset of "talkies" brought the popular studio tours to a standstill. Producers and directors could no longer work with the chatter and noise of strangers and excited fans on their sets. Sound films meant quiet sets, and quiet sets meant no more studio tours.

It wasn't until 1961 that the public could mingle with the stars again. Grey Line Bus Tours signed an exclusive deal with the studio to set up a tour called "Dine with the Stars." The bus driver would take movie fans on a driving tour of the lot, complete with commentary. The tour would end with lunch in the studio commissary right alongside the actors. Not surprisingly, the actors quickly learned to avoid eating at the time the tour bus was out front.

Three years later, by July of 1964, the studio opened its gates for a different kind of tour. For $6.50, two adults and one child could take a leisurely tour of the lot on the "Glamour Tram." The studio purchased two luxury trams and employed two drivers and two guides to cover the tours. Needless to say, the popularity of the tour grew so quickly that the studio needed to buy more trams, and fast!

Of course, that novel idea of Universal founder Carl Laemmle to open his studio to the people in 1915 has now grown into one of the most popular, most exciting tourist attractions/theme parks in the world. Universal Studios not only operates its original theme park in California, but in recent years exact replicas of the park have opened in Florida, Spain and Japan.

It's somewhat sad to think that a man, an immigrant, with the vision and courage to open his own movie studio in his adopted country was eventually forced out of the organization that he so lovingly created. But that's exactly what happened.

On April 22, 1936, 500 members of the film community filled the "Fiesta Room" of the Ambassador Hotel to honor "Uncle Carl" at an elaborate testimonial dinner. The crowd was a who's who of Hollywood royalty. In attendance were the brothers Cohn, William Wyler, D.W. Griffith, Jerome Kern, Irene Dunne, John Huston, Max Factor, Bela Lugosi, Oscar Hammerstein, Sigmund Romberg, Robert Young, Merle Oberon, David Niven and Louise Rainer, just to name a few. In *City of Dreams*, by Bernard F. Dick, it was reported that Irving Thalberg served as the master of ceremonies. He publicly praised Carl as "a man who never stole a star, director or player from another company in all the years of operation."

Carl Laemmle left that evening with a smile, a warm heart, a scroll signed by members of the Producers Association, an inlaid walking stick, and an ink stand in the form of the Universal studio—*his* studio—gates.

On August 29, 1936, Universal's creditors took over the studio for $4.5 million. Some fifteen hundred invited guests helped celebrate the transfer of power. Charles R. Rogers became the head of production, and J. Cheever Cowdin took over as president. The takeover was largely due to the studio's 1935/36 combined loss of $1.098 million.

Carl Laemmle was a businessman. He understood that a business needed to make money in order to survive. He begged, borrowed and reshuffled (while he was still in control) in order to save his company from imminent disaster. He simply ran out of time. As a businessman, he understood the take-over. As a man, he was crushed.

On September 24, 1939, just three years after his forced retirement, "Uncle Carl" died of a heart attack at his Benedict Canyon Drive home. Some say he died of a broken heart. He was 72 years old. Five minutes of silence was observed at all movie studios across the country.

Shortly after the 1936 reshuffle, the goody-two-shoes quality of the films churned out by Universal's young star player, Deanna Durbin, helped pull the studio back from their first run-in with bankruptcy. *Three Smart Girls* (1936) featured fourteen-year-old Deanna Durbin's debut performance, and thanks to the low production cost of just over $200,000, the film's profits of $1.6 million made the new studio bosses very happy indeed.

Over the course of the next decade, and with another 21 box office hits to her name, it was fresh-faced Deanna Durbin who helped keep the studio afloat. It was a financial burden that would fall onto the shoulders of future Universal performers well into the latter part of the 1950s. The future well-being of the studio rested on the financial success of each new film release. Failure was not an option!

Author Bernard F. Dick (1997) gives his opinion as to why the studio fell on hard times: "Universal's films needed a longer time to find acceptance—and that acceptance would not always come from moviegoers but from film scholars, who rarely acclaim a film at the time of its release. The typical Hollywood chestnut is roasted into mealiness;

Universal's chestnuts needed more time to burst open, which did not always coincide with their release dates."

In 1946, a decade after the ousting of "Uncle Carl," Universal Pictures merged with International Pictures. Together they became Universal International. Despite the name change and ongoing financial troubles, the studio's legacy included some of the most influential films in Hollywood history, such as *The Hunchback of Notre Dame* (1923), *The Phantom of the Opera* (1925), and *All Quiet on the Western Front* (1930). Their horror characters, Dracula, the Mummy, the Wolf Man, the Invisible Man, and, of course, the Frankenstein Monster were all Universal monsters who went on to make back-to-back films and mega-dollars for the studio.

It's not often we see Marjorie laughing. After all, it's her job to make *us* laugh!

Eventually, Abbott and Costello ran into the Universal monsters, and the combination of horror and comedy worked a treat with audiences. In contrast, Ma and Pa Kettle were always the main stars of their films; the studio didn't feel the need to have Pa meet up with Frankenstein or Dracula.

The Kettles' support came from behind the camera in the form of six gifted men — Charles Lamont, Edward Sedgwick, Charles Barton, Leonard Goldstein, Lee Sholem and Virgil W. Vogel. Together, they were the silent geniuses.

Leonard Goldstein was a mid-forties, enthusiastic executive producer with Universal International Studios when he got the idea to make Ma and Pa Kettle the star attractions in their very own film series. Goldstein had served as an executive producer on *The Egg and I* (1947), and it was his personal observations of audience reactions to the Kettles in that film that switched a light bulb on in his head.

A more subdued demeanor.

Sitting in a darkened theater with only the light from the screen to illuminate the people around him, Goldstein went from one cinema to another, anonymously observing one common factor. In an interview conducted for a UI production report (October 8, 1949), he said, "I noticed something intriguing at the previews of 'The Egg and I.' Every time the Kettles appeared on the screen, the audiences would perk up and lean forward in their seats. Main and Kilbride were stealing this picture and it suddenly occurred to me. Why not a low budget series based on the Kettles?"

How's this? Marjorie poses for yet another wardrobe test.

As a thank you for giving the studio the idea for the series, Goldstein was awarded the lucrative job of producer on the newly penned Kettle adventures. The studio recognized his enthusiasm for the series and the characters, and in their eyes there was no one better suited for the job.

Leonard Goldstein was born in Bisbee, Arizona, in 1903, and after completing his education in Los Angeles, California, he worked as booking agent for the Million Dollar and Metropolitan theaters in Los Angeles. By 1928 he made the move east to New York City. Once there he floated between jobs until landing a secure position as an executive assistant to Ben Goetz at Consolidated Film Industries. After three years (1933–1936) he left this position to work for producer George Hirliman. Goldstein was to be his general manager. It was a big step up from his previous position of executive assistant.

Goldstein earned his first screen credit at the age of 33, as associate producer on *Daniel Boone* (RKO, 1936). He quickly advanced his career, moving on to become personal assistant to Damon Runyan and then production executive with Columbia Pictures.

By 1946, just as International Pictures merged with Universal to become Universal International, Goldstein became executive producer and eventually producer of over 30 films with the new company. Historically, he's best known for his work on the Ma and Pa Kettle film series, as well as the equally popular, Francis the Talking Mule series.

By 1952, Goldstein resigned from Universal International in favor of working for rival studio 20th Century–Fox. But, after completing his contract with Fox, he left the studio to form his own independent film company with his twin brother, Robert.

Leonard Goldstein's life and career was tragically cut short when he died as a result of heart failure in 1954 at the age of 51. In his half-life he did more for film history than other producers accomplished with an entire career's worth of opportunities. In hindsight, he was so prolific, so innovative toward the latter part of the 1940s, it was as if he knew he was living and working on borrowed time.

Charles Fred Lamont started out as an actor in 1919 but quickly moved behind the camera three years later. In the early days he was given the tag "the boy director" because of his baby-faced appearance. It was a name that he desperately tried to shake by gluing on a fake moustache each morning before reporting to work.

By the looks of her, Marjorie has just seen the latest Kettle picture.

By 1922 Lamont was directing one- and two-reel comedies for the likes of Mack Sennett and Al Christie. In fact, he is widely credited for discovering one of the best-loved child actors in film history—the little girl with the curls, Shirley Temple. While scouting dance halls for some children to put in the background of one of his shorts, he met little five-year-old Shirley. Realizing she was far too cute and far too talented to consign to the background, he went home and wrote a special song and dance sequence just for her. The rest, as they say, is history.

By the mid–1930s Lamont began directing features for various studios until he finally secured a permanent position with Universal Pictures in the latter part of that same decade. He gave the best sixteen years of his life to the studio, becoming one of the most prolific American directors of our time.

During his career, Charles Lamont gave direction to some of the most influential actors and acts in Hollywood history, including Buster Keaton, Shirley Temple, Charley Chase, Harry Langdon, Polly Moran, the Three Stooges, and Abbott and Costello. He was also the most influential director on the Ma and Pa Kettle film series. He directed five of the nine Kettle films. Charles Fred Lamont succumbed to pneumonia on September 12, 1993. He was 98 years old.

The other Charles, Charles Barton, also started his career as an actor. Although uncredited for his modest performance, he can clearly be seen as the soldier flirting with Clara Bow in *Wings* (1927). *The County Fair* (1920) and *Beau Geste* (1939) rounded out his three-film acting career; not unlike Charles Lamont, Charles Barton felt more comfortable behind the camera. Once there he not only made his mark in film, but in television as well, with his name becoming synonymous with some of the most highly rated sitcoms in small-screen history.

Barton directed Marjorie in two of her most popular films, *The Wistful Widow of Wagon Gap* (1947) and *Ma and Pa Kettle at the Fair* (1952). He was also at the helm for many of the successful Abbott and Costello features, too. As if that wasn't enough, Barton directed such legendary television shows as *Amos 'n' Andy* (1951), *Leave It to Beaver* (1957), *Zorro* (1957), *Dennis the Menace* (1959), *Hazel* (1961), *McHale's Navy* (1962), *Petticoat Junction* (1963), *The Munsters* (1964) and, last but not least, *Family Affair* (1966). He died on December 5, 1981, as a result of heart failure. He was 79 years old.

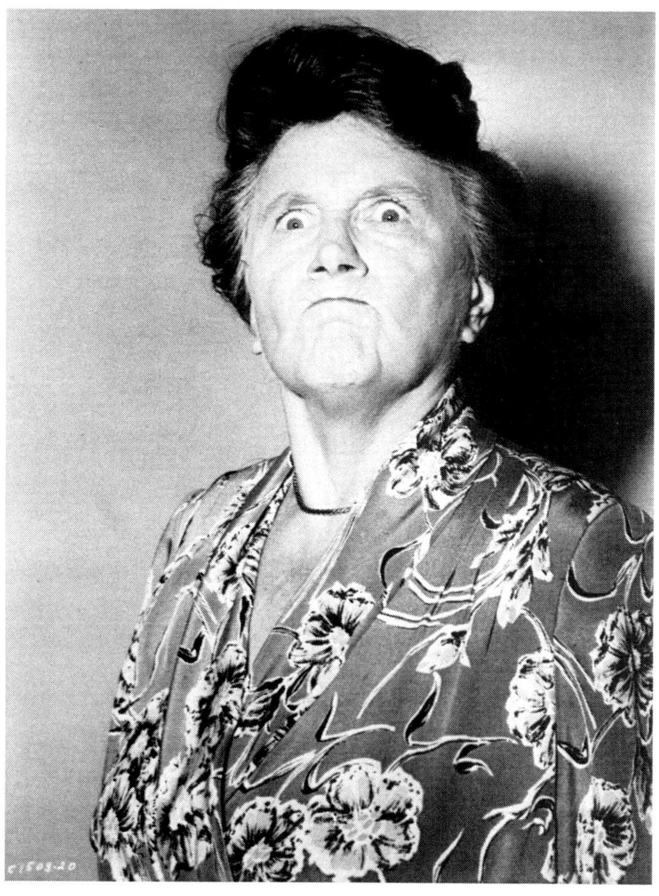

Don't mess with Ma Kettle!

Noted silent and early sound director Edward Sedgwick jumped in to direct *Ma and Pa Kettle Back on the Farm* (1951); while Lee "Roll 'em" Sholem directed Percy Kilbride's last film, *Ma and Pa Kettle at Waikiki* (1955). In directing over 1000 shows (both film and television) within his 40-year career, Sholem was known for never having gone over schedule, ever. It's a perfect record unsurpassed by anyone else in the industry. He died on August 12, 2000 at the age of 87.

Last but by no means least was Virgil W. Vogel. After making a lengthy career at Universal Pictures as editor, he pressured studio bosses into letting him try his hand at directing. Hoping to "shut him up," they threw him a script called *The Mole People* (1956) and sent him on his way. After the unlikely success of such a film, Vogel moved from the editing room to the director's chair permanently. His second directorial effort came on the last Kettle feature, *The Kettles on Old MacDonald's Farm* (1957).

Despite the final film being the weakest of the series, it's unfair to lay all the blame on Vogel. After all, by that time the series was tired; it had simply run out of steam. Sadly, not even Lamont or Barton could have saved this one.

Vogel went on to make his own mark on the small screen, directing a laundry list of shows, including forty nine episodes of *The Big Valley* (1965) and various episodes of *Wagon Train* (1957), *Bonanza* (1959),*The FBI* (1965), *Mission Impossible* (1966), *The Streets of San Francisco* (1972), *Barnaby Jones* (1973), *Police Story* (1973), *The Six Million Dollar Man* (1974), *Police Woman* (1974), *Magnum P.I.* (1980), *Knight Rider* (1982), *Airwolf* (1984), *Miami Vice* (1984) and *Quantum Leap* (1989), just to name a few. His impressive television credentials more than demonstrate his ability as a director, which only goes to prove that a good director cannot make something out of a bad script. And *The Kettles on Old MacDonald's Farm* (1957) was exactly that.

So, after starting his working career in the editing room, Virgil W. Vogel ended up spending forty years behind the camera as director. He reluctantly retired in 1994, dying a little under two years later. He was 76 years old.

Carl Laemmle was the founding father of Universal Pictures, but over a period of close to ten years it was the talent of the six aforementioned men that molded the Kettles into one of the most-loved families in the movies. Together they made history. Together, they were the men behind the magic.

SIX

Ma and Pa Kettle, Inc.

Two years after the box-office success of *The Egg and I* (1947) Ma and Pa Kettle were back on the big screen, and this time *they* were the stars. *Ma and Pa Kettle* (1949), as it was originally titled, is now known as *The Further Adventures of Ma and Pa Kettle* (1949). Because of the varying titles, it often gets referenced as two different films, but in actual fact it is one and the same.

With two additional children, bringing their brood up from 13 to 15, the Kettles must defend their farm after being served with an eviction notice. After Pa wins a new house in a tobacco slogan contest, all of their problems seem to be over; but the Kettles never were ones for modern conveniences, and the new house has every new gadget going. This is where the real problems begin...

Pa admits to entering the contest because each entrant was guaranteed to receive a new tobacco pouch. That's all he wanted; he didn't expect to win. The audience is introduced to several new characters in this installment, including the friendly Indian neighbors Geoduck (Lester Allen) and Crowbar (Chief Yowlachie), willing helpmates to Pa.

Lester Allen was a noted circus performer and veteran of vaudeville, burlesque and the stage. Having appeared in many Paramount shorts from 1932 through 1933, and with a now-certain recurring role in the Kettle Film series, his life and career were cut tragically short. While crossing Ventura Boulevard in the San Fernando Valley on November 6, 1949, he was struck and killed by a car. He was 11 days shy of his 58th birthday. For reasons unknown, his scenes, together with Crowbar's (Chief Yowlachie), were deleted from the next Kettle film, *Ma and Pa Kettle Go to Town* (1950).

Despite the characters of Geoduck and Crowbar appearing in subsequent Kettle films, Chief Yowlachie, the original Crowbar, never played that character again. He was a veteran of 72 films and lived until March 7, 1966; however, it seems *his* portrayal of "Crowbar" died right along with Lester Allen's portrayal of "Geoduck." Teddy Hart, of *Three Men on a Horse* stage fame; Oliver Blake, a former Shakespearean actor; Stan Ross, famed deadpan actor; Victor Potel; and John Berkes all played Pa's bumbling Indian pals throughout the series.

The Further Adventures of Ma and Pa Kettle (1949) revolves around the Kettles struggling to cope with modern conveniences, and it's these "fish out of water" situations that serve as a basis for the laughs in all the Kettle features. A little romance is thrown in when the eldest Kettle son, Tom (Richard Long), marries Kim (Meg Randall).

The film ends with Pa winning yet another contest, opening the door for a second film — if the public took to this one. And take to it they did! The public loved the film, and Universal immediately set to work on writing the second screenplay. The sequel was to be released in 1950, just one year after *The Further Adventures of Ma and Pa Kettle.* It truly was a production line — a very profitable production line that spanned an entire decade.

The promotional poster for *The Further Adventures of Ma and Pa Kettle* (1949), the first solo Kettle caper in the long-running series.

A serious sinus condition, an ailment that Marjorie would suffer her entire life, flared up during filming of *The Further Adventures of Ma and Pa Kettle,* but being the trouper that she was, not a day's shooting was missed because of her illness. Physicians were brought in and she was ordered to take a break, but, knowing how much it would cost the production for her to do so, she asked that a compromise be reached. Marjorie inhaled powdered penicillin at frequent intervals for the duration of the shoot, and as soon as filming had finished she was ordered straight to bed.

It's ironic that two of Universal International's biggest box-office pairs were mismatched and dysfunctional, but completely lovable in their own special way. Abbott and Costello and Ma and Pa Kettle helped see the studio through the 1940s financially; yet, more importantly, they helped see audiences through a decade of war and post-war troubles with a lot of laughs.

It was bad story buying that got Universal into its financial mess in the first place. The studio bought a load of expensive dramatic Broadway plays with thoughts of bringing them all to the silver screen. But, after making two of these plays into film flops, the

A revolving bar is just one of the fancy gadgets featured in the new electronic home that Pa wins for his family in *The Further Adventures of Ma and Pa Kettle* (1949).

studio found itself with a shelf full of dramatic scripts on hand, and a public that didn't care to see any of them — it was imminent financial disaster.

By Christmas of 1940 Universal wasn't about to see in another year. Its 25-year run had seen both success and failure, like all businesses, but this time it needed a miracle to pull them from the brink of collapse. Surprisingly, that miracle came in the form of a tall, derogatory con man and a short, chubby innocent. They were Abbott and Costello, known affectionately to all as Bud and Lou.

Their early films, such as the high-grossing *Buck Privates* (1941) cost just under $200,000 to produce, yet the studio return was over two million. Their stream of 1940s comedy films not only saved Universal from bankruptcy, they made the studio a tidy profit, just as Ma and Pa Kettle would do in the latter part of the same decade.

In the early 1940s, as the country was gripped by war, audiences wanted to forget their troubles and laugh. The heavy dramatic "message" plays that Universal had foolishly purchased were the last things filmgoers wanted to see. For the better part of four decades no dramatic film ever pulled Universal out of trouble; they only got them into it.

Marjorie is all smiles in this promotional photograph for *Big Jack* (1949); in reality, working with Wallace Beery made her miserable.

In 1931 it was the horror classics *Dracula* (1931) and *Frankenstein* (1931) that saved Universal from bankruptcy. In 1936 it was the lavishly produced musical *Show Boat* (1936) that barely kept the studio doors open.

As already stated, Bud and Lou and Ma and Pa Kettle were the next big money-makers; and it was the much loved comedy genre that allowed the studio to continue making movies, period. Drama and Universal just didn't mix, at least not onscreen (the studio certainly had its fair share of drama off-screen). Those dramatic Broadway scripts became *very* expensive doorstops.

The success of the Kettle film and the profits the studio raked in because of it made Marjorie reluctant to continue with the series. Yes, she was under contract, and if she refused to appear in any future Kettle film MGM would put her on indefinite suspension. Both MGM and Universal were profiting greatly from the films; Universal received the bulk of the money, but MGM was getting a nice piece of the pie because Marjorie was its contract player. Her bitterness at receiving her standard salary, with no bonus as a thank you for making the Kettle series a success, caused Marjorie to consider risking her career and taking the suspension as a matter of principle.

In an *Indianapolis Star* interview (March 2, 1969), Marjorie said, "When they sent

Marjorie rushes to the aid of Wallace Beery in *Big Jack* (1949).

me the script for the first 'Ma and Pa Kettle' movie, I turned it down. But, I was under contract with MGM at the time and they told me I had to go to Universal and do it. After the success of that one, the scripts just kept on comin' and I kept on doin' 'em." In the end she concluded, "I would rather make people laugh than anything else," and continued with the series.

As this new chapter began, MGM decided to bring Marjorie back to her home studio for a final pairing with Wallace Beery. Just as the Kettle door opened (to Marjorie's delight), this one was about to close—in more ways than one.

Big Jack (1949) was a box-office flop, and Beery was gravely ill for the duration of the production. Beery made no secret of his dislike for Marjorie; in fact, the *Indianapolis Star* (March 12, 1978) reported that shortly after completion of *Big Jack* he confided to a reporter, "If I have to make another picture with her [Marjorie] I'll have a heart attack!" His prediction came true. A heart attack claimed his life just a few days later.

His sudden death and the decades that passed since did nothing to soften Marjorie's feelings for Beery either. On May 17, 1974, at a lavish 50th Birthday Celebration for her studio, Metro-Goldwyn-Mayer, she forewarned interviewer Army Archer, "Don't you go expecting me to say anything nice about Wallace Beery, because I won't!"

Wallace Beery is buried at the Forest Lawn Memorial Park in Glendale, California.

Before and After: Ma Kettle gets a full day of beauty treatment in New York City in *Ma and Pa Kettle Go to Town* (1950).

His memorial plaque at lot 2086 in the Vale of Memory bears a true copy of his signature, his birth and death dates (1885–1949), and the inscription, "No man is indispensable, but some are irreplaceable."

In *Ma and Pa Kettle Go to Town* (1950) the Kettles leave their farm and take on a group of New York City gangsters. Location shooting at many of New York's famous landmarks meant that the cast and crew were working away from the studio lot for the very first time. With the profits from the first Kettle film being so high, the studio upped the ante on this one. The Kettles left their country home and were introduced to the hustle and bustle of city life. Not just any city — New York City! The film shows that you can take the Kettles out of the country, but you can't take the country out of the Kettles.

Marjorie's makeover scene completely transforms Ma from ugly duckling to elegant swan. Included in her makeover was a new, neater version of her upswept "owl's nest" hairstyle, false eyelashes, cupid-bow lips, and a well-girdled Parisian gown. Pa's expression as he reacts to his normally plain wife dressed up in a designer dress with perfectly groomed hair and false eyelashes is hilarious.

Her new ensemble was certainly a far cry from her familiar house dress. Ma's outfit consisted of a $400 black and white tie-silk gown, $125 Rex hat and $40 Saks shoes. As soon as Marjorie was done in wardrobe, she walked to a full-length mirror to take a peek at her character's new look. She stood there, silent, looking herself up and down from head to toe. The hair and makeup team were anxiously waiting for her to say something, anything. Marjorie was rarely silent. Finally she turned around to face everyone and said three words: "My feet hurt!"

Marjorie graciously accepted the primping as a part of the role, and she hobbled over to the sound stage in her high heels for rehearsals. She blushed crimson red when, at the sight of her, the entire crew gave a collective wolf whistle. Not content with leaving it at that, producer Leonard Goldstein and director Charles Lamont officially proclaimed her, "Miss Glamor Girl of 1949." The set still photographer even offered to take a series of sweater and cheesecake shots. Marjorie took their teasing in stride. After the completion of the scene, a UI production report (January 18, 1949) stated that Marjorie politely asked if she could take the outfit home, "just to be able to walk around the house in it," she said.

The new, glamorous Marjorie must have impressed one male admirer, because every day for two weeks a bouquet of flowers was delivered to her dressing room. No card identified the sender. Marjorie was so curious about the identity of her secret admirer that she checked all of her friends on the studio lot, as well as those away from the studio. None admitted to being the sender of the flowers. Surrounded by the sweet perfume of numerous bouquets, Marjorie smiled and was quoted in a UI production report (April 22, 1953) as saying, "I'm a little old for this sort of thing, but it sure is romantic."

By week three, with the flowers still arriving and Marjorie being no closer to uncovering her admirer's identity, a UI production report (May 12, 1953) stated that she went so far as to engage a private detective to get to the bottom of the situation. "Look, I enjoy receiving flowers as much as the next person, but I'm fed up with this mystery. If the fellow who is sending me these bouquets is too bashful to reveal himself, I mean to force him into the open," she declared.

The first week of flowers from her mystery admirer was flattering; by week two she became slightly annoyed; by week three she was determined to find him once and for all. "I thought maybe it might even be Percy Kilbride who was giving me a bouquet," said Marjorie in an interview with UI (May 16, 1953). "But when the flowers kept coming I knew it was nobody on the picture who was sending 'em. I don't care what it costs me to find out who the sender is. A girl has got to be careful of strange men nowadays." It's not known if Marjorie ever uncovered her mystery man.

The American Mothers' Committee of New York named Ma Kettle honorary screen mother of the year (1950); and, thanks to many other nationwide publicity events, *Ma and Pa Kettle Go to Town* (1950) became a highly anticipated film.

Of course, in the film there's no fancy makeover for Pa. As usual, Percy spends most of his time in his long flannels, thereby probably becoming the actor most likely to appear onscreen in his underwear! It all started with *The Egg and I* (1947), where 270 feet of film was shot with Pa in his "longies." In *The Further Adventures of Ma and Pa Kettle* (1949), some 450 feet of film featured Pa in his unmentionables; and in *Ma and Pa Kettle Go to Town* (1950), over 600 additional feet of film recorded Pa in his "signature outfit."

Percy became known as the best "undressed" actor in the business. In his semi-annual inventory of his professional wardrobe for income tax purposes, Percy listed four ordinary suits of clothes, one derby hat, six pairs of shoes and thirty-two suits of long

An unlikely serenade...

underwear. Thankfully, his underwear (the neck to ankle variety) was personally owned, and used strictly for his portrayal of Pa Kettle. Although distinctly "un-regal" in appearance, Pa Kettle's suits tallied $25 apiece. A New York tailor made the suits to fit Percy's rail-thin frame, and on demand they would be flown air-express whenever needed. Still, it was Percy's underwear that became Pa's "signature" attire.

Amusingly, given the comfort factor of working in his underwear, Percy didn't think to add to his breezy wardrobe when it came time for lunch. He'd just stroll into the Universal Studios commissary and, with every overly-dressed actor's eyes upon him, casually order and eat his lunch. A collective laugh would ring out at the sight of this scrawny, 126-pound, elderly man eating his lunch, stone-faced, in his underwear! No one enjoyed the gag more than Percy; after all, he was in the laugh business, and if he could continue to entertain people on his break from filming, so be it. In reality, Percy Kilbride was a faultless dresser, the polar opposite of Pa Kettle.

The reviews for *Ma and Pa Kettle Go to Town* were favorable, with one publicity release (UI, March 27, 1950) reading as follows: "The new Kettle film has virtually the same cast as the first, co-starring Marjorie Main and Percy Kilbride, with Meg Randall and Richard Long providing the romantic interest and fourteen younger Kettle kids boiling through scene after hilarious scene.

"The story, of stouter thread and swifter pace than the first in the series deals with the Kettles winning a trip to New York after submitting a prize slogan for a cola drink. When a bank robber seeks refuge in the old Kettle shack and decides to serve as baby sitter for the incredible Kettle kids while the elderly couple goes to New York, the fun begins, and it doesn't let up until the film's fadeout.

"The chase for a black bag containing a fortune in stolen money, which the unwitting Pa has been duped into taking to New York for delivery to a pal of the bank robber, has not been matched on the screen, for sock suspense-comedy, in many a day. The entire family and single seaters as well, will get their money's worth out of this latest Kettle laugh-fest."

The humor surrounding *Ma and Pa Kettle Go to Town* wasn't confined to the screen. The film's pressbook (a booklet sent to exhibitors by the studios offering promotional materials and gimmicks) included a number of humorous contest suggestions, a few of which are included here:

Jingle Contest for Box Office Tingle

In the picture, Ma and Pa Kettle win a jingle contest and a trip to New York.... So, shape one of your newspaper or radio sponsorship — or use your lobby and heralds. Invite contestants to complete the following jingles:

"Ma and Pa Kettle" it's clear
Are folks who shed nary a tear
With barrels of fun
For everyone
(Their movies are full of good cheer).
Laughter can cure any ill
For Mary, or Bobby or Bill
"Ma and Pa Go To Town"
And they kill every frown
(Much better than taking a pill).
The Kettles are with us again
Percy Kilbride and Marjorie Main
Just look and compare
You'll find that this pair
(Are sweeter than sweet sugar cane).

Title card for ***Mrs. O'Malley and Mr. Malone*** (1951).

(NOTE: The last line in each jingle was the suggested tag line and served as an example for the creative contestant. The winning entries, along with their own original endings, were to be displayed at the box office, with free tickets to the new Kettle movie as the prize.)

Resemblance Contest

Conduct a contest on your stage by inviting local couples to assume the identity of Ma and Pa Kettle. Prizes, promoted through local merchants, go to the couple whose costume and make up most closely simulates the appearance of the Kettles.

A Loot Hunt Taken Right Out of the Picture

Part of the plot of *Ma and Pa Kettle Go to Town* centers around a black bag filled with loot from a bank robbery. You can use this angle for a citywide stores tie-up, based on the old "treasure hunt stunt." You can refer to it as the "Ma and Pa Kettle Loot Hunt." Place a number of black bags similar to the one used in the picture in the windows of as many stores as you can get to cooperate. The first ten contestants who bring in the complete list of the stores whose window displays the bag are adjudged winners, and given suitable prizes, which you promote from the merchants operating.

Largest Family Gets Baby sitter

Conduct a search to find the local Ma and Pa who have the most children. As their prize, supply a baby-sitter so that "Ma and Pa may go to town." Sitter may be theater manager or other local dignitary, such as mayor, police chief, etc....

Ma and Pa Kettle Go to Town was such a box-office success that Universal planned to release one Kettle film each and every year. In between playing Ma, Marjorie would go back to playing the mother or the maid in other productions. Her popularity as Ma Kettle made her an audience draw card, as it seemed that anything with Marjorie was good for a lot of laughs—guaranteed.

In *Summer Stock* (1950) Marjorie plays Esme, the vigilant maid at Judy Garland's Connecticut farm. This lavish MGM musical, with a dash of comedy thrown in, was stock MGM formula for the day, but with Judy Garland singing, and Marjorie doing her bit to make the audience laugh, *Summer Stock* was a box-office success.

In trying to muster a successful film series of their own, MGM decided to try its hand at putting Marjorie into a comedic whodunit entitled *Mrs. O'Malley and Mr. Malone* (1951). Marjorie plays a housewife, Mrs. O'Malley, who wins a radio contest and boards a train East in order to collect her prize. At the Chicago stop, Mr. Malone (James Whitmore), a criminal lawyer, boards the train; he's on the trail of some crooks who have knowledge of some missing cash. Mrs. O'Malley's love of mystery books endears her to Mr. Malone, and Marjorie and Whitmore team up to find the crooks. Despite the short running time of a little over an hour, *Mrs. O'Malley and Mr. Malone* just didn't carry the same audience appeal as the Kettle film series.

So, it was back to the farm for Marjorie—literally. Filming her first scene in the new Kettle picture, it was reported in a UI accident report (February 17, 1950) that Marjorie stepped onto the front door of their rickety farmhouse, inhaled the crisp air, and fell right through the porch! Four set workers were required to haul Marjorie up through the rotted planking. Marjorie was not injured; in fact, she joked, "I'm gonna have to get Pa to fix that."

The third entry in the Kettle series was entitled *Ma and Pa Kettle Back on the Farm* (1951). This time, Tom (Richard Long) and Kim (Meg Randall) are about to make Ma and Pa first-time grandparents. Still living in their modern house, Ma and Pa are desperate to make a sophisticated impression on Kim's well-to-do parents. The baby's birth causes all sorts of problems when Kim's mother steps in and implies that Ma knows nothing about raising babies. A family feud breaks out, and, after taking their respective parents' sides, Tom and Kim break up.

The young couple's split forces the Kettles and their Boston in-laws to agree to disagree on baby rearing, with their main aim now to get their children back together. As expected, and thanks to their parents, Kim and Tom reunite just in time for the credits to roll.

Incidentally, *Ma and Pa Kettle Back on the Farm* teamed Meg Randall and Richard Long as an onscreen husband-and-wife team for the fifth time within an 18-month period. Apart from the three Kettle calamities made up until this point, they were paired together as Mr. and Mrs. in *Criss Cross* (1948) and *The Life of Riley* (1949).

Baby-faced Richard Long is best known for his role as Tom Kettle on the big screen, but he carved out quite a career for himself as a television actor, too. His most noted roles were on *77 Sunset Strip* (1960–1961), the long running western series *The Big Valley*

Title card for *Ma and Pa Kettle Back on the Farm* (1951).

(1965–1969), and as the star of the whimsical *Nanny and the Professor* (1970–1971), playing opposite Juliet Mills.

His fresh-faced good looks hid a multitude of personal pain, beginning with the tragic death of his first wife, Suzan Ball, second cousin to Lucille Ball. A fellow actor and dancer, Suzan suffered a blow to her leg during a dance number on *East of Sumatra* (1952). Nothing much was thought of the minor incident until 1953 during the production of *War Arrow* (1953) when doctors discovered that several tumors had developed in the same leg. Soon after the diagnosis Suzan slipped on a wet floor in her home and broke the very same leg. Doctors immediately operated, but the tumors had gone too far; the amputation of her right leg was now a necessity to save her life. Before the operation, just a few weeks before Christmas of 1953, Suzan and Richard became engaged. By early January, Suzan underwent the operation to amputate her leg. As soon as she was strong enough (by that April), Suzan and Richard were married. Wearing an artificial limb, and with her promising dancing career now over, Suzan made the brave decision to at least try to continue her acting career.

By May of 1955 Suzan was looking forward to, and rehearsing for, a television drama spot when she suddenly collapsed on the set. Tests revealed that the cancer thought to

A scene from ***Ma and Pa Kettle Back on the Farm*** **(1951).**

be contained with the amputation of her leg had now spread to her lungs. It took three months for the disease to claim her life. On August 5, 1955, Suzan passed away. She was just 21 years old, and Richard was devastated. He began to numb his pain with alcohol, and as a result it became a lifelong demon he found difficult to control.

By 1957 Richard had fallen in love and was newly married for a second time. Mara Corday, also an actress, bore him three children. She was widowed by his untimely death on December 21, 1974. At just 47 years of age, the ever youthful Richard Long succumbed to a series of multiple heart attacks.

Richard Long plays Tom Kettle, the eldest and most socially acceptable Kettle kid in the Ma and Pa Kettle series.

Marjorie stars as the richest woman in the west in *The Law and the Lady* (1951).

Ma and Pa Kettle Back on the Farm (1951) only featured three of the original 15 kids introduced in *The Egg and I* (1947). Teddy Infuhr, Eugene Persson and Diane Florentine were originally the babies of the bunch, yet in this installment they're the oldest kids. The rule seemed to be that as soon as the kids grew as tall as Percy they were out and replaced by newcomers.

Because the Kettles move back into their original shack in *Ma and Pa Kettle Back on the Farm,* studio workmen had to "reverse renovate," so to speak. Replacement rust was reapplied in places where it had worn off; three boards were loosened in the front porch which had been nailed down as a safety precaution; hip high weeds were planted to give the Kettle farm that unkempt look; and the front door was "fixed" so it would fall off when opened. Unfortunately, the chicken coop was a little too real, even for a Kettle dwelling. Upon stepping out of the hen house the entire structure collapsed on top of Percy's head. Fortunately, he wasn't hurt, just a little shaken.

Marjorie had a birthday during production, and filming halted for an entire afternoon of celebration. In addition to receiving gifts and an enormous birthday cake, Marjorie was remembered by the veterans of the 96th Infantry Division, who claimed her as their own Queen during World War II. They proved they still loved her by sending from Chicago a huge floral display in the shape of the 96th's shoulder patch.

After making *Ma and Pa Kettle Back on the Farm* (1951), Marjorie appeared in five more productions before taking on the next Kettle adventure. All five were fairly

Marjorie as Mrs. Cabot in ***Mr. Imperium*** (1951).

Marjorie, a brunette Debbie Reynolds, and a loosely clothed Lana Turner (in order to hide her real-life pregnancy) in ***Mr. Imperium*** (1951). Shortly after filming wrapped, Lana Turner lost the baby she was carrying.

Marjorie in a high end pose for *The Law and the Lady* (1951).

forgettable. *The Law and the Lady* (1951), *A Letter from a Soldier* (1951) and *Mr. Imperium* (1951) were her final productions for 1951, while *It's a Big Country* (1952) and *The Belle of New York* (1952) helped Marjorie pass the time before the next big Ma and Pa Kettle adventure for 1952. Incidentally, *Ma and Pa Kettle at the Fair* (1952) would end up being the highest grossing film of the Kettle series.

SEVEN

The Kettles Continued

Marjorie now felt that staying on the studio lot for the duration of a film shoot better prepared her for her role. For 30 days, the average time it took to complete a Kettle feature, she'd set up house in her dressing room/bungalow.

In a UI production report (May 6, 1950) she said, "I used to have Deanna Durbin's swank cottage, but they made it into offices, so now I shack up right next to the studio fire department. Makes it pretty nice too, because in the evenings, I play a bit of nickel-dime poker with the boys on duty." She was popular with the swing shift policeman as well. Anytime up until midnight (Marjorie's bed time) the officers were welcome to stop by her studio bungalow and help themselves to the pot of hot coffee that was always brewing.

Marjorie grew to love her role as Ma Kettle, and one of the reasons was that each picture represented an opportunity to catch up on some extra sleep. "Those glamor girls wouldn't dare nap on the set," she told a UI publicity reporter (June 21, 1950). "If they do, they have to get fussed over by makeup men and hairdressers for an hour before they can go back to work."

The next Kettle feature was no exception. Shot in the usual 30 days, it gave Marjorie a total of 60 hours of on-the-job nap time as she squeezed in at least two hours of between-scenes snoozing per day. As a result, she looked messier than ever, and no one cared; in fact, it made things easier for everyone. It was an authentic look that no makeup or hairdressing department could match, and Marjorie always considered her naps "work related." It contributed to her Ma Kettle look. "The longer and harder I sleep, the better I look for the part I play," she told UI reporters (June 12, 1950).

Ma and Pa Kettle at the Fair (1952) has Ma entering the contests this time. When faced with needing money for her daughter Rosie's (Lori Nelson) college education, Ma decides to enter the baking contests at the annual county fair. With cash prizes to be had, Pa guarantees his creditors a 50 percent take in Ma's future fair winnings in return for a broken-down horse. Ma wins the jam contest but is eventually disqualified when it's learned that she made a mistake and entered the horse race, not the jam contest. Without a valid entry she is ineligible to win.

As she gets ready for the baking contest, Ma can't for the life of her figure out why her usually light bread is so heavy. Unbeknownst to her, Pa stored his cement in her flour

"Come an' git it!" was the familiar call when dinner was ready in the Kettle household.

tin, which caused her to bake bricks instead of bread. Crowbar and Geoduck unknowingly help Pa's chances by feeding the other racehorses Ma's cement bread.

Using fresh flour — without Pa's cement additive — she wins the baking contest, but she still sees no cash thanks to Pa's promise to his creditors of a share in Ma's prize money. With no money and only one thing left to do, Ma keeps the nag in the horse race — with Pa as jockey!

The happiest mismatched couple in Hollywood history — Ma and Pa Kettle.

Just as Pa looks like winning the race, Ma finds out the town have all bet against him and their nag. Knowing the town will go bankrupt if Pa wins the race, she takes off her pantyhose and uses them as a slingshot to make Pa's horse break into a gallop, which, in turn, loses him the race. Both Ma and Pa are thrown in jail after the cement bread sabotage gets out, but they're soon released after everyone finds out that Ma single-handedly saved the town from bankruptcy. Ma apologizes to Pa for causing him to lose the race, but she confesses, "If the town went broke, Pa, you'd have nobody to borrow from." For their sacrifice, the prize money from the winning horse is given over to the Kettles. Rosie goes to college, and all is well with the world.

In an interview in *The Astounding B-Monster Archive*, Lori Nelson, who plays Rosie Kettle in several of the films, commented on her screen parents. "They were pretty much the same characters they played on the screen," she said. "Percy was a very intelligent man, however. Very quiet and sweet. Marjorie was rough and gruff and boisterous."

Ma and Pa Kettle at the Fair is considered to be one of the best films of the entire Kettle series. The actors are comfortable with their characters and the stories are still fresh. This is the Kettles in their prime! An audience sneak preview on March 6, 1951, at Warner Theatre in California produced such preview card comments as:

"We need more of these harmless types of pictures; fun is needed, not guns!"

"My sides hurt from laughing."

"Indians were a scream!"

"Very entertaining and a relief from war pictures."

"It's good to laugh and forget our troubles with a picture like this."

A classic shot of Percy Kilbride as Pa Kettle.

The test audience was made up of 78 males and 39 females. Twelve were children, with the majority of audience members falling into the 18–45 age group.

At 61 years of age, Marjorie was still in high demand, but at this point in her career she was starting to hint at slowing down. "From here on out I'm going to take it easy," she stated in a UI production report (September 21, 1952). "I've been doing five pictures

An enormous cake celebrates Percy Kilbride's 50th year in the entertainment industry, circa 1952.

a year for 15 years. As far as I'm concerned, those days are over. One or two pictures a year for me is all I'm looking for." One or two films these days would be a busy work year for an actor, but back in Marjorie's day she'd be working just two or three months of the year in order to fulfill her self-imposed lighter schedule.

All of Marjorie's between-pictures time was spent in Palm Springs, where she had moved on doctor's orders to relieve the pain of the serious sinus condition that had plagued her for years. Three major operations failed to alleviate the problem; her only relief was the dry desert air. "The dry air at Palm Springs makes me feel great," she told a UI reporter (February 23, 1950), "but I'm getting a little tired of sand in my shoes!" Marjorie's Palm Springs home was three hours away from the Universal City studio; her Cheviot Hills home was barely an hour away.

Just as Marjorie was slowing down, the Kettle pictures started to slow down with her. Unfortunately, like with most long-running series, the later Kettle films started to lose the spark they once had. The good films are worthy of a belly laugh, the mediocre films are worthy of a smile, and, sadly, the latter films are just worthy of being forgotten altogether. Part of that decline is a direct result of the retirement and subsequent death of Percy Kilbride. His decision to retire from acting after *Ma and Pa Kettle at Waikiki* (1955) should have ended the series. But greedy studio production heads had other ideas.

Marjorie was forced to appear solo in *The Kettles in the Ozarks* (1956), and Parker Fennelly stepped into the role of Pa Kettle for the last film, *The Kettles on Old Macdonald's Farm* (1957). It's unfair to say that his performance was bad; he just wasn't Percy Kilbride. Percy was Pa, and he was irreplaceable.

Despite his success as Pa, Percy Kilbride never understood why *he* was the one to become typecast in the hillbilly role. Though Marjorie is best remembered today as Ma Kettle, throughout her working life she moved from one production to the other, making back-to-back movies and then jumping right back into her Ma Kettle role with ease. Percy, on the other hand, waited patiently for the yearly Kettle film to begin production — he had no choice, as there were few, if any, offers in between.

The one consolation of being a character actor was never being blamed for a movie flop. In a UI production report (January 14, 1946) Percy agreed; "Character actors from the New York stage don't have to die to go to heaven, they go to Hollywood. After all, when a picture doesn't work out too well, the character actor is never blamed. It's always the producer, or the director, or the stars who take the criticism."

Despite her regular work schedule, Marjorie was receiving fewer studio perks than Percy. It was a situation that she resented, but she didn't dare blame Percy. In a UI production report (July 2, 1950), Marjorie credited Percy as, "The best deadpan actor in the business, and a true gentleman. I can't think of anyone I respect more than my partner." It was a compliment publicly repeated by Marjorie for as long as the couple worked together.

It was again time for audiences to get their yearly dose of the Kettles. In *Ma and Pa Kettle on Vacation* (1953), Ma and Pa leave the familiar surroundings of the farm for a well deserved vacation, in of all cities, Paris. The trouble starts when naive Pa agrees to deliver a letter for a stranger that he meets on the plane. As a result, he gets himself involved in an international spy ring. Their daughter-in-law's stuffy parents accompany the Kettles to Europe, and all hell breaks loose as the group gets caught up in the middle of a racket involving intelligence secrets.

Again, Marjorie did several films in between her Ma Kettle role. *Fast Company* (1953) billed Marjorie as the star of the film, yet its success was only mediocre at the box office. Next came the Lucille Ball–Desi Arnaz classic *The Long, Long Trailer* (1954). In this light comedy about newlyweds who take an unforgettable cross-country adventure in a brand new trailer, Marjorie once again played the nosy neighbor role to perfection and stole the show. The last film for Marjorie before putting on her Ma Kettle house dress again

The title card for *Ma and Pa Kettle on Vacation* (1953).

was *Rose Marie* (1954), a remake of two previous versions that MGM had filmed years before. In a minor part, Marjorie plays Lady Jane Dunstock.

Despite the fact that they hold the record for the longest wed couple in screen history, Marjorie and Percy rarely saw each other out of costume. So when Marjorie treated herself to a movie and was strolling along Hollywood Boulevard to the nearest soda fountain afterward, it came as a shock when she spotted a familiar looking fella about a half a block ahead. According to a UI press release (November 10, 1953), Marjorie said, "There was something vaguely familiar about the way the fella carried himself, something about the tilt of his derby hat that struck a chord of memory." Marjorie hurried her steps in order to catch the familiar stranger and hesitantly tapped the man on the shoulder, saying, "Are you — is this P-Percy Kil — ." The man turned and stared at her with a blank expression. Then suddenly they both recognized each other at once. After a shared laugh, they went to the soda fountain together.

The year 1954 was officially the end of an era for Marjorie. Her MGM contract had expired, and for the first time in 14 years she was a free agent. There was to be no extension this time. Despite the expiration of her second seven-year contract Marjorie went straight back to Universal for *Ma and Pa Kettle at Home* (1954). She was given an exclusive Universal contract, a one-picture deal for the duration of the film.

Marjorie gets all dressed up in *Ma and Pa Kettle on Vacation* (1953).

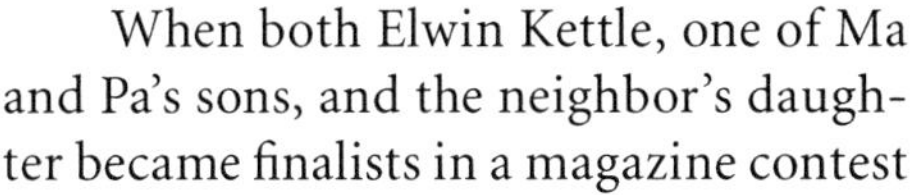

When both Elwin Kettle, one of Ma and Pa's sons, and the neighbor's daughter became finalists in a magazine contest entitled "My Life on a Typical American Farm," the judges make plans to visit the two in order to better determine who the winner should be. With a four-year, fully paid scholarship to agricultural college at stake, Ma and Pa give their broken down farm a full makeover — as only they could. Their renovation shortcuts are soon revealed when a rainstorm hits and literally washes away their repairs. Despite the neighbor's farm being superior, the judges determine that any family who'd go to such lengths to win the prize should be declared the winners, too. They declare the competition a draw and the four-year scholarship is split into two, two-year scholarships. Another happy Kettle ending.

Veteran character actor Oliver Blake portrayed the Indian Geoduck for the fifth time in the series. Victor Potel, Johnny Hawkes and Lester Allen had all passed away since their earlier performances as Pa's redskin helpmates. Emery Parnell came back for a sixth time to portray the lovable, if not a little persistent, salesman Billy Reed; and for the first time in many a Kettle caper there was no part for Esther Dale as the gossipy Birdie Hicks.

All of the original Kettle kids had outgrown their roles by now, and a whole new batch of brats were cast. With the new brood coming, Universal International released a statement (October 23, 1954) saying, "Marjorie Main has mothered more kids in movies than any other feminine star in the history of Hollywood."

Incidentally, the 15 Kettle kids were made up of eight boys and seven girls. Despite Ma and Pa constantly mixing up their names— or forgetting them altogether — they were Tom, George, Ted, Ben, Willy, Billy, Danny, Henry, Sara, Nancy, Susie, Ruthy, Sally, Rosie and Eve.

One of eight lobby cards issued for *Ma and Pa Kettle on Vacation* (1953).

To everyone's astonishment, Marjorie turned out a batch of edible cookies during the production of *Ma and Pa Kettle at Home.* According to a story in a UI production report (September 27, 1954), amazed cast and crew members flocked to the ramshackle Kettle kitchen after Percy Kilbride announced that he was actually eating one of the cookies after a comedy take. "I can't understand it," said Marjorie. "I mixed 'em and baked 'em just like always in a 'Kettle' picture, but for some reason they turned out right tasty." Filming resumed after the last cookie was devoured.

A UI production report (October 13, 1954) stated that, before one early morning call, Marjorie swept onto the sound stage, saw a dignified gent, who might have been a producer or businessman, and said, "Where did I park my car? I know I left it between two sound stages, but I don't remember which ones. Please, go and find it for me like a good fellow." Leaving the unknown gent scratching his head, she stormed into her dressing room, calling, "Darling," "Honey," and "Yoo-hoo" to round up hairdressers, wardrobe mistresses and makeup men. Minutes after cyclone Marjorie had done that, she spotted the dialogue director. "Yoo-hoo, Mr. What's-your-name?" she shouted, "I need to practice my lines. Help me, won't you?"

In a mid-fifties UI press release (March 19, 1955), director Charles Lamont smiled at the orderly confusion that Marjorie exuded when she walked onto a set. "When she squints up her eyes and smiles," he said, "she can get away with anything. I don't know of any other star who can get so much out of people without ever really demanding anything."

Ma swipes the chickens from the table in preparation for the evening meal in a scene from *Ma and Pa Kettle at Home* (1954).

On August 24, 1953, at the Warners Theatre in California, *Ma and Pa Kettle at Home* (1954) received favorable test audience reviews. An audience of 23 males and 64 females, 28 of which were children, marked their preview cards with such comments as:

"That was the best picture I have seen for many a day — all scenes were funny."

"As a teacher and educator, I rejoice to see such a wholesome picture for our youngsters who need clean entertainment — even we adults need it!"

"Why don't you make more Ma and Pa Kettle pictures?"

"It was truly great and had many important ideas and lessons in it."

"It should be in 3-D."

"One of the better Ma and Pa pictures"

By 1954 the Far Western Housewives Association had branded Marjorie with the title of "Most Untidy Housekeeper of the Year." It was an "honor" bestowed upon her for the third year running. Perhaps this is the reason why, over the course of the long-running series, she was sent enough gadgets and household appliances to outfit several homes.

Among the goods received were gas and electric refrigerators and stoves, automatic window washers, push-button door opening and closing fixtures, disappearing folding beds, armchair-control heating and cooling devices and light switch controls, electric table setters, and — one of the most bizarre — an automatic bed maker. Many of the gadgets

Marjorie mixes it up — in more ways than one — in *Ricochet Romance* (1954).

came with a letter from their manufacturer asking Marjorie to conspicuously place their product in her latest picture.

Regarding one batch of goodies, a UI production report (April 23, 1953) quoted Marjorie as saying, "I'm keeping a head and back scratcher, and I gave Percy a shave-while-you-sleep gadget." The rest of the appliances Marjorie distributed amongst the film crew, friends and neighbors. Anyone who could use it, and wanted it, was welcome to it. Marjorie's generosity rewarded her with the nickname "Ma Bountiful" among the crew.

Ma and Pa Kettle with most of their brood in ***Ma and Pa Kettle at Home*** (1954).

J.W. Williamson makes another interesting observation about the Kettle film series in his book *Hillbillyland*: "Ma and Pa are forever going into snooty society [*Ma and Pa Kettle Go to Town,* 1951, and *Ma and Pa Kettle on Vacation,* 1953] or snooty society is forever seeking them out, for example Alan Mowbray playing Alphonsus Mannering in *Ma and Pa Kettle at Home* (1954), and through the very simple, poor, rural, unmodernized goodness in their hearts, the Kettles always stumble through to victory."

Percy Kilbride had now forewarned the studio that he'd do one more Kettle film and that'd be it. While still trying to lure him into sticking with the role, they set up a plan B, just in case they failed to convince him. Universal hoped that lightning would strike twice when they paired Marjorie and Chill Wills together for *Ricochet Romance* (1954). Their plan didn't work. The hopeful new screen team just didn't have the same chemistry that Marjorie and Percy did, and the disappointing box office take trumpeted that fact, loud and clear.

Percy was still adamant that *Ma and Pa Kettle at Waikiki* (1955) was going to be the film after which he'd hang up his derby for good. His decision to retire from acting at age 66 made the studio understandably nervous. Not even a $1 million offer (an unheard

Marjorie, as Pansy Jones, pictured with Chill Wills in ***Ricochet Romance*** (1954).

Title card for ***Ricochet Romance*** (1954).

Ma Kettle in ***Ma and Pa Kettle at Waikiki*** **(1955). Although Marjorie is pictured in a traditional Hawaiian grass skirt, it was eventually replaced with a skirt made of tea leaves after Marjorie complained that this one was "too revealing."**

of amount for the time) to star in a television spin-off of the Kettles (with or without Marjorie) could sway him. He was a man of his word; he'd worked long enough, and *Ma and Pa Kettle at Waikiki* was his final farewell. As a tribute, Percy is featured prominently in his last Kettle film, with the story revolving entirely around Pa.

When Pa mouths off about his exceptional business skills to his sick Hawaiian cousin, he's asked to take over his cousin's pineapple processing plant until he's well enough to return. It takes some convincing, but Ma, Pa and daughter Rosie (Lori Nelson) all head off to Honolulu to help keep the pineapple farm running while cousin Kettle recovers. On his first day on the job, Pa accidentally blows up the assembly line.

With Pa depressed and thinking he can't do a thing right, a rival pineapple grower takes advantage of Pa's broken spirit by luring him to another island with the promise of hidden treasure. Believing it's a perfect opportunity to redeem himself, gullible Pa heads off to "treasure island." In doing so, he leaves the pineapple plant unattended — exactly what the crooks had hoped for. On arrival at the new island, Pa meets up with a Hawaiian family that eerily mirrors his own.

After realizing Pa has disappeared, Ma tracks him to the island, catches the crooks and saves the day, as usual. Before going back to the farm and their kids, it's discovered that Pa's accidental explosion wasn't a disaster after all. He unwittingly created a new formula that can be put to good use at the plant; suddenly, Pa is honored as a Hawaiian hero.

The Kettles are treated to a traditional Hawaiian farewell, and Ma trades her house dress for a grass hula skirt! Appropriately, the last scene of the film shows Pa giving Ma an affectionate kiss on the cheek before fade-out. In reality, it was a kiss goodbye. Both Percy and Pa had now officially retired.

A UI production report (February 25, 1955) stated, "Funniest sight of the week at Universal International was witnessed by wardrobe women when Marjorie Main got into a hula costume for a fitting before starting her co-starring role with Percy Kilbride in *'Ma and Pa Kettle at Waikiki'* (1955).

"Reason for the laughter that filled the wardrobe department was an involuntary hula dance executed by Marjorie when the costume was fastened by her. Because a regulation grass skirt was deemed too 'immodest' to suit Miss Main's taste, a costume made entirely of tea leaves was flown from Hawaii for her to wear in the picture. In order to preserve the tea leaves, the costume must be kept in a refrigerator.

"It was iced tea that clung to Marjorie's quivering flesh when she donned the costume, and her wriggling, bordering on an authentic hula movement, was funny enough to convulse the wardrobe workers."

After 40-plus years in the business, it took until 1955 for Marjorie to be recognized in an edition of *Who's Who in America*. She was on the set of *Ma and Pa Kettle at Waikiki* when informed of the honor. In a UI production report (February 25, 1955) she said, "My late husband, Dr. Stanley L. Krebs, was listed for many years in *'Who's Who,'* but I never thought while he was alive that one day, I too would be honored. He was a brilliant man in several fields of science and it was to be expected.

"But what have I done to be included in such a listing? As far as I can see, I screeched at Wally Beery in a series of movies for some years and for the last five years I've been screeching at Percy Kilbride in the 'Ma and Pa' Kettle series. I don't see how that qualifies me for listing in 'Who's Who.' I certainly don't set any shining example as a housewife in these movies. I set the plates on the table for Pa and the 15 kids and hoot, 'Come an' git it!' and they put me in *'Who's Who.'* It sure beats me!"

Modest Marjorie failed to include the fact that her starring roles on the screen had made millions laugh for more than fifteen years, and that her characterizations of a slatternly homespun mother of a lively brood of kids had never been clouded by any evidence of selfishness or lack of integrity. Finally she admitted, "During more recent years, I hoped I would, someday appear in '*Who's Who.*' I feel now as though I have been of some purpose and that my existence has been justified."

Marjorie's *Who's Who in America* (p. 436) listing appears as follows:

> MAIN, Marjorie, actress; b. Acton, Ind., Feb 24, 1890; d. Rev. Samuel Joseph and Jennie (McGaughey) Tomlinson; student Franklin (Ind.) Coll.; grad Sch. of Expression, Hamilton Coll., Lexington, Ky., 1909; student dramatic art, Chicago and N.Y.; m. Dr. Stanley LeFevre Krebs, Nov. 2, 1921 (died 1935). Teacher dramatic art, Bourbon Coll., Paris, Ky., 1 yr.; appeared New York stage, vaudeville, stock cos., road shows, radio and Chautauqua; has made over 80 motion pictures, 1937—including: *Dead End, The Women, The Egg and I* (Acad. nomination); a series with Wallace Beery, and 'Ma' in the Ma and Pa Kettle series. Home: 3066 Patricia Av., Los Angeles 64; also 1280 S. Calle Rolph St., Palm Springs, Cal.; Rimrock Rd., Idyllwild, Cal.

Ma and Pa Kettle at Waikiki (1955) was plagued by quite a few problems during the course of production. Apart from Percy's imminent departure from the series, a number of secondary problems held up production for a time, including a feast of traditional Hawaiian poi (boiled and mashed taro root) that was to be consumed in the final scenes at the luau.

Prop men took samples of the poi to be used in the film around to several of the cast and crew members to sample it. In a UI production report (February 25, 1955), prop man Bud Laraby said, "The poi made several people quite ill. Custard photographs just like it, and it tasted a lot better, too."

Another scene called for Marjorie to soak her feet in a pan of steaming water. But the moment she removed her feet from the water, she would break into a fit of sneezes. Marjorie was terrified of catching cold. Something had to be done, and fast, to change the situation. Finally, after three takes an enterprising prop man came to the rescue with a heating pad concealed beneath the pan and a tub full of transparent plastic bubbles to replace the water. With warm feet and no sneezing, Marjorie was able to complete the scene in one take.

The initial special effects crew of eight men was swiftly expanded to 16 to keep up with the gags in the script. The explosion in the pineapple factory came off with such realism that the camera lens ended up covered with crushed pineapple and papaya. The entire sequence had to be reset and reshot the following day.

Another UI production report (February 25, 1955) states that Marjorie had a terrible time remembering her lines for one particular scene. A line of dialogue in the script read simply, "That's what you say, Birdie Hicks," and this was the line of contention.

For the scene a giant wind machine is turned on by the special effects man and the entire crew heave everything from cabbage to kitchen calendars in Marjorie's direction. The melee starts and Marjorie shouts, "That's what you say, Bennie Hicks."

"Cut!" says the director, "The name is Birdie Hicks, Marjorie."

The camera rolls again; Marjorie waits for her cue and gives out with, "That's what you say, Betty Hicks!"

Cut!" says the weary director, "Try it again. At least we're using a woman's name now."

The third take looks perfect with bonnets, carrots, aprons and table cloths all flying around the room in a fine sequence until Marjorie's line comes up and she tops herself with, "That's what you say, Sara Bernhardt!"

In a fit of laughter, Marjorie said, "And just to think, I started in the theater playing Shakespeare!" Incidentally, Esther Dale reprised her role as the nosy "Birdie Hicks" for the seventh time in the series.

Seven of the original Kettle kids returned for *Ma and Pa Kettle at Waikiki.* Elana Schreinger, Donna Leary, Ronnie Rondell Jr., Beverly Mook, Jackie Jensen, Margaret Brown and George Arglen all passed through five grades in the studio school while moonlighting as a Kettle kid.

Director Lee Sholem was a well liked, patient, unselfish director. All good traits to have when directing a Kettle picture. More often than not, a mix of 15 children, any number of farm animals and a variety of gags that may or may not work required a sense of humor and a lot of patience. Sholem had the perfect personality for this. He was receptive, good natured and ahead of his time in believing that being the director didn't necessarily mean that he knew it all. He was more than happy to hear of a funny gag, from anyone, be it cast, crew or child. Everyone was encouraged to speak up with an idea, and if it was good enough it would be incorporated into a scene.

Because *Ma and Pa Kettle at Waikiki* had a Hawaiian theme, a red badge of distinction, aptly titled the "Poi Medal" (Personal Order Intelligentsia), was rotated daily to the person coming up with the funniest gag or new bit of business. At the end of the day the winner got to keep the silver dollar attached to the medal.

Everyone was happy with the arrangement — with the exception of Marjorie and Percy. After all, they were usually the ones on the receiving end of the "bright ideas." The first winner of the "Poi Medal" was a special effects man. He had the idea of setting up a cabbage to fall on top of Marjorie's head at the climax of a particularly harrowing scene that already called for her to be drenched by a fire extinguisher, covered with flour by an air conditioner that Pa had installed backwards, and knocked off her feet by at least half a dozen of her children.

Percy made a winner out of a prop man on the second day of filming in the pineapple factory sequence. Percy was sitting on a long conveyor belt covered with pineapples when the prop man got the idea of turning the belt on and having Percy make his exit along with the fruit. (While avoiding motion sickness in this scene, Percy somehow managed to make himself sea sick in the rocking hammock that he used between takes.)

By the end of production, a sound technician, dialogue coach and a camera operator had all submitted worthy ideas that were incorporated into the final scenes, making the project more of a group effort than most. *Ma and Pa Kettle at Waikiki* (1955) was the last good Kettle picture. Percy Kilbride's exit marked the beginning of the end, in more ways than one.

By 1955, the price of a television set had dropped considerably. Instead of costing half the price of a car, they were suddenly the price of a couple of tires. It was no longer considered a luxury item, and the affordability of this new invention meant that 67 percent of American households owned a television by 1955. By 1960 that figure had jumped to 87 percent. During this time, box office sales plummeted, and studio bosses were understandably *very* nervous.

Just as sound had threatened and eventually taken the place of silent films, television threatened the future of feature films, period. History tells us there was room for both. Sadly, this time it was radio that suffered the fate of progress.

EIGHT

The Beginning of the End... Literally

It was a tough decision, but the studio had enough confidence in Marjorie to continue the Kettle series without Percy Kilbride. *The Kettles in the Ozarks* (1956) introduced Pa's brother, Sedge Kettle, played by Arthur Hunnicutt. His character traits follow those possessed by Pa: the male Kettle idleness, vagueness and the sly penchant for getting most of what he wants in spite of these seeming handicaps were all present; however, he wasn't Percy. There was no replacing Pa.

The new male lead only served as a constant reminder of how missed Percy/Pa was in the film series. Marjorie did all she could to promote Hunnicutt's role as the possible new blood that could extend the series indefinitely. "If this goes over with audiences, Arthur and I will do some more. Sometimes the stories are corny, but I'd stand on my head to make people laugh. That's all I have to live for. I don't want to retire," she told the *Indianapolis Star*.

Despite Marjorie's claim that she had no plans to retire, in reality she was only two feature films away from doing just that. The disappointing box office take for *The Kettles in the Ozarks* halted all chances of Arthur Hunnicutt continuing his role as Sedge Kettle, and it did nothing to help along Marjorie's wish to continue with the series she had grown to love.

The spiraling public opinion of a Kettle caper without Percy Kilbride showed in the (August 3, 1955) test audience preview cards taken from the Panorama Theater in California:

"The many references to Pa Kettle are ridiculous. I waited throughout for him to come into the picture. Why build up a character without using him?"

"Marjorie Main is excellent as Ma, but give her and her crew better material."

"Don't bother admitting it to the public. It's a menace!"

"Please stop making children think all people are idiots and fathers are lazy."

"This is our first preview and hope that unlike radishes, it never repeats!"

"I liked the first Ma and Pa Kettle pictures made, but this one I had to walk out on before it was over."

"We were charged too much for this preview [$1.00]."

Arthur Hunnicutt and Una Merkel share a scene with Marjorie in *The Kettles in the Ozarks* (1956).

"One of the best Kettle pictures, but it's too bad Pa couldn't be in it."

"Where is Percy Kilbride?"

Given the overall negative opinion of the test audiences on *The Kettles in the Ozarks,* studio bosses were very nervous—and they had reason to be. This was the beginning of the end, and deep down they knew it.

The studio had spared no expense in trying to make the latest Kettle picture a success. For instance, the cornfield was probably the most expensive corn ever raised for a production. The field, set on the back lot of Universal International, had to be raised when it was still a bit too cold, especially at night.

There wasn't enough time to grow a mature crop from seed, so the studio bought and transplanted young hothouse shoots. Then, to protect them from the cold, a special heating system was installed in the ground. This consisted of lines of resistance wire sheathed in lead, one wire along each row of plants. The cost of the underground wire installation constituted a big enough item of expense, but an additional five men were employed as nursemaids to the corn, watering them separately by hand with watering cans morning, noon and night.

In a *Valley Times* article (March 5, 1956), Marjorie was still positive about the future

This publicity pose was used on the title card for ***The Kettles in the Ozarks*** **(1956).**

of the Kettle series. "There is something immensely satisfying about working in a series like this," she said. "That's especially true when you play a character like 'Ma Kettle,' who's both likable and amusing. After all, the main function of an actress is to give pleasure to the people. I've been an actress a long time and I've played many a fine part, but even I was surprised at the warmth and evident affection with which I was greeted wherever I went after I started playing 'Ma Kettle.'

"Aside from this warm regard from the public, another reason I've enjoyed so much working in this series is the comfortable feeling I get from working with pretty much the same people all the time. I suppose that sort of thing depends on what type person you are. Some actresses may enjoy

A portrait shot of an older Marjorie.

On the set of *Friendly Persuasion* (1956), Gary Cooper finds Marjorie just as funny as the rest of us do.

working with new people all the time. As for me, I have a kind of family feeling about the cast and crew of these 'Kettle' pictures and I'd love to have them around for as long as I continue to work."

Friendly Persuasion (1956) was Marjorie's last non–Kettle motion picture. Marjorie plays the bullying Widow Hudspeth, who does all she can to find husbands for her three less-than-desirable daughters. An all-star cast included Anthony Perkins, Dorothy

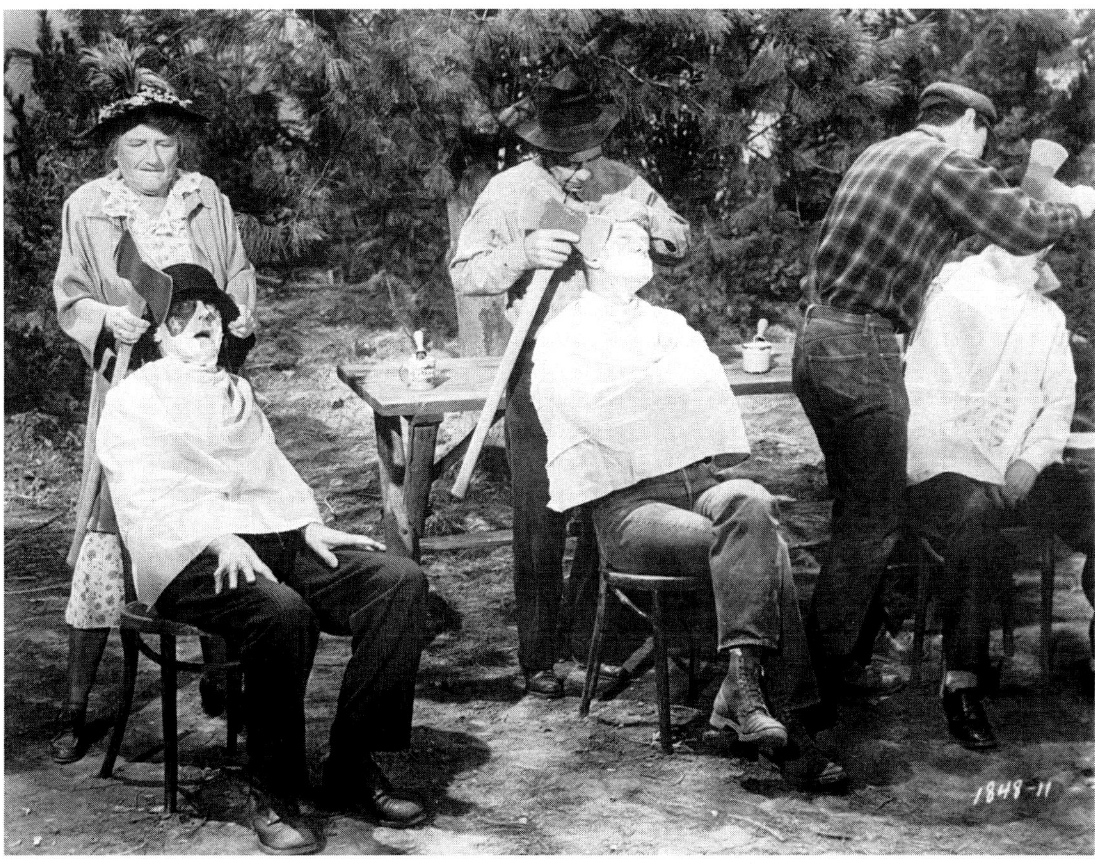

Parker Fennelly, as Pa Kettle, looks a little nervous as Ma gets to work in a shaving contest in *The Kettles on Old MacDonald's Farm* (1957).

McGuire and Gary Cooper. In an *Indianapolis Star* interview (March 2, 1969), Marjorie spoke lovingly of her leading man: "Gary [Cooper] was such a wonderful man, I almost fell in love with him."

Just like with Percy Kilbride, it seemed that one last Kettle adventure would be a suitable end to Marjorie's long film career. *The Kettles on Old MacDonald's Farm* (1957) was the last of the Kettle films, and, appropriately, it was Marjorie's last feature film before her retirement. This time the studio *replaced* Percy Kilbride with Parker Fennelly. Parker did his job well and, to his credit, didn't try to imitate Percy's Pa. He brought his own personality to the role. But Parker was no Percy, and in all fairness, there was no actor that could fill Percy's shoes. Percy gave life to the character, and anyone who attempted the role was just a poor imitation of the original.

Once again the preview cards taken from an April 5, 1957, preview screening at the Paradise Theater in California were peppered with mixed comments and confusion as to where the old Pa Kettle had gone:

"I think the other Pa Kettle, Percy Kilbride, was much better."

"Why the new Pa Kettle?"

"I don't like this Pa."

"I think the series has run dry."

Marjorie with Gary Cooper in *Friendly Persuasion* (1956).

"They ought to ship it to Arabia!"

"It was comical, but I have seen better Kettle pictures."

"As with all the Ma and Pa Kettle pictures, this was a riot."

Without a doubt, the onset of television played a large part in the declining box-office sales for all movies, not just the Kettle series. Marjorie tried working within the new "fad," but after appearing in only a handful of television shows, most notably *The Sacramento Story* and *Wagon Train*, she decided she was too old and the television business too fast. Content with the fact that she'd at least tried it, she happily retired at age 66. Coincidentally, Percy Kilbride retired at the exact same age.

In an interview conducted for a UI production report (November 12, 1955), Marjorie was asked to give her advice to young women wanting to make their mark on the motion picture industry. "Be a comedienne," she emphatically stated. "Dramatic actresses are a dime a dozen. Everybody's trying to be a Bette Davis or an Ann Blyth. What this country needs is more lady comics. There are plenty of funny men on stage and screen, but how many women?" asks Marjorie.

"Well, you can count them almost on the fingers of your hands—Betty Hutton, Marie Wilson, Gracie Allen, Joan Davis, Eve Arden, Judy Holliday, Lucille Ball, Judy Canova and Cass Daley. Comediennes are as scarce as multi-millionaire boyfriends. If you want to hit the show business jackpot, learn to make 'em laugh instead of trying to make 'em cry."

Title card for *The Kettles on Old MacDonald's Farm* (1957).

Marjorie lived out her retirement comfortably and, despite having homes in Palm Springs and Idyllwild, she rarely left her Los Angeles residence. In an interview for the *Indianapolis Star* (March 2, 1969), Marjorie was asked if she'd consider returning to the screen. "I'd like to work with the old timers again," she said, "but they aren't making pictures. And I don't think I'd fit in with the new young set. I wouldn't be at ease with them."

She may have had little desire to continue her acting career on television, but Marjorie certainly enjoyed eating her dinner in front of it. Her favorite programs were news shows and, not surprisingly, old movies. In the same interview with the *Indianapolis Star* (March 2, 1969), she said, "I see so many old friends that have passed on. It's like renewing old acquaintances. Besides, my early career is starting all over again. All the pictures I made years ago are now showing up on television."

In a 1958 interview with Jean McMurphy of the *Los Angeles Times*, Marjorie reminisced about the universal appeal of the Kettle series. "The Kettles' are playing all over the world now," she said somewhat surprised. "When I was in Europe a few years ago, I saw my picture on a billboard outside the theater across from my hotel in Venice. I went in to see the show. There I was all right. But Ma was speaking faultless Italian! She was perfectly charming, quite watered down."

Residents of Marjorie's home town of Acton, Indiana, always held a special place in

In a candid moment on the set of *The Kettles on Old MacDonald's Farm* (1957), a brave Marjorie challenges former French heavyweight fighter George Carpentier to an impromptu boxing match.

their hearts for the small-town girl who made good. Despite her hectic career, Marjorie would travel back to Indianapolis whenever she could. Ill health and advancing age forced her to decline some of those home town invitations, but the townsfolk remembered her warmly. Mrs. Rachel Pfendler, the Acton postmistress, knew her well. She made this statement to Joe Adams of the *Indianapolis Star* (August 17, 1958): "Marjorie was just as harum-scarum and lovable then [before her fame] as in her pictures. It was always a pleasure to meet her on the street or at parties."

Incidentally, the state of Indianapolis honored Marjorie with a variety of awards during her lifetime. The Franklin College Alumni Council made her an honorary member; the Indiana Foundation of Southern California honored her for her "contribution to Americanism"; and her tireless home town appearances to sell war bonds raised a staggering $50,000 in one night!

For the price of one $18.75 war bond the buyer received a ticket to see Marjorie on stage. This was in December of 1942, long before audiences knew her from *The Egg and I* (1947) and the Kettle franchise, yet Marjorie still had enough star power to sell out an entire stadium. After hearing that a mere 1,500 war bonds had been sold in exchange for tickets to see her, Marjorie publicly announced in the *Indianapolis Star* (December 12, 1942) that those sales just weren't good enough. "They tell me that 1,500 war bonds have been sold to get tickets to see and hear me," Marjorie said. "But that's not good enough. Where I come from you can't get anywhere on less than a full house." That brief public announcement caused such a rush for tickets that the show quickly sold out. Good-hearted Marjorie agreed to come back for a second night. "You can never sell too many war bonds," she beamed.

One personal appearance that Marjorie wouldn't dare miss was the annual Hollywood Christmas Parade. Every year, long into her retirement, Marjorie could be seen perched atop a float, waving and smiling to the cheering crowd.

Marjorie was an advocate of women aging gracefully, without "talking themselves into that middle age blur," as she would describe it. "Heaven knows," she said in a UI production report (August 29, 1949), "I was no example of charm and wit either on the screen or off, but I do think that too many girls take middle age and old age for granted. They just lie back and enjoy being blah! Paint and powder and fine clothes and a snazzy hairdo are only half an answer to this business of staying young after forty-five," she said. "It's what goes on inside your skull that really counts." Marjorie insisted that girls whose wrinkles had started to play havoc with their libido had one distinct advantage on their side, and that is experience. "A gal who's lived," she said, "has something to talk about. Experience is a great weapon to keep the rest of the world interested. Men like to talk to a woman who thinks for herself and has something to say. If she's got the ability to look on life as an adventure, it'll always come out in the form of charm."

Known for her personality rather than her looks, Marjorie let out a huge guffaw at the idea that sex is everything. In the same UI production report (April 8, 1957), she said, "Skin deep beauty couldn't keep any man but the dumbest interested for very long." Her recipe for staying young, or at least young at heart, was to read good books, develop the art of thought and conversation, don't let yourself get slovenly and don't get "that half century inferiority complex!"

Marjorie enjoyed her life in her own special way. She had the means to live luxuriously, yet she chose to live comfortably; she had the star power to make ridiculous demands, yet she chose to do for herself. She was an independent farm girl who just happened to be employed by a film studio in Hollywood. She thought herself no better than the woman she sat next to on the bus or the man she'd offer to share her hot cakes with in a drugstore.

Yes, she was a little offbeat, and as she got older it's fair to say that she was even a little eccentric, too; but compared to a majority of her peers, working with Marjorie Main was fun. She was professional, unaffected by her fame and fortune, and, until the day she died, deep down was still Mary Tomlinson — a country girl from a modest little farm in rural Indiana. Despite her success as an actress, that's what she was proudest of.

Sadly, Marjorie Main lost her battle with lung cancer at St. Vincent's Hospital in Los Angeles on April 10, 1975. She was 85 years old. She's buried next to her husband at Forest Lawn Memorial Park, Hollywood Hills, California.

In 1954 Marjorie made arrangements for her husband's remains to be moved from Mount Carmel Cemetery in Littlestown, Pennsylvania, to Forest Lawn Memorial Park, where she had purchased plots for both of them. "I've been lonely so much of my life, I'd like to be with him in death," she told the *Indianapolis Star* (March 2, 1969).

Aside from "Marjorie Main," her memorial plaque bears her stage name of Marjorie, her birth name of Mary Tomlinson, and her married name of Krebs:

MRS. MARY TOMLINSON KREBS
"MARJORIE MAIN"
1890–1975

To prove just how much Marjorie had crossed over into being "Ma" in real life, many of her newspaper obituaries didn't even carry her real name in the headline. Most of them read, "'Ma Kettle' dies at 85." And honestly, she would have been nothing but proud of that tribute.

Marjorie's will, dated January 19, 1961, officially proves how alone she really was in the world. The opening paragraph reads, "I declare that I had no child; my husband Dr. Stanley LaFevre Krebs, and my parents have died. I had no brother or sister, except my brother, Samuel Tomlinson, who has died and has no descendant." Her will goes on to say that, "I further declare I have no living spouse, ancestor, descendant, brother, sister, nephew or niece."

With that said, the bulk of Marjorie's estate was bequeathed to various organizations, including the Oxford Group, Moral Re-Armament, M.A.A., INC. and Leland Stanford Junior University.

Marjorie summed up her role as Ma Kettle better than anyone else. The *Indianapolis Star* (April 20, 1947) quoted her as saying: "Ma Kettle was the grandest character role I've ever played. She was frowzy, but not repulsive, tough, but never vicious, big-hearted, impulsive, maternal, and her only faults were the result of circumstances over which she had no control — like Pa Kettle's shiftlessness and his failure to discipline his numerous children. Honestly, I don't think I could have ever played that part if I hadn't lived on a farm in Indiana."

Carl Lewis of the *Indianapolis Star* (March 31, 1947) said, "Marjorie Main didn't need to act as Ma Kettle. And she is the first to admit it. She just plays herself — she talks with the same raspy voice off screen as she does on. She fiddles with her hair and her hats and is an all-round good fellow. She admits that she learned a lot about playing rural characters from her own observations of life on a farm in rural Indiana."

Marjorie Main and Percy Kilbride were parents to 15 children onscreen and to the rest of the world they're considered the most loved parents that Hollywood ever created. It's a remarkable legacy to leave behind, especially considering neither one of them had children of their own.

NINE

Percy and Pa

The Midwestern Practical Nurses Association named him "Hollywood's Most Eligible Bachelor" of 1949, and it was a title that Percy just couldn't comprehend. "What woman would want to marry Pa Kettle?" he said, bewildered (UI, February 26, 1949).

A bachelor all his life, Percy admitted in a UI interview (October 19, 1954) to coming close to marriage on a few occasions: "I've been mighty close to getting hitched, and sometimes I'm heartsick at the thought that I never went through with it. The responsibility of a family might have given me the push that would have made a big star of me."

But he *was* a big star. He was no Clark Gable or Cary Grant, but in his own special way Percy Kilbride has made his mark in history as the most lovable lazy husband that a girl could ever hope for. Percy had character, and it was that quality that made him one of America's most successful "character actors."

An actor — any actor — has two big fears they hope to avoid throughout their working life. The first fear is not getting enough work to survive, and the second is being typecast in a role that won't allow producers or an audience to see them as anything but one particular character. Unfortunately, Percy got stuck with the latter.

It's no curse to be known exclusively as Pa Kettle in today's world, but back when Percy was actively looking for work it most certainly was. While Marjorie reinvented her "mother roles" for other films, Percy would often have to be content to sit it out until the yearly Kettle film began production. "The trouble with Percy is that he plays Pa too well," Marjorie said in a UI production report (February 28, 1952).

Percy's depiction of Pa was especially brilliant since the two men were polar opposites in both personality and appearance. Percy was an immaculate dresser. He'd show up for work on the studio lot wearing a full suit, complete with waistcoat, hat and pocket watch. Pa, on the other hand, had holes in his disheveled clothes and held his pants up with a piece of twine. Percy kept his Hollywood Hills apartment in spotless condition, whereas Pa lived like a squatter, and was reluctant to clean or fix anything around the house.

In fact, Percy was so fastidious that Marjorie was too embarrassed to allow him inside her house of paper piles and the like. After Percy's retirement, Marjorie missed having him around the movie set; but despite her best intentions, she never did get around to having him visit for lunch. Her main reason for dragging her feet on the

Oh, oh... Pa's in trouble again!

invitation was the fact that her house was always in such disarray. "I've been intending to ask Percy around for a visit for a long, long, long time," Marjorie told the *Los Angeles Times*. "But somehow or other I just can't get my house straightened up. Percy's just so neat."

Percy never married and had no children, whereas Pa was most definitely married, with fifteen children! Percy was an extremely intelligent, independent man, always reading and learning new things, whereas Pa was a simpleton, content with letting others do for him. Percy was generous with his time and money, whereas Pa was always looking to "borrow" or beg something from someone.

One particular example pointing out the difference between Percy and Pa came after a personal appearance that Percy made promoting one of the Kettle films. It was Universal International's policy to pay for all on-the-road expenses when their actors did promotional work for their films. While some actors took advantage of studio money, Percy was honest — to the very last cent. On his return to the studio he handed his modest $3.10 bill to the accounting department and quietly explained that the 10 cents was for the purchase of a soft drink that he'd bought on the way home.

The assorted farm animals that city-raised Percy was to work with, and look at home amongst, terrified him. The milking scene in *Ma and Pa Kettle Go to Town* (1950) was especially nerve-wracking, since he was called upon to physically milk the cow. First off, Percy refused to go near the harmless creature until its feet and tail were securely tied. With that done, Percy nervously pulled up his milking stool, grabbed the udders and

A good ol' fashioned ear twang gets Pa's attention in a promotional shot for *Ma and Pa Kettle at the Fair* (1952).

tugged a couple of times; but alas, no milk. After several takes, Percy just couldn't draw milk from the cow, so with some clever editing, and with the help of a double's hand, on film Pa Kettle looks to be an experienced dairy farmer.

The only part of Percy that was really *in* Pa was the slow drawl to his voice, but even there he slowed down his natural tone to enhance the aura of Pa's slothful manner. For Percy, playing Pa Kettle really *was* acting.

During the production of *Ma and Pa Kettle Go to Town,* Percy was chosen by a noted sculptor as a model for the first known bust of Uncle Sam because of his uncanny resemblance to that mythical symbol of America. The Boy Scouts of America ordered the finished bust for their national headquarters.

It was also during the production of *Ma and Pa Kettle Go to Town* that a UI press release (February 12, 1950) stated that Percy had officially worn his signature derby hat in fifteen legitimate stage plays and twelve motion pictures. Percy was asked to dye the derby black (it was originally brown in color) for movie camera purposes as the deeper color photographed better in a black-and-white picture.

Percy's favorite hat has quite the story behind it. Said at the time to be one of the last of the famous Al Smith derbies, it was gifted to him by the politician back in 1930. "There isn't another one of these famous skimmers in existence," boasted Percy to a UI reporter (December 2, 1953).

Battered and slightly moth-eaten, the derby was a daily fixture on Percy's head, both

Ma lets her hair down, literally, to kick up her heels with Pa.

onscreen and off. The hat had been presented to Percy at a Lamb's Club luncheon honoring politician Al Smith in 1930. At the same time, Smith presented duplicates to magician Howard Thurston and band leader Ben Bernie. Both of these performers lost their souvenir hats prior to their respective deaths. Over the years, several people tried to acquire the hat as a collector's item. The highest offer came from a Detroit theater owner who offered to write him a check for $1,000. Percy politely declined the offer.

Just look at those eyes!

"Howdy folks!"— Percy as Pa Kettle, circa 1954.

Percy and Marjorie shared their "first date" during the production of *Ma and Pa Kettle Go to Town* (1950). They created a sensation when photographers spotted them having dinner at a popular night spot on Sunset Strip. Was there a new Hollywood romance brewing? No, they were good friends out for dinner, nothing more. Still, they did hold the record for being Hollywood's longest-running onscreen married couple.

Marjorie and Percy were a formidable publicity duo when it came time to promote the latest Kettle installment. In those days, radio was the biggest promotional tool, and they'd travel the country together doing interviews and making guest appearances. Whatever it took to promote their latest Kettle feature, they'd do it.

A radio interview in Wichita, Kansas, proved particularly daunting, especially for Percy. He was asked an in-depth question about soil cultivation. It was a question to which Pa would obviously know the answer, but, again, Percy was far from being Pa, in many ways. The tricky farming question left Percy speechless. Seeing Percy's discomfort, Marjorie stepped in to save him, just as Ma would have (Parish, 1973). "First, I would like to know something. As a farm child, I was told that more chicks were produced from brown eggs than white ones. Is that true?" she asked. Her interesting question became such a topic of discussion, the original soil cultivation question was forgotten altogether. Percy breathed a sigh of relief and later thanked Marjorie for saving him from looking foolish on the air.

Totally unaffected by his fame, Percy would tip his hat to the ladies and be the first to say "good morning" to a stranger. Put simply, he was an old-fashioned gentleman. His gentle, calm demeanor was a blessing on a movie set, especially on a movie set with a couple of dozen farm animals, 15 children, and 15 "stage mothers" all linked to those children! Regarding the old Hollywood axiom "Never work with children and animals," the Kettle productions seemed to have missed that memo.

Between scenes Percy was content to quietly rehearse his lines in his dressing room until he was needed. Marjorie, like Ma, would be bustling from one person to another, laughing and joking around. When it came time for Percy to be back on set, Marjorie would just holler, "HEY, PERCYYYYYYY!" and that was his cue to get back to work.

Marjorie would only report to the set when she was needed, and she was superstitious about reading any part but her own. In an interview with the *Indianapolis Star* (September 18, 1949), she said, "I never read my own movie scripts. It spoils the preview for me. I like to be surprised by the story." Early in her career she would learn everyone's lines. Age and experience taught her differently.

Bob Pritchard, whose job it was to handle the mixing dials on the Kettle films, had a tough time tweaking the volume in order to capture Ma's bellow and Percy's soft twang. In a UI production report (March 11, 1953) he explains, "Marjorie Main, as Ma, has a foghorn voice. She must let it out in order to put over the character. Her co-star, Percy Kilbride in the role of Pa, on the other hand, has the softest voice on the screen today. Getting the proper amount of volume for both voices is the hardest job I've ever tackled. The sound boom man must be the nimblest in the business. He's busy every second, pulling the mike back from Marjorie and shooting up close to Percy. It's real work — but it's worth it when we hear the finished product in a projection room. No doubt about it, they're the hardest comedy team that we've ever had to record. But the sharp contrast in their personalities, as depicted by their voices alone, is what has made them so popular."

Born in San Francisco, California, on July 16, 1888, Percy Kilbride started his career in the theater as an usher. He then moved to backstage work and eventually took to acting. After five years at the Central Theater in San Francisco, he like Marjorie toured the country with a stock company. As a young actor his burning ambition was to appear on a Broadway stage; he had the talent to make it in the Big Apple, but just didn't stay around long enough to score a part. "I never had enough money to hang around New York and wait for a good part," he told a UI reporter (January 29, 1952). "I had to keep working, and at the time, that meant hitting the road."

Ironically, the bulk of his stage performances, which Percy once estimated to be close to 1000, were mostly dramatic, with even some romance roles thrown in! It wasn't until the end of his stage career, before entering film, that he tried his hand at comedy. By his 50th year, one opening night in 1938, Percy's dream of appearing on a Broadway stage became a reality. It was a long apprenticeship, but the success of the play *Those We Love* was well worth the wait. From that point on there was no going back; Broadway was home.

His next Broadway play, *Post Road,* gave him a small part and was a moderate success; but it was his third Broadway performance, in *George Washington Slept Here,* that proved to be the pinnacle of his stage career. Percy played the role of the eccentric caretaker, and his performance was so good that Warner Brothers considered no one else for the same role in the 1941 film version. That role was Percy's springboard from stage to screen, and he never looked back.

Ironically, Marjorie was a member of the audience at one of Percy's early stage per-

After fifteen kids, Ma and Pa still look at each other adoringly.

formances. She was so impressed she marked his name in the theater program as an actor she'd like to work with someday. The rest, as they say, is history.

A UI production report (June 25, 1956) asked Percy to sum up why he thought the Kettle films were so popular. Percy said, "I think it's because anybody, even the lowliest bum, can feel superior to the Kettles." In the same studio production report, Marjorie was described as "scratching her head" and saying, "I'll be hanged if I can understand why so many people like the 'Kettle' comedies. Critics don't like 'em. Nobody seems to like 'Kettle' comedies but the people."

During the production of *Ma and Pa Kettle at Waikiki* (1955), Marjorie received a fan letter from a housewife in Little Rock, Arkansas. A UI production report (November 12, 1953) stated that she thanked Marjorie, not for any particular performance that she had enjoyed but for "showing my husband the facts of life about raising kids." Her letter continued, "I have six kids of my own and I get sick and tired of seeing these movies where there are six or seven children in the family, the house is always spotless, and the mother looks like she just stepped out of a beauty parlor." Marjorie wrote back and thanked the woman for her letter, but expressed an opinion that, "if the lady's husband isn't reconciled to the facts of life after being the father of six children, he never will be!"

Many people have tried to figure out why the Kettle series was so popular, and realism seems to be the most common answer. A UI production report (April 6, 1953) stated, "One of the theories for the Kettles' popularity is that the blowzy Ma and the ineffectual Pa, as portrayed by Percy Kilbride, represent some sort of American myth. But that theory doesn't stand up when it's considered that the comedies are amazingly popular as far away as Australia."

The official studio document summarized the topic by saying, "Any or all of the theories thought of can be credited in accounting for the great popularity of the 'Kettles,' but credit must be given where credit is due. It must be considered that Percy Kilbride does a very funny characterization, with his dead pan, outlandish dignity and nasal drawl, and that Marjorie Main knows her business equally well."

A dapper Percy Kilbride as he appeared off-screen, away from the Kettle farm.

After completing *Ma and Pa Kettle at Waikiki,* Percy thoroughly enjoyed his retirement. He'd often spend his days catching up with old theater buddies, and he wouldn't miss his nightly walks along Hollywood Boulevard. He lived a quiet, unassuming life alone (the male equivalent to the way Marjorie lived her life). A horrible automobile accident claimed his life while he was doing what he loved most of all—walking and talking with a friend.

On September 21, 1964, Percy was taking his nightly walk through his neighborhood with fellow actor and long-time friend Ralf Belmont. While crossing busy Hollywood Boulevard, at precisely 9:10 p.m., an out of control car struck them both. Ralf Belmont was killed instantly. Percy was taken to a nearby hospital, where he survived almost three months; but on December 11, 1964, he died on the operating table at 12:05 a.m. during emergency brain surgery. He was 76 years old.

Like Marjorie, Percy had no children. He never married; yet, ironically, he is known as one of the most lovable husbands and fathers that Hollywood ever produced. Years later (Hadleigh, 1994) Marjorie still became choked up when she remembered her onscreen husband: "That was one of the saddest days of my life, when I found out that Percy was hit, and then when he passed on. He was such a sweet soul."

Percy William Kilbride is buried in the Golden Gate National Cemetery, a military cemetery in San Mateo County, California. His memorial says nothing of his acting career, but it does mention his war service. Percy had been a private in Company B of the 317th Infantry in World War I. Like most veterans, it was a chapter of his life that he rarely spoke about. His headstone reads:

PERCY W. KILBRIDE
CALIFORNIA
PVT CO B 317 INF
30 DIVISION
WORLD WAR I
JULY 16, 1888
DECEMBER 11, 1964

TEN

Dr. and Mrs. Krebs

Dr. Stanley Lefevre Krebs, or "Doctor," as Marjorie would call him, was a former minister and devoted lecturer on psychology. He spent most of his life touring the country, and the world, lecturing people about the mind and how it works. He was ahead of his time in his thinking, and for that reason he was considered somewhat of an oddball.

The 14 years of marriage that he and Marjorie shared were mostly spent apart, or at least that was the case after the first couple of years had passed. In those early years of marriage, the "honeymoon period," Marjorie traveled the country with her husband. She'd help him organize his paperwork, make lecture bookings and generally be with him for moral support as they moved from town to town. She even gave up acting for him, which was surprising, considering how much she battled her own father to become an actress in the first place.

In a letter to Marjorie, dated November 20, 1923, Dr. Krebs makes a note that he is writing while on a train, between towns. His dislike for Marjorie's chosen profession is blatantly evident, and he doesn't hold back in telling her so. In trying to convince his wife to accompany him on stage while on his lecture circuit, he writes, "This field is more literary, astute and refined than mimicking life in an imaginary drama on the stage. Real life is better and of a higher order and importance than mimicking life and acting out stories." He continues with the somewhat snobbish statement that "his business" appeals to a "higher type of people."

Marjorie went along with her husband's wishes, at least for a couple of years anyway. Their 26-year age gap meant that Dr. Krebs was at the tail end of his career, and after a couple of solid years on the lecture circuit as newlyweds the couple eventually settled in New York. After a period of rest, Dr. Krebs would be itching to get back on the road again, so he'd travel for a few months before settling back in New York for a rest before his next tour. By this time, Marjorie had returned to the stage (with her husband's reluctant permission), and her increasing work load meant that she was now unable to accompany him on his travels.

It is around this time, in the early '30s, that Dr. Krebs' correspondence to Marjorie turns toward the bizarre. In reading his responses to Marjorie's letters (her correspondence to him is lost), she seems to be accusing him of possessing a roving eye. It was quite the accusation, considering he was now a man approaching 70 years of age.

Dr. Krebs was a well respected doctor of the mind, but Marjorie had the ability to confound him no end. In reading his letters, most of the time he was utterly confused about their relationship; and when it came to money, Marjorie was the one in charge of the purse strings. Dr. Krebs had to account for every dollar he spent, in writing, right down to the last cent!

A rare late 1800s portrait photograph of Marjorie's husband, Dr. Stanley L. Krebs. Courtesy of The Academy of Motion Picture Arts and Sciences.

The first of his letters typed on "The Langwell Hotel" of New York stationary (August 10, 1934) is a cryptic two pages regarding a love triangle gone wrong. Any capitalization or underlining of words is exactly how the letter appears in its original form. It reads:

"Darling Worrying One—

"You must remember, too, that 'C' occasionally kissed Jim on the cheek and after a year or two, occasionally on the lips, you would clap your hands together and exclaim, 'Isn't that fine. I love anyone who loves Jim.' We can't blame HER, therefore, if she thought and still thinks you had opened your heart to receive her into your life and Jim's in an unusually intimate way.

"And now, when I gently but firmly strive to eliminate her so as to remove her to the distance she held before we met all three of us at the Club, no one on earth could blame her for repudiating us, in such a systematic deception which we will thus prove we exercised all these years with her. What a story she COULD tell, if she is incensed so to do, about Toots and Cutem! And where would Toots and Cutem stand THEN?....And yet, I must strive to eliminate her entirely, because I simply cannot endure the thought of your suffering because of suspicions that would undoubtedly roll through your soul if she 'looked after me' during your absence as you asked her to do.

"At the time, I admired you for being so trusting and liberal and great of soul, and still admire the spirit you then manifested. But I don't blame you NOW for being suspicious, for you MADE Jim go too far with her, much farther than he himself WANTED to go, and that HAS SPOILED ALL, spoiled a BEAUTIFUL situation that had grown up naturally, normally, and rightly, and sweetly.

"It never entered even REMOTELY in my mind that OUR love was endangered, for I never felt it was, ours was central and supreme, and everything in my life revolved around that FACT. But NOW, because of what you URGED to be done, you get a feeling towards me very near hatred—you threaten never to write anymore (think of such a thing!), and yet I have your letter stating that very thing in black and white, and going so far as threatening also to divorce me.

"But, I here and now wash my hands of ALL RESPONSIBILITY for whatever may happen to 'C' and to you when it dawns on her mind that I am trying to shake her loose, so as to have nothing more to do with her, in order to reproduce this most cherished and sweet atmosphere of devoted love that existed between you and me before we knew her. I wish you would preserve this statement because I am keeping a carbon copy of it.

"On reading your letters over again I see you want only the yellow bank slips returned, so I will keep the bank book until you write for it. The amount you have in the bank is $367.81, I have not, as you see, drawn a cent since you left.

"I am so eager to hear what has happened to you since you got to Hollywood. You certainly will have lots to write about.—Loving kisses, Cutem."

This letter gives an insight into the tumultuous and unconventional relationship that Marjorie and Dr. Krebs shared for the duration of their 14-year marriage. The woman referred to as "C" in the letter seems to have been a woman known only as "Ceil." Nothing is known about her except for the fact that she did write a brief note to Marjorie telling her that she'd received two letters from "Stanley" regarding the "situation."

In the note, after accusing Marjorie of having *"ulterior motives,"* Ceil ends by telling Marjorie that under the circumstances it is best if she just ceases all communication with both of them. There's no further correspondence from "Ceil" in the group of letters found, so it is unknown whether their "shared" relationship continued.

In his letter, Dr. Krebs mentions that Marjorie asked "C" to "look after him" during her absence. It's a sentence that discreetly alludes to sexual favors, but it seems both Dr. Krebs and Marjorie were involved with "C" at some point in time, and they were all more than just friends.

In another letter, dated February 26, 1935, Dr. Krebs again speaks of Marjorie's relationship with "Ceil":

"Before you went to Hollywood and while there I thought you were wonderful, and so did your good friend, Ceil, the one woman who knows more about you than any other woman on earth, but now...well...you seem to be shrinking in your very soul. Am I to blame?

"Remember what I said to you about Ceil, that you are to handle her alone, without my aid. I will write ONLY when you ask me to, and send you a carbon copy of what I say—all to keep her sweet TOWARD YOU, not only for business reasons, but also because you declared more than once that you do love her for her own sake, personally. I personally don't WANT to write her, only at YOUR orders. Remember this..."

There have been ongoing rumors of Marjorie's bisexuality for years, and in an interview with film historian Boze Hadleigh, published in 1994, toward the end of her life, she was surprisingly candid about both her marriage to Dr. Krebs and her sexuality. Marjorie admitted that her marriage had had its "ups and downs," and that she did, at times, consider divorce.

Despite her claims in many of her interviews that she enjoyed a happy marriage, she later clarified that fact with Hadleigh, telling him, "Dr. Krebs wasn't a very practical man. I didn't figure on having to run the show, I kinda tired of it after a few years. We pretty much went our own ways but we was still in the eyes of the law, man and wife."

As the conversation edged toward the topic of lesbianism, Hadleigh asked Marjorie about the stigma of being gay in Hollywood, especially during the strict studio system of her era. She responded, "I think the 'different' people should be honest with their relatives, if they want to. That's practical. At work, it's not. But if they're really your loved ones..."

Hadleigh delved further, asking her if she had parents or siblings, would *she* tell them? Her response was surprising. "I wouldn't have to tell 'em. I'd show them — I'd just show up with my lady friend, and if I'd had it to do all over, I might live with her. When I was younger, I'd like to have lived with her," she confessed.

Marjorie went on to say that "her lady friend" was someone special, but she dodged Hadleigh's question of whether there was just one someone or more than one woman in her life. "That's for me to know, and you to find out.... Now, I've gone as far as I dare," she smiled coyly.

Despite ending the interview there she was now officially on the record as admitting to at least one lesbian affair during her lifetime. It has been widely reported that Marjorie had a long-standing affair with fellow actress Spring Byington. Despite her four-year marriage to Roy Carey Chandler, which resulted in two daughters, Byington was said to be an active lesbian.

A dedicated actress on both stage and screen, Byington is perhaps best known as the mother in George Cukor's classic coming of age drama *Little Women* (1933). Just as Marjorie specialized in the gruff, tough-love mother roles, Byington was notably the opposite. Throughout her lengthy career she was often cast in the sweet, flighty mother roles.

Without naming names, and for the first time in her life (long after her career was behind her), Marjorie had nothing to lose by "coming out," so to speak. Perhaps that was the reason for her openness, yet Hadleigh admits that she may have regretted her frank admissions later. Several of his requests for another interview went unanswered, and Marjorie's death a few years later closed that door forever.

In a typed letter dated Tuesday, February 26, 1935, on Hotel Foeste, Sheboygan, Wisconsin, stationary, Dr. Krebs wrote a message at the top of his letter: "Please read this letter slowly, thoughtfully." It seems Marjorie's letter had accused her husband of cheating on her with a "red headed woman" at a party years ago. For some reason, she decided it was time to open old wounds. This is Dr. Krebs' response to her accusations:

"Dear Troubled Sweetheart O' Mine —

"Life for the best of us consists of ups and downs. (Kenosis and apotheosis of Jesus) I was up with all love and eagerness to get back to you and your love and arms, counting the days now, dreaming of the Culinary Corner and your snuggling love, when, crash!, came your letter written Thursday and mailed Saturday about the red headed woman of the Bacharach party of years ago, and condemnation after condemnation heaped upon poor me — and for absolutely nothing. I remember IMPORTANT events and forget very naturally unimportant trifles, I tell you all important events, but cannot tell what slips my mind and what is of no moment whatsoever.

"In the spirit of fun, jollity and play I danced with her for not more than one or two minutes, at most, in the presence of THREE WITNESSES, who enjoyed the fun as much as I or she did, and when we sat down at the table none of the party gave it a second thought. It was a trifle that had slipped over the falls and was far down the stream of life to the ocean of oblivion, when, lo and behold, you go and rush after it, dig it up, bring it back to the present, and make a mountain of suffering for yourself and a waste of time for me writing all this out of that piffle and piss-abed speck. You ought to be ashamed of yourself and kick yourself all around the room for such boundless, childish, dirty and rotten suspicions.

"But, you seem to LIKE to find suspicions, you seem to love them, to hanker after them, you seem to relish the feeling of worms crawling over the surface of your sweet soul (sweet and otherwise dear to me as my own soul, as you know only too well). Suspicions are EASY, LAZY, MORONIC. Any fool can make them.

"Here is an example:

"(1) You sat up until 2.00 AM alone on a park bench with a man who tried to "make" you and whom you liked at the time. NO WITNESSES.

"(2) You came in one night, in the wee hours of the morning from an artist's apartment and were drunk with the hair and your dress disheveled. If there was anything to make a husband suspicious THAT WAS.

"(3) You flirted with a Y.M. in a blaze of glory, infatuated by his eyes, face, body and voice, and went out nights with him.

An early publicity pose for her new studio, MGM. She was contracted to the studio for fourteen years.

"Now in either case and all of them I could have suspicions. I asked you what you did in each case, and you told me some things, but I simply HAD to just BELIEVE what you said, you could not and did not furnish PROOF that what you said to me was the truth. I had to just BELIEVE it, didn't I?—But I never referred to either case thereafter, I never flung suspicions in your face, I never be-labored you with them, nor hammered your soul sore with flinging them at you, did I? (Except when you got angry in one of our discussions or fights, and then YOU suggested recourse to these facts to rebut your charges against me.) But I never brought these cases up of my own choice and desire. I just BELIEVED what you said and forgot it all, which led to peace and our unspotted love.

"Jesus well said, 'Let the dead bury their dead,' but you dig them up from their graves in a past which God Almighty can't change, items that are over the falls and are far down the stream toward oblivion, you hook up and spread their suspicious slime over OUR LOVE, so sweet and so precious a thing as that. The 'greatest thing in the world' as a well known author, Drummond, has called it in his famous book.

"Have you never heard this saying?—'If you have nothing good to say about a person, say nothing at all.' The worst is, you make YOURSELF so unhappy and so miserable by these unfounded thoughts, and therefore, make me miserable. What good does it all do? I'm miserable when YOU are. Like it? Do you love and revel in misery for both of us?

"Unless you get wise, I will certainly expect a storm about Alice in Milwaukee. Your suspicions will most likely be aroused by something that is said or happens that I will forget because it mounts to nothing. She is a case for suspicious minds to revel suspiciously in. She is pretty, accomplished in her way, active, clever, esteemed by this large community in Milwaukee, and I'll bet dollars to doughnuts that you will go nuts over my visit here. Say in one or two months, or in three or four years, and raise hell about her in our family between you and me. You'll imagine that I am secretly in love with her and am trying to hide it from you!

"Think of it!—We sat up together alone in the corner of a hotel lobby, chatting and whispering so that others in the lobby could not overhear what we were saying, and kept this up until midnight, nay until 1:00 AM., by the time she got her taxi in the snow storm. There is plenty of ground for SUSPICIONS to grow up like WEEDS, but not a single shred or splinter for sound common sense thought to worry or trouble about.

"Listen dear one—I have given you my heart and mind, both of them are yours, and all of each. I have no more to give. If you are not satisfied with that gift, and long for something else, we will have to talk it all over SERIOUSLY when I get home and decide what is best to do.

"I expect to get home Thursday, March 7th, arriving at 6:00 PM, if I make a connection at Pittsburgh, which is doubtful, owing to the condition of the roads. If not, then at 10:30 PM and IT may be later. So, don't bother yourself to come out to the bus depot to wait for me.

"Still lovingly, devotedly, wholly yours, Cutem.

"PS: I have written you long and detailed letters of my doings, but it seems in vain, it but has aroused your suspicions, and I, little fool that I must be, thought I was giving you pleasure and satisfaction. So, short letters from now on, young lady.

"PPS: On re-reading your letter, I find I have omitted one point you mention, and if I had FORGOTTEN to take it up, you would have raised hell, of course, thinking it was INTENTIONAL on my part. Here is what it is:

"You say: 'I know in your travels you have temptations, all I want is,' and right there, your sentence ends and your letter ends, abruptly like the book of Acts. I do not have any more temptations in travel than YOU do. A pretty girl like you would and must have men 'approaching' them, and even walking down Broadway you have them after you. Well, if I am seated in a car or bus and see a pretty girl in the seat ahead, would you call it a temptation to talk to her? Or, do you think I am tempted to either squeeze her hand or kiss her, or something more? Well, if I should feel that way sometimes, I have never persuaded it or yielded. Is that what you wanted when you said, 'all I want is?'

"I suppose you have in mind that came of the girl you humbled yourself to go see at the Hudnut factory. Her mother sat beside her all the way in the bus, as I told you. What I said to one, I said to both of them. They asked for my lecture and book circulars and I sent them a note saying if they wanted more information I would see them both or either one at lunch and go into my work in detail, for both of them seemed bright and interested. THAT is how I recall what happened with them, AND that is how I recall what happened with them. Is THAT temptation, or what you mean by temptation? They were BOTH business women, and had I got them interested in the Assembly YOU would have been told about it. But it had not gone that far, nothing came of it, and when you found the notes of it in my diary or date book, I told you ALL this. But, you were drinking and would not understand or believe me, you SUSPECTED all sorts of things that hadn't a scintilla of probability in them, and forced a loss of TIME on my part and a loss of DIGNITY on your part in the estimation of those women — running down there to interview them about your husband!

"Once and for all, let me say I did not feel those women were 'TEMPTING' me to anything BAD or IMMORAL or RISKY or DANGEROUS. If I would have told you about it, you would have certainly thought it was VERY important, far more important than it was. I tell you ALL IMPORTANT things, but you go into DETAILS to me and always make a far longer story of what happens to you when I return from my trips than I do or can of what happens to me. You often jokingly say, 'Is that all you have to tell? Well, I would have taken an hour to describe it.'—Just like Alice Moe, two hours to tell what I would have told in ten or fifteen minutes. You women, I suspect, are all the same in this matter. Well, I am not, I have more profound and important matters to occupy my mind. And THAT'S THAT.

"I note in all your letters to me these days you call me, 'My Dear.' And I appreciate that title, but you USED to say, 'Baby,' 'Cutem,' 'I miss you so,' 'I long for your return,' etc. Not one word like that this trip. Well, if after all I have given you and been to you, your love is dwindling or shrinking, I can do no more than I have done or am doing!"

The most informative passage in this letter is Dr. Krebs' reference to Marjorie's "drinking." Marjorie's claim of being a teetotaler was most likely studio hype. Promoting a wholesome image for their stars was a trait that all studios (especially MGM) were particularly known for, even for their character actors.

What's more, Marjorie's own admission of at least one lesbian affair, with the likelihood of others, together with this new information about Marjorie "drinking," completely discredits the image that she worked so hard to portray to the public. But, in all fairness, these letters were not meant for public viewing.

Dr. Krebs writes his next letter to Marjorie on Friday, March 1, 1935. His typed letter is on New Hotel Randolph stationary, Milwaukee, Wisconsin.

"My Dear–

"I have written you love letters, every one of them, since I left you and you saw me off on the 9:05 A.M. bus, two weeks ago. All of mine were love letters, because I love you is the simple but invaluable reason, none higher, nor deeper, and true. But your letters to me have been formal, 'My Dear,' 'Love, Margie'—and that was all.

"Well, I am thankful for that much, but you USED to say more endearing things that, IF YOU have changed, I HAVE NOT. But since the receipt of that red-head SUSPICION letter (which you did not sign nor finish) I have decided to treat you as you treat me. I have worked HARD every inch of this long journey, cramped in busses most of the trip, and all for you, writing, planning business here and making lists of business names, clubs, for immediate work when I return, working over my notes for the book, reading Eddington's belief in Deity, answers to it, making new notes, relaxing at a movie every now and then, talking with Alice to keep her interest alive in the future Assembly. I have worked HARD, I repeat, and THIS coldness on your part is my reward. Tell me, what CAN I do to please you? WHAT DO YOU WANT ME TO DO? I beg you to answer this, that at least you can do and I certainly think is my due. I eagerly await your answer. Love, Cutem."

This was a more forceful, more demanding letter from Dr. Krebs. Marjorie still has

A rare glamor portrait of Marjorie.

him running in circles, but he's shifted in his stance of explaining every little thing to her; instead, he's demanding answers as to why her demeanor has changed toward him. His next letter is of a similar tone, again written on New Hotel Randolph stationary, Milwaukee, Wisconsin. No date.

"My Dear–

"Have you any idea what a satisfaction it is to your correspondents to DATE your letters? Have you no calendar in sight or handy? Perk up in this matter, my suspicious dear (I wish I could drop out that adjective — I don't like it).

"I wonder what you do these days. You never say you make rounds, or anybody calls or phones, as you USED to tell me. Are you saving it all until I get back?

"So, as you don't tell me anything you do, I'll do the same to you and see how you like it. Even this short note is longer than the letters you write me. Love, Cutem.

"P.S. Thanks for sending on the business mail so promptly. But, not a single word in any of your letters about wanting me back, wanting to see me, missing me, anxious to have me back, etc."

Marjorie's ongoing suspicions of her husband's on-the-road indiscretions seemed to eat her alive. In this selection of letters that Dr. Krebs wrote home, most of them carried an in-depth explanation of his actions. All of them contained continuing pleas for her love and forgiveness. In one letter, written from Madison, Wisconsin, he advises Marjorie of his imminent return home, saying, "When I get home I'll just stay in another room until you feel right toward me, for I shall never try to compel you to endure me."

Aside from these letters, among the rare papers were at least 50 IOU's, all written by Dr. Krebs to Marjorie, bar one. Despite Dr. Krebs' busy schedules and tours, it seems he made little or no money to support them. These bizarre promise notes are written on a variety of different scraps of paper; some are handwritten, some are typed. Most notes refer to Marjorie as "MM," and all are signed "Cutem," Marjorie's pet name for the doctor.

June 25, 1931—"Received of 'Marjorie' the sum of ten dollars for half of a new summer suit of mohair. Cutem."

October 5, 1931—"Received from 'Marjorie' one hundred dollars, to be paid back as soon as possible. Cutem."

June 9, 1932 — "Received from 'MM' (sweet thing) the sum of forty dollars for trip to St. Paul. Cutem."

May 29, 1933 — "'MM' gave me $25.00 for room rent, her newspapers, and my cigars. Cutem."

July 8, 1933 — "'MM' gave me $30.00 for room rent ($25.28) and $4.72 for meals. Cutem."

July 29, 1933 — "'MM' gave me five dollars for meals, etc., Cutem."

November 18, 1933 — "Received from 'MM' fifty dollars for three weeks room rent and meals. Cutem."

June 23, 1935 — "'MM' loaned me ten dollars for my lecture trip. Cutem."

The most telling promise note was written by Dr. Krebs on, June 17, 1935, just three months before his death. In it he admits to his failure as a provider. With just a hint of sarcasm, he wrote, "I boasted I could make our living by lecturing, but for various reasons I failed. So, Marjorie loaned [the word "gave" is crossed out and replaced with "loaned"] me $75.00 for which I sincerely thank her. Cutem."

The earliest transaction between husband and wife is dated August 15, 1927. This is the only receipt for monies loaned *to* Marjorie. Signed by Dr. Krebs, it's a receipt for a loan that Marjorie had paid back in full. It reads, "Received of my wife, Marjorie, ten dollars that I had loaned her for buying one share of oil stock. Stanley L. Krebs."

In an undated letter on Hotel De France stationary, 142–146 West 49th Street, New York, N.Y., Dr. Krebs writes to Marjorie about her stage career, money, and about allowing him to come back home. "Please though, understand me, and let me come back," he writes on the last page.

Unfortunately, there are only five pages of this particular letter in existence, which is a shame, considering its informative content. The first four pages deal primarily with Dr. Krebs encouraging and coaching Marjorie in her stage work. It's a strange topic of discussion, since he was always so blatantly against her chosen profession. The last page, the incomplete one, once again deals with Dr. Krebs paying Marjorie back monies owed. He writes, "You know my unfortunate situation at present, owing to these two big bad checks. But, please be patient, you will get your money back as soon as I can do it."

The bulk of the letter reads as follows:

"Darling Mine (believe it or not, it is so),

"No personal matter was meant you see. It was an effort, the only one I knew of that was left, to help you get what you love — a stage job. Selling yourself to these men who buy and sell the emotional, requires somewhat of a different salesmanship than selling a pair of shoes (which can be seen and examined), but spirit, spark, reserve power cannot be seen, per se.

"So, the present situation in the theatre is a different situation which neither you, nor Ameila, nor Dorothy could explain — why you didn't land a job. You called, and faithfully, they saw you, things were doing ok, and yet no job landed such as you desired. You asked me to explain it, and this explanation was my answer:

"Mental Metabolism: In mental metabolism, anger, real anger is stirred, and then the resulting psychological reaction (energy, spark, spirit, temperament — call it what you will), reserve power, driving force (call it what you will) is applied not to the cause or person, who provoked the anger, but to one's daily work — it flushes such work with unwanted energy, intensity, and effectiveness. So, I had to arouse real anger in you, or make no effort at all. Hence I said all the ugly things that I could think of at the time.

"In the few moments you can talk to your prospective employer on the stage, this new increment of reserve power would show and awake you. Remember, although, they would not understand the cause or nature of it. But, 'she has a power about her,' they would say, and, 'we must use that girl.'

"Secondly: To intensify your talk at such a strategic moment with the agency or producer, I also brought into your angry mind the glimpse of what it would be like for you if you did not have me to fall back upon; you see, then you would be compelled to earn your daily bread. Would not that thought or dilemma also increase the intensity of your appeal to the managers and producers? Would you not put more appeal into your voice? Remember, 'hardship, develops talent.'

"In short: The unexplained mystery may be that you have not gone after the job quite earnestly enough, deeply enough, soulfully enough to make you a marked and remembered girl amongst the mob; you may have been indifferent in your talk, possibly from being tired, too.

"This reserve power from the two causes operating in you would cause you, for example, to say to Mr. Hopkins, 'Yes, Mr. Hopkins, I can get work, but I prefer to work under your instructions and for you far more than anyone else, and that is why I'm holding out.' Tell Paul Porter the same thing. Tell it to them earnestly (not carelessly or lightly), with vibrato in your voice or even tears in your eyes. Tell it as though your next meal or very life depended on it, or as though it would be the last thing you would ever say on this earth.

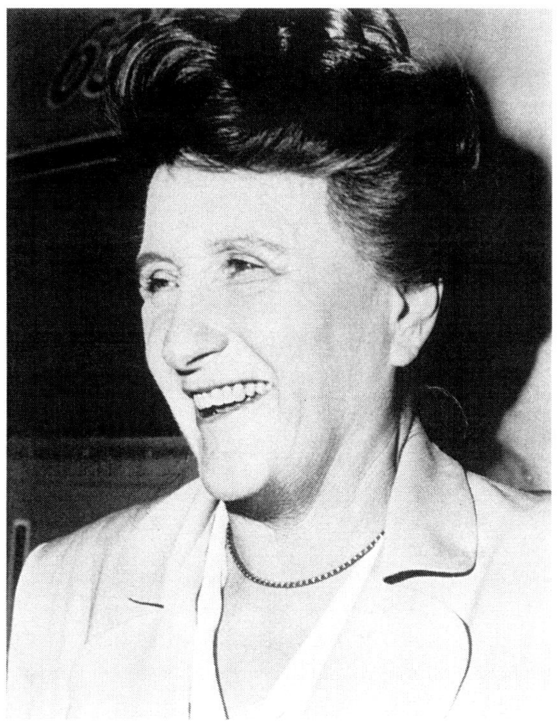

Away from the movie camera, Marjorie is all laughs in this candid close-up.

"What I am trying to do, dearest (and suffering to do it) is to help you in a situation that you all (Amelia and Dorothy) confess is different and even mysterious; help you to the thing you love and by your own legitimate powers stored up to the enth degree. These men who sell emotion to the public must first find it and buy it, and as they like to see it and hear it in these who present themselves before them.

"Please, though understand me, and let me come back. I am most unhappy without you, miserable in fact. But, I cannot come back until you understand the real cause of the recent explosion. I don't..."

As frustrating as it would be to have the last page torn out of an engrossing book, the letter ends there. Marjorie appears to have been struggling with her career in the theater during this period. Dr. Krebs' advice on assertion indicates that a young Marjorie was not nearly as confident as the crusty characters she later portrayed on the silver screen.

As rocky as their marriage seems to have been, all evidence points to Dr. Krebs being a faithful husband. It's unclear if Marjorie's paranoia stemmed from a marital indiscretion that she knew to be true, or was just all in her head. In one letter's handwritten post script proclaiming Dr. Krebs' loyalty he wrote, "Sweetheart, your wish is my law." There are aspects to this union that will probably never be understood. It is lost to time, buried with the two people who understood it best, Dr. and Mrs. Krebs.

In a UI production report (March 3, 1952), Marjorie expressed her own views on marriage, saying, "Marriage is a great deal like the used car business. A smart woman no more expects to be swept off her feet than a salesman expects the customer to come in and demand an automobile. In either case, the first step is the easy one. The real test comes in getting him to keep up the payments after he's read the fine print in the contract."

Filmography and Film Facts

Marjorie Main's extensive filmography is listed here, starting with her earliest screen appearance in *A House Divided* (1931), right through to her last film role as the lovable Ma Kettle in *The Kettles on Old MacDonald's Farm* (1957).

Marjorie Main tallied an impressive 85 films over a 26-year period in the movie industry. In most cases, interesting facts about the productions and co-stars, together with behind the scenes trivia, will be included for each film. (*The Internet Movie Database, The Internet Broadway Database* and over a decade of Universal International production reports were the primary sources for the film facts and trivia.)

1. *A House Divided* (1931)

Director: William Wyler
Screenplay: John B. Clymer and Oale Van Every
Cinematographer: Charles Stumer
Studio: Universal Pictures
Running time: 71 minutes
Black and White
Genre: Drama

Cast

Walter Huston	Seth Law
Douglass Montgomery	Matt Law (as Kent Douglass)
Helen Chandler	Ruth Evans
Mary Foy	Mary
Vivien Oakland	Bess
Lloyd Ingraham	Doctor
Marjorie Main	**Woman at Wedding**
Charles Middleton	Minister
Frank Hagney	Big Bill
Walter Brennan	Musician
Richard Alexander	Sailor (uncredited)
Mary Gordon	Townswoman (uncredited)

When an older man marries a younger woman, only to fall in love with her new husband's son, the bizarre love triangle becomes the talk of the small fishing village they occupy. It's a gossipy tale, with Marjorie appearing as a wedding guest in a minor role.

Trivia: Working title was *Heart and Hand.* Based on the story "*Heart and Hand*" by Olive Edens.

Lead actor Walter Huston is the father of actor John Huston, and the grandfather of actress Angelica Huston. The Huston family rewrote the Hollywood history books. All three generations have the distinct honor of winning an Academy Award.

2. *Hot Saturday* (1932)

Director: William A. Seiter
Screenplay: William A. Seiter
Cinematographer: Arthur L. Todd
Studio: Paramount Pictures
Running time: 73 minutes
Black and White
Genre: Drama
Release dates: October 28, 1932

Cast

Nancy Carroll	Ruth Brock
Cary Grant	Romer Sheffield
Randolph Scott	Bill Fadden
Edward Woods	Conny Billop
Lilian Bond	Eva Randolph
William Collier Sr.	Harry Brock
Jane Darwell	Mrs. Brock
Rita La Roy	Camille
Rose Coghlan	Annie Brock
Oscar Apfel	Ed W. Randolph
Jessie Arnold	Aunt Minnie
Grady Sutton	Archie
Stanley Smith	Joe
Dave O'Brien	Guest
Marjorie Main	**A town gossip**
Nora Cecil	A town gossip

Ruth (Nancy Carroll) is an innocent small-town girl whose life is almost destroyed by gossip mongers who make it their business to spread rumors about her. Cary Grant plays the part of "Romer Sheffield" in one of his earliest screen roles. Marjorie plays one of the town gossips.

Trivia: Randolph Scott and Cary Grant were co-stars in this one. The two were close friends and roommates for much of the 1930s. To this day, the Hollywood rumor mill has been abuzz about just how "close" they really were.

Randolph Scott was honored with his own country song in the 1970s. *Whatever Happened to Randolph Scott?* was a top–20 hit for the Statler Brothers in 1973.

Leading lady Nancy Carroll would later go on to star as Betty MacDonald's mother in the television version of the popular film *The Egg and I* (1951–1952, TV).

Poster tagline: "They Gave Her A Bad Name ... And She Lived Up To It!"

3. *Take a Chance* (1933)

Directors: Monte Brice and Laurence Schwab
Screenplay: Laurence Schwab, Monte Brice and B. G. DeSylva
Cinematographer: William Steiner
Studio: Paramount Pictures
Running time: 82 minutes
Black and White
Genre: Comedy
Release Date: November 25, 1933

Cast

James Dunn	Duke Stanley
Cliff Edwards	Louie Webb

June Knight	Toni Ray
Lillian Roth	Wanda Hill
Charles "Buddy" Rogers	Kenneth Raleigh
Lilian Bond	Thelma Green
Charles Richman	Andrew Raleigh
Dorothy Lee	Consuelo Raleigh
Robert Gleckler	Mike Caruso
Lona Andre	Miss Miami Beach
Marjorie Main	**Woman**

Based on the Broadway play of the same name, the film just didn't live up to the Ethel Merman stage version. The most notable thing about it is an uncredited appearance of Vivian Vance (Lucille Ball's lovable television neighbor) in the chorus of the musical number "Eadie Was a Lady." In the credits, Marjorie is simply listed as "woman," a clue to the brevity of her appearance in this production. She can be spotted briefly in a crowd scene.

Trivia: Cliff Edwards is commonly referred to as "the most well known, unknown actor in Hollywood." Aside from his years of vaudeville and film work, he was an accomplished musician and the voice of Disney's Jiminy Cricket character. The classic song "When You Wish Upon a Star" is also sung by Edwards. He died broke and alone in 1971 (age 78); however, Walt Disney Productions paid for all funeral costs in honor of his timeless work for the studio.

Lead actress Lillian Roth was married and divorced eight times. Actress Susan Hayward portrayed her on the screen (and was nominated for an Academy Award) in the biopic *I'll Cry Tomorrow* (1955). It was a moving story about Roth's lifelong battle with alcoholism.

Despite Mary Pickford and Douglas Fairbanks being commonly referred to as "Hollywood Royalty," it was Charles "Buddy" Rogers who became Pickford's life partner. They were married for forty-two years, and were parted only by her death in 1979.

4. *Art Trouble* (1934)

Director: Ralph Staub
Screenplay: Jack Henley and Dolph Singer
Cinematographer: E. B. DuPar
Studio: Warner Brothers
Running time: 21 minutes
Black and White
Genre: Comedy/Short
Release Date: June 23, 1934

Cast

Harry Gribbon	Art Student
Shemp Howard	Art Student
Beatrice Blinn	Girl at nightclub
Leni Stengel	Girl at nightclub
Hope Landin	(uncredited)
Marjorie Main	**Woman Who Sits on Painting (uncredited)**
James Stewart	Mr. Burton (uncredited)
Gayne Whitman	(uncredited)

This fun short follows two brothers who are sent to Paris by their parents to study art. They hatch a plan to pay two guys to take their place; but when the phony brothers win a local art contest, that's when things go haywire. Again, Marjorie has a brief comedic scene, without so much as a character name to her credit.

Trivia: A fresh faced, twenty-six-year-old James Stewart appears here in his screen debut. Along with Marjorie, Stewart goes uncredited; however, they both went on to star in future films with their names *above* the title.

5. *Crime Without Passion* (1934)

Directors: Ben Hecht and Charles MacArthur
Screenplay: Ben Hecht and Charles MacArthur
Cinematographer: Lee Garmes
Studio: Paramount Pictures
Running time: 70 minutes
Black and White
Genre: Crime/Drama
Release Dates: August 18, 1934 (premiere); August 30, 1934 (nationwide)

Cast

Claude Rains	Lee Gentry
Margo	Carmen Brown
Paula Trueman	Buster Malloy
Whitney Bourne	Katy Costello
Leslie Adams	District Attorney O'Brien
Charles Kennedy	Police Lieutenant Norton
Stanley Ridges	Eddie White
Esther Dale	Miss Keeley, Gentry's secretary
Greta Granstedt	Della
Fuller Mellish	Judge
Ben Hecht	Reporter
Charles MacArthur	Reporter
Marjorie Main	**(uncredited)**
Alice Anthon	(uncredited)
Fanny Brice	Extra in Hotel Lobby (uncredited)
Helen Hayes	Extra in Hotel Lobby (uncredited)

A successful lawyer must establish an alibi for himself after the shooting death of his girlfriend during a heated argument. Marjorie, Fanny Brice and Helen Hayes all play uncredited bit parts in this film. They all appear briefly in several of the crowd scenes. If you study the film carefully, you can spot them without causing too much eye strain.

Trivia: With a birth name of María Marguerita Guadalupe Teresa Estela Bolado Castilla y O'Donnell, it's no mystery as to why actress Margo chose a one-word stage name for her acting career.

Poster Tagline: "He had tired of her — and for that he was sorry. He was tied to her — and for that he hated her!"

6. *Music in the Air* (1934)

Director: Joe May
Studio: Fox Film Corporation
Screenplay: Howard Young and Billy Wilder
Cinematographer: Ernest Palmer
Running time: 85 minutes
Black and White
Genre: Comedy/Musical
Release Date: December 13, 1934

Cast

Gloria Swanson	Frieda
John Boles	Bruno Mahler

Douglass Montgomery	Karl Roder
June Lang	Sieglinde
Al Shean	Dr. Lessing
Reginald Owen	Weber
Joseph Cawthorn	Uppman
Hobart Bosworth	Cornelius
Sara Haden	Martha
Marjorie Main	**Anna**
Roger Imhof	Burgomaster
Jed Prouty	Kirschner

In this lighthearted musical romance with Oscar Hammerstein songs scattered throughout, Frieda (Gloria Swanson) and her lover Bruno (John Boles) each try to make the other increasingly jealous with a series of flirtations involving a younger couple. Most of Marjorie's performance was cut from the film.

Trivia: Marjorie recreated her stage role of Anna in this film adaptation.

This was Gloria Swanson's "comeback" performance; however, the lackluster box-office sales on the film so devastated her that she retreated from acting for another seven years.

The film was based on the play of the same name, written by Oscar Hammerstein II and Jerome Kern.

7. *Naughty Marietta* (1935)

Directors: Robert Z. Leonard and W.S. Van Dyke
Producers: Hunt Stromberg and W. S. Van Dyke
Screenplay: Frances Goodrich, Albert Hackett, John Lee Mahin and Rida Johnson Young
Cinematographer: William Daniels
Studio: MGM
Running time: 105 minutes
Black and White
Genre: Drama/Musical
Production Dates: December 4, 1934–February 7, 1935
Release Dates: March 8, 1935 (premiere, Washington, D.C.); March 22, 1935 (New York City, New York); March 29, 1935 (nationwide)
Awards and Nominations: 1936 Academy Awards, Won, Best Sound Recording, Douglas Shearer; 1936 Academy Awards, Nominated, Best Picture.

Cast

Jeanette MacDonald	Marietta
Nelson Eddy	Captain Richard Warrington
Frank Morgan	Governor Gaspar d'Annard
Elsa Lanchester	Madame d'Annard
Douglass Dumbrille	Prince de Namours de la Bonfain, Marietta's Uncle (as Douglas Dumbrille)
Joseph Cawthorn	Herr "Schumie" Schuman (as Joseph Cawthorne)
Cecilia Parker	Julie
Walter Kingsford	Don Carlos de Braganza
Greta Meyer	Frau Schuman
Akim Tamiroff	Rudolpho
Harold Huber	Abraham "Abe"
Edward Brophy	Ezekial "Zeke" Cramer
Zari Elmassian	Suzette (voice)
Jane Barnes	Casquette Girl (uncredited)
Margaret Bloodgood	Casquette Girl (uncredited)
Ralph Brooks	Suitor (uncredited)

William Burress	Petshop Keeper (uncredited)
Olive Carey	Madame Renavant (uncredited)
Adriana Caselotti	Dancing Doll (uncredited)
Jean Chatburn	Casquette Girl (uncredited)
Edmund Cobb	Mercenary Scout (uncredited)
William Desmond	Gendarme Chief (uncredited)
Billy Dooley	Marietta's Drunken Brother (uncredited)
Mary Doran	Casquette Girl (uncredited)
Minta Durfee	(uncredited)
Margo Early	(uncredited)
Kay English	Casquette Girl (uncredited)
Patricia Farley	Casquette Girl (uncredited)
Mary Foy	Duenna (uncredited)
Roger Gray	Jacques the Suitor (uncredited)
Catherine Griffith	Prunella the Maid (uncredited)
Frank Hagney	Mercenary Scout (uncredited)
Ben Hall	Mama's Boy (uncredited)
Edward Hearn	Mercenary Scout (uncredited)
Richard Hemingway	(uncredited)
Delos Jewkes	Barber (uncredited)
Edward Keane	Major Bonnell (uncredited)
Walter Long	Pirate Leader (uncredited)
Mary Loos	(uncredited)
Wilfred Lucas	Announcer (uncredited)
Marjorie Main	**Casquette Girl (uncredited)**

In their screen debut together, MGM's singing lovebirds, Jeanette MacDonald and Nelson Eddy, fall in love and sing of their happiness to all who'll listen. On the eve of her arranged marriage, Princess Marie (Jeanette MacDonald) trades places with her maid, Marietta, and sails to New Orleans on a cargo ship. She is taken hostage by pirates, and then saved by the handsome Captain Richard Warrington (Nelson Eddy). They soon fall in love.

Meanwhile, in France, a country is searching for their missing Princess. When a reward is offered for information, her uncle and fiancé sail to America in order to bring her back. Upon learning that his new love is a member of royalty and has been ordered back to France to marry a man she doesn't love, Captain Warrington (Nelson Eddy) must save the Princess all over again.

Marjorie's performance is uncredited.

Trivia: The film is based on the 1910 operetta of the same name.

Frank Morgan shaved his moustache for his role in the film. As a result, he was clean shaven for the first time in seventeen years.

Director Robert Z. Leonard resigned after the first day of shooting.

Two years after Adriana Caselotti appeared as the "dancing doll" in this uncredited part she gave life to one of the best known characters in Hollywood history; Walt Disney chose her for the voice of Snow White in his first full-length animated feature film, *Snow White and the Seven Dwarfs* (1937). He was so obsessed with maintaining the mystery of the voice, his contractual arrangement with her stated that she would under no circumstances appear as "the voice of Snow White" anywhere. So, despite being the voice of one of the most loved storybook characters ever, Adriana Caselotti was an unknown name to the movie-going public. But after Walt Disney's death and the expiration of her contract with the studio, Adriana was free to appear anywhere and everywhere, and she did. Well into her old age she took great pleasure in greeting wide-eyed children with her sweet Snow White voice.

Adriana's own obsession with Snow White was evident by the decor in her Beverly Hills home. Both inside and out, her house was filled with figurines and memorabilia relating to the character. Her wishing well and life-sized Snow White and the Seven Dwarfs figurines were the center pieces of her lavish garden. Her answering machine greeted callers with her recording of "I'm Wishing." Adriana Caselloti literally became Snow White. The character was her life and career, and she embraced it with open arms.

Adriana gave voice to Juliet in *The Wizard of Oz* (1939), but it was an uncredited part and the only time she ever voiced a character other than Snow White.

Poster Taglines: "MGM's Great Musical Romance!" "Jeanette MacDonald and Nelson Eddy together for the first time!"

8. *Love in a Bungalow* (1937)

Director: Ray McCarey
Producer: E. M. Asher
Screenplay: Austin Parker, Karen DeWolf and James Mulhauser
Cinematographer: Milton R. Krasner
Studio: Universal Pictures
Running time: 67 minutes
Black and White
Genre: Comedy/Romance
Release Date: July 1, 1937

Cast

Nan Grey	Mary Callahan
Kent Taylor	Jeff Langan
Louise Beavers	Millie
J. Scott Smart	Wilbur Babcock (as Jack Smart)
Minerva Urecal	Mrs. Kester
Hobart Cavanaugh	Mr. Kester
Richard Carle	Mr. Bisbee
Marjorie Main	**Miss Emma Bisbee**
Margaret McWade	Miss Lydia Bisbee
Robert Spencer	Tracy
Arthur Hoyt	A man
Florence Lake	The "Ga-Ga" Prospect
Armand "Curly" Wright	Janitor
Dell Henderson	Manager
Otto Fries	Policeman
William "Billy" Benedict	Telegraph boy
Sherry Hall	Clerk in Bisbee's Office
Edward Earle	Clerk in Bisbee's Office
Arthur Yeoman	Clerk in Bisbee's Office
James T. Mack	Clerk in Bisbee's Office
John Iven	Clerk in Bisbee's Office
Burr Caruth	Clerk in Bisbee's Office
Bobby Watson	Barker

Nan (Mary Callahan) and Kent (Jeff Langan) concoct a plan to pose as newlyweds in order to win a radio contest. What follows is a lightweight comedy farce as they race to gather a dog, a cat and a couple of kids—the required "happy couple" components needed to qualify for the $5000 cash prize. They are, of course, found out, but miraculously manage to talk their way into keeping the prize — and each other — anyway.

Marjorie plays Miss Emma Bisbee, an eccentric spinster. She has a minor role in a comedic scene with her character's sister, Miss Lydia Bisbee (Margaret McWade), also a spinster. *Hollywood Reporter* (undated, 1937) said, "Margaret McWade and Marjorie Main as elderly spinsters add precious bits of real fun."

9. *Dead End* (1937)

Director: William Wyler
Producer: Samuel Goldwyn
Screenplay: Lilian Hellman
Cinematographer: Gregg Toland
Studio: United Artists / Samuel Goldwyn Company
Running time: 93 minutes
Black and White
Genre: Crime/Drama
Release date: August 24, 1937
Awards and Nominations: Academy Awards, 1938, Nominated, Best Actress in a Supporting Role — Claire Trevor, Best Art Direction — Richard Day, Best Cinematography — Gregg Toland, Best Picture — Samuel Goldwyn and Merritt Hulburd.

Cast

Sylvia Sidney	Drina
Joel McCrea	Dave
Humphrey Bogart	"Baby Face" Martin
Wendy Barrie	Kay
Claire Trevor	Francey
Allen Jenkins	Hunk
Marjorie Main	**Mrs. Martin**
Billy Halop	Tommy
Huntz Hall	Dippy
Bobby Jordan	Angel
Leo Gorcey	Spit (as Leo B. Gorcey)
Gabriel Dell	T. B.
Bernard Punsly	Milty
Charles Peck	Philip
Minor Watson	Mr. Griswald
James Burke	Mulligan
Ward Bond	Doorman
Elisabeth Risdon	Mrs. Connell
Esther Dale	Mrs. Fenner
George Humbert	Pascagli
Marcelle Corday	Governess

This Depression-era story of the gangs of New York and the poverty stricken environment that spawned them went on to become the inspiration of some 80-plus films starring "the Dead End Kids," "the Eastside Kids," "the Little Tough Guys" and "the Bowery Boys."

Featuring A-list stars such as Humphrey Bogart and James Cagney, this simple tale of life on the streets launched careers and a series of films that spanned two decades. When "Baby Face" Martin (Humphrey Bogart) returns to his former neighborhood after a stint in reform school, he finds out that his mother, Mrs. Martin (Marjorie Main), wants nothing more to do with him and his girlfriend Francey (Claire Trevor), a prostitute in the latter stages of syphilis. His unwelcome homecoming leads to a whole new influx of crime and violence, one that "Baby Face" Martin begins and ends with his bitter and angry approach to life.

Working title: *Cradle of Crime.*

Trivia: Based on the play of the same name, written by Sidney Kingsley.

To avoid the wrath of the censors, Francey's prostitution and her subsequent illness was implied, and never openly explored. Humphrey Bogart appeared in two other "Dead End" films after *Dead End—Angels with Dirty Faces* (1938, starring alongside James Cagney) and *Crime School* (1938).

The original "Dead End" gang was made up of Billy Halop, Huntz Hall, Bobby Jordan, Leo Gorcey, Gabriel Dell and Bernard Punsley.

Daily Variety (30 July, 1937) said, "Marjorie Main does one great and terrible scene as the mother of the killer who, when he comes to see her, reviles him as a murderer."

Hollywood Reporter (30 July, 1937) said, "Sidney Kingsley's great play reaches the screen with all of the power of its thought-provoking drama intact. There are no compromises with the basic theme of the original. It remains a grim slice of life, ending, as it begins, in futility. A highly effective theatrical reenactment, 'Dead End' is magnificently played by each and every member of its tremendous cast and flawlessly directed by William Wyler."

Samuel Goldwyn was up to his usual eccentric behavior on this film leaving director William Wyler ready to call King Vidor to ask him where he could get one of those "NO MORE GOLDWYN PICTURES!" signs for *his* desk.

In the darkened projection room at Goldwyn's house, director William (Willie) Wyler, writer Garson Kanin, Goldwyn's chief editor, Danny Mandel, and a couple of studio secretaries all nervously gathered around Samuel Goldwyn to watch the final cut of *Dead End*.

From the outset, Goldwyn was clearly unhappy with the pace of the film. Wyler's style was apparent from the opening scene. He was slowly building the audience to an eventual climax that would carry one hard punch, but Goldwyn grew impatient with each passing scene. He had no time to watch for subtle hints; he wanted to show it for what it was—without all these cryptic clues. He wanted all irrelevant scenes cut from the picture. The only problem was, what Goldwyn saw as "irrelevant" Wyler saw as crucial.

At this point in time, the picture was at the point where Humphrey Bogart, playing Baby Face Martin, walks into a bar with his no-good friend Hunk, played by Allen Jenkins. They both order a whiskey. The bartender pours them a shot glass each and then puts the bottle down in front of them. Just as he's about to walk away, he takes a second look at the unsavory pair. His instincts cause him to come back, take a pencil from behind his ear and casually mark the level of whiskey in the bottle before walking away.

All of a sudden, Goldwyn shouted, "Stop it!" as he maniacally pressed the button to signal to the projectionist to stop the picture. "I said stop it!" he screamed again. Eventually the film faded out and the lights went up in the room. All eyes were on Goldwyn. This was BIG! He never stopped films. In Garson Kanin's *Hollywood*, he recalls the rest of the conversation:

"'That's out,' said Goldwyn, 'The bottle business. It doesn't mean a goddam thing!'

"At this point Wyler was out of his chair and on his feet. 'What the hell are you talking about, Sam? That's the most important scene in the whole reel.'

"'It's OUT!' Goldwyn screamed again.

"Wyler sighed, 'But why Sam?'

"'Because,' said Goldwyn, 'it's too complicated. Nobody will understand it.'

"Wyler pleaded, 'A child can understand it.'

"Suddenly, as if he was cued to do so, Samuel Goldwyn's twelve year old son, Sam Jr., appeared in the hallway. The shouting match halted and everyone turned to the wide eyed child. 'Come in, Sammy,' Goldwyn said, gesturing with his hand for his son to step into the room, 'I have something I want you to see.'

"Goldwyn signaled for the scene to be rolled back, the lights went down and as soon as the scene was over, the film faded and the lights came up again. It was apparent to everyone in the room that Goldwyn was hell bent on proving Wyler wrong by asking his own child to analyze the scene for him.

"Goldwyn turned to his son, 'Well, did you understand that, Sammy? The bottle business?'

"'Sure, Pop,' Sammy responded confidently.

"Goldwyn stared at him open mouthed, 'You did?!'

"Wyler grinned, half confident of victory, yet half disbelieving that it was the word of a twelve year old that was deciding the fate of his 'artsy' scene.

"'Let me hear you explain it to me then?' Goldwyn said.

"'Well,' said Sammy. 'The guy puts down the bottle, but then ... he sees that these other two guys are ... sort of like gangsters ... so he doesn't trust them ... so he makes a mark on the bottle so he'll know how much they took.'

"Wyler triumphantly clapped his hands together. The kid got it! And, it wasn't just any kid, it was Samuel Goldwyn's kid! There was no sweeter victory, or so he thought!

"There was a long pause from Goldwyn. The whole room waited anxiously for his response. He eventually turned to Wyler and gruffly mumbled, 'Ahhhh, what the hell does a child know!'

"Wyler flopped into his chair, exhausted!"

Samuel Goldwyn was a tornado, a cantankerous character who enjoyed a battle of words with almost everyone he came into contact with. He drove directors crazy, not just with his tyrannical behavior, but with his bizarre expressions that were commonly referred to as "Goldwynisms." Some of his most infamous quotes are (IMDB):

"Include me out."

"When I want your opinion, I'll give it to you."

"A verbal agreement isn't worth the paper it's written on."

"Anyone who sees a psychiatrist should have their head examined!"

"I had a great idea this morning, but I didn't like it."

"Hospitals are no place to be sick. I'm bored out of my brain."

10. *Stella Dallas* (1937)

Director: King Vidor
Producer: Samuel Goldwyn
Screenplay: Victor Heerman and Sara Y. Mason
Cinematographer: Rudolph Mate
Studio: Samuel Goldwyn Company / United Artists.
Running time: 105 minutes
Black and White
Genre: Drama
Release Date: August 5, 1937 (New York City, New York)

Awards and Nominations: 1938 Academy Awards, Nominated, Best Actress—Barbara Stanwyck; 1938 Academy Awards, Nominated, Best Actress in a Supporting Role—Anne Shirley.

Cast

Barbara Stanwyck	Stella Martin Dallas
John Boles	Stephen Dallas
Anne Shirley	Laurel Dallas

Barbara O'Neil	Helen Morrison Dallas
Alan Hale	Ed Munn
Marjorie Main	**Mrs. Martin**
George Walcott	Charlie Martin
Ann Shoemaker	Miss Phillibrown
Tim Holt	Richard Grosvenor III
Nella Walker	Mrs. Grosvenor
Bruce Satterlee	Cornelius "Con" Morrison
Jimmy Butler	Cornelius "Con" Morrison (grown up)
Jack Egger	John Morrison
Dickie Jones	Lee Morrison
Jessie Arnold	Ed's Landlady (uncredited)
Harry Bowen	(uncredited)
Harlan Briggs	Mr. Beamer (uncredited)
Laraine Day	Girl at Resort (uncredited)

This sentimental classic stars Barbara Stanwyck as Stella Dallas, a woman from the wrong side of the tracks who marries money, but can't quite shake off her old lifestyle.

After Stella snares a rich husband, Stephen Dallas (John Boles), the birth of their daughter, Laurel (Anne Shirley), soon becomes the focus of Stella's life, to the detriment of her marriage.

Stella spoils her daughter, giving her everything that she herself lacked in life — to the point where her daughter's new rich friends and lifestyle make Stella realize that Laurel would be better off without her as a mother.

The sacrifice that Stella makes to benefit her daughter's future is a noble one, yet it goes down as one of saddest moments in screen history. The final scene of Stella standing in the rain among a crowd of strangers, trying desperately to catch a glimpse of her daughter's society wedding, is truly heart wrenching.

In arguably one of her best roles, Barbara Stanwyck was nominated for a Best Actress Academy Award for her portrayal of Stella, and Anne Shirley was given equal consideration with a Best Supporting Actress nomination for her portrayal as Laurel. Marjorie briefly is seen in the first few scenes, playing Barbara Stanwyck's mother.

Trivia: The story, based on the best-selling book *Stella Dallas*, had been filmed previously (as *Stella Dallas* in 1925), and was later remade (again as *Stella Dallas*) in 1990.

Samuel Goldwyn bought the movie rights for the bargain price of $15,000. King Vidor took on the task of director. By the end of production, Goldwyn had made the legendary director a nervous wreck.

According to Hollywood biographer Arthur Marx, Goldwyn would storm onto the set like a tornado, yelling and screaming. He'd bellow that the rushes were the worst he'd ever seen, and the picture was "a mess." After disrupting the set and upsetting the cast and crew, he'd leave as quickly as he came. Without fail, Vidor would get a phone call from Goldwyn the same night, apologizing for his irrational behavior. He'd end the conversation by telling Vidor that he'd watched the rushes again, and they were actually "quite good." Still, Goldwyn would create the very same scene the following week, and the week after that, right up until production ended.

Goldwyn's unpredictable outbursts were such a common occurrence throughout the production that, by the end of shooting, a frazzled Vidor had put a permanent sign on his desk that read "NO MORE GOLDWYN PICTURES!" in bold letters. Despite *Stella Dallas* receiving rave reviews and amassing several Oscar nominations, Vidor stuck to his word; he never did another Goldwyn picture.

Barbara Stanwyck is often mentioned as

"the Best Actress Who Never Won an Oscar." Her performance in *Stella Dallas* (1937) is as Oscar-worthy as any performance before or since; yet the coveted award of Best Actress for 1937 went to Luise Rainer for her role in *The Good Earth.* It was Rainer's second Oscar out of just three films. She received the same award the year before for her role in *The Great Ziegfeld* (1936). Rainer's second award turned out to be a controversial victory over her more experienced peers—Janet Gaynor, Greta Garbo, Irene Dunne and, of course, Barbara Stanwyck. In perhaps the most honest Oscar-loser comment of all time, Stanwyck lamented, "My life's blood was in that picture. I should have won." (Smith, 1988)

All four losers were equal favorites to win the award. Stanwyck's nomination for *Stella Dallas* was the first of a total of four Best Actress nominations earned throughout her prestigious career. Stanwyck's *Stella Dallas co-star,* Anne Shirley, lost her one and only chance of taking home a gold statue for Best Supporting Actress when Alice Brady won for her role in *Old Chicago* (1937).

The *Hollywood Spectator* (July 31, 1937) reviewed Marjorie's performance favorably: "Drab, slovenly, long-suffering, the impression we get of her in the home in which Stella was raised, makes reasonable everything which later is developed in Stella's character. Miss Main is an artist and her contribution to the picture is out of all proportion to the length of her part."

A radio serial based on the characters from *Stella Dallas* ran for twenty years.

Poster tagline: "The Emotional Classic of the Screen."

11. *The Man Who Cried Wolf* (1937)

Director: Lewis R. Foster
Producer: E. M. Asher
Screenplay: Charles Grayson and Sy Bartlett
Cinematographer: George Robinson
Studio: Universal Pictures
Running time: 68 minutes
Black and White
Genre: Crime
Release date: August 29, 1937

Cast

Lewis Stone	Lawrence Fontaine
Tom Brown	Tommy Bradley
Barbara Read	Nan
Marjorie Main	**Amelia Bradley**
Robert Spencer	Reporter
Robert Gleckler	Captain Walter Reid
Forrester Harvey	Jocko
Billy Wayne	Halligan
Jameson Thomas	George Bradley

In an interesting twist on "the Boy Who Cried Wolf" theory, Lawrence Fontaine (Lewis Stone) confesses to a series of murders that he didn't commit in order to convince the police that he's insane. It's all a master plan to get away with the one murder that he does intend to do himself. After the murder, he, of course, confesses to police; and, just as he planned, the police don't believe him for a minute. As the tag line goes, "He was too perfect in a 'perfect crime!'

Marjorie plays Amelia Bradley, the sister of the murder victim.

Trivia: The film is based on the story "*Too Clever to Live*" by Arthur Rolhsfel.

Leading actor Lewis Stone was a veteran of over 200 films, both silents and sound. He is perhaps best remembered for his portrayal of lovable Judge James Hardy in the popular series of films featuring

Mickey Rooney as Andy Hardy, the Judge's son.

After running outside to move along some mischievous teenagers who were taking pleasure in destroying his meticulously kept flower beds, Stone died of a massive heart attack. He was 73 years old and still working at the time of his tragic death.

Poster taglines: "He Was Too Perfect in a 'Perfect Crime.'"

12. *The Wrong Road* (1937)

Director: James Cruze
Producer: Colbert Clark
Screenplay: Gordon Rigby and Eric Taylor
Cinematographer: Ernest Miller
Studio: Republic Pictures
Running time: 62 minutes
Black and White
Genre: Drama/Romance
Release date: October 11, 1937

Cast

Richard Cromwell	Jimmy Caldwell
Helen Mack	Ruth Holden
Lionel Atwill	Mike Roberts
Horace McMahon	Blackie Clayton
Russ Powell	Chief Ira Foster
Billy Bevan	McLean
Marjorie Main	**Martha Foster**
Rex Evans	Victor J. Holbrook
Joseph Crehan	District Attorney
Arthur Hoyt	Beamish, the banker
Syd Saylor	Big Hobo
Selmer Jackson	Judge
Chester Clute	Dan O'Fearna

When young lovers Jimmy (Richard Cromwell) and Ruth (Helen Mack) are sent to prison for embezzling $100,000 from the bank where Jimmy worked, Mike Roberts (Lionel Atwill), an insurance company detective, helps the pair recover the missing cash and, in the process, rebuild their lives.

Marjorie played Mrs. Foster in another of her stereotypical mother roles.

Trivia: Leading actor Richard Cromwell appeared in many 1930s films. He was the first husband of actress Angela Lansbury, but they divorced after barely a year of marriage. Cromwell succumbed to cancer on October 11, 1960. He was fifty years old.

13. *The Shadow* (1937)

Director: Charles C. Coleman
Producer: Wallace MacDonald
Screenplay: Arthur T. Horman and Milton Raison (story)
Cinematographer: Lucien Ballard
Studio: Columbia Pictures
Running time: 59 minutes
Black and White
Genre: Mystery
Release date: December 22, 1937

Cast

Rita Hayworth	Mary Gillespie
Charles Quigley	Jim Quinn
Marc Lawrence	Kid Crow
Arthur Loft	Sheriff Jackson
Dick Curtis	Carlos
Vernon Dent	Dutch Schultz
Marjorie Main	**Hannah Gillespie**
Donald Kirke	Peter Martinet

Dwight Frye	Vindecco
Bess Flowers	Marianne
William Irving	Mac
Eddie Fetherston	Woody
Sally St. Clair	Dolores
Sue St. Clair	Rosa
John Tyrrell	Mr. Moreno

When Mary Gillespie (Rita Hayworth) takes over Col. Gillespie's Circus after her father's death, her determination to restore it to its former glory is shared by her publicist lover, Jim (Charles Quigley). However, when the sleazy equestrian star, Peter Martinet (Donald Kirke), is murdered during his performance, the eyes of suspicion fall on everyone. Could it have been the work of the mysterious shadowy figure that has been seen on the circus lot?

After Vindecco, Martinet's disfigured assistant, divulges clues about Martinet's death to Mary, *his* death soon follows. Despite his feelings for Mary, Jim turns her over to the authorities; but he returns to the circus, vowing to uncover the identity of the mysterious shadowy figure once and for all.

In a minor role, Marjorie plays Rita Hayworth's lovable Aunt Hannah.

Trivia: This is the first film in which Margarita Carmen Cansino was billed as Rita Hayworth!

The Shadow was released as *The Circus Shadow* in the U.K. Joan Crawford starred in the campy 1968 remake, *Berserk!*

14. *City Girl* (1938)

Director: Alfred L. Werker
Producer: Sol M. Wurtzel
Screenplay: Robin Harris, Frances Hyland and Lester Ziffren
Cinematographer: Harry Jackson
Studio: 20th Century–Fox
Running time: 63 minutes
Black and White
Genre: Crime
Release date: January 7, 1938

Cast

Phyllis Brooks	Ellen Ward
Ricardo Cortez	Charles Blake
Robert Wilcox	Donald Sanford
Douglas Fowley	Ritchie
Chick Chandler	Mike Harrison
Adrienne Ames	Vivian Ross (uncredited)
Irving Bacon	Porter (uncredited)
Lynn Bari	Waitress (uncredited)
Brooks Benedict	Pete (uncredited)
Wade Boteler	Police Radio Announcer (uncredited)
Lon Chaney Jr.	Gangster (uncredited)
Chick Collins	Customer (uncredited)
Heinie Conklin	Cook (uncredited)
Edgar Dearing	Detective Lieutenant (uncredited)
Ralph Dunn	Mac, Policeman (uncredited)
Jack Gargan	Bookie (uncredited)
Harold Goodwin	Chaney's Aide (uncredited)
Eddie Hart	Bookie (uncredited)
Milton Kibbee	Doctor's Assistant (uncredited)
Charles Lane	Dr. Abbott (uncredited)
Robert Lowery	Greenleaf (uncredited)
George Lynn	Steve (uncredited)

George Magrill	Plainclothesman (uncredited)
Marjorie Main	**Mrs. Ward (uncredited)**

This simple 1930s crime drama is about a waitress who's forced to get information from a District Attorney by a low-life racketeer. Complications arise when she falls in love with the DA.

Both Marjorie and Lon Chaney Jr. go uncredited in this one.

15. *Boy of the Streets* (1938)

Director: William Nigh
Screenplay: Gilson Brown, Rowland Brown (story) and Scott Darling
Cinematographer: Gilbert Warrenton
Studio: Monogram Pictures
Running time: 76 minutes
Black and White
Genre: Drama
Release date: January 8, 1938

Cast

Jackie Cooper	Chuck Brennan
Maureen O'Connor	Norah
Kathleen Burke	Julie
Robert Emmett O'Connor	Rourke
Matty Fain	Blackie
George Cleveland	Tim "Flannel-Mouth" Farley
Marjorie Main	**Mrs. Brennan**
Bill Elliott	Dr. Alben (as Gordon Elliott)
Guy Usher	"Fog Horn" Brennan
Don Latorre	Tony
Paul White	Spike

Prints of this street kid drama seem to have disappeared, so a basic plot outline is all that exists today. *Boy of the Streets* stars Jackie Cooper an over-confident street kid who worships his no-good father.

Trivia: Playing the part of Nora, this was Maureen O'Connor's debut role; however, she wouldn't be seen onscreen again until 1960. After 22 years away from the acting profession, her comeback was less than impressive — an uncredited part in *Expresso Bongo* (1960).

16. *Penitentiary* (1938)

Director: John Brahm
Producer: Robert North
Screenplay: Martin Flavin (play), Seton I. Miller and Fred Niblo Jr.
Cinematographer: Lucien Ballard
Studio: Columbia Pictures
Running time: 74 minutes
Black and White
Genre: Drama
Release date: February 5, 1938

Cast

Walter Connolly	Mathews
John Howard	William Jordan
Jean Parker	Elizabeth
Robert Barrat	Grady
Robert Allen	Doctor (uncredited)
Stanley Andrews	Capt. Dorn (uncredited)
Billy Arnold	Fingerprint Man (uncredited)

Ward Bond	Prison Barber (uncredited)
Ralph Brooks	Man (uncredited)
Earle D. Bunn	Machine Gunner (uncredited)
William Chapman	Art Dupuis (uncredited)
George Chesebro	Guard (uncredited)
Kernan Cripps	Conductor (uncredited)
Marjorie Main	**Katie (uncredited)**

Little is known about this 1938 crime drama; however, it was remade as *Convicted* in 1950, with Glenn Ford in the lead role. In the later film, a prison warden believes in the innocence of one of his prisoners and makes it his business to prove the man should be set free. There's no reason to believe the remake would be far off the plot line of the now-lost original.

Trivia: Penitentiary was filmed on location in Anamosa, Iowa.

17. *King of the Newsboys* (1938)

Director: Bernard Vorhaus
Producer: Bernard Vorhaus
Screenplay: Horace McCoy (story), Samuel Ornitz (story), Peggy Thompson and Louis Weitzenkorn
Cinematographer: Jack A. Marta
Studio: Republic Pictures
Running time: 65 minutes
Black and White
Genre: Drama/Romance
Release date: March 18, 1938

Cast

Lew Ayres	Jerry Flynn
Helen Mack	Mary Ellen Stephens
Alison Skipworth	Nora
Victor Varconi	Wire Arno
Sheila Bromley	Connie Madison
Alice White	Dolly
Horace McMahon	Lockjaw
William "Billy" Benedict	Squimpy
Ray Cooke	Pussy
Jack Pennick	Lefty
Mary Kornman	Peggy
Gloria Rich	Maizie
Oscar O'Shea	Mr. Stephens
Marjorie Main	**Mrs. Stephens (uncredited)**

This predictable love story revolves around Jerry (Lew Ayres), the blue collar boyfriend of Mary Ellen (Helen Mack), who leaves him after falling for the lavish lifestyle that a gangster can provide for her. Heartbroken, Jerry sets out to prove to his girlfriend that he too can become a money-making success—and legally, unlike the slum gangster that she's left him for.

He succeeds in setting up a newspaper distribution company; and in the throes of his new-found success, he still wants Mary Ellen (Helen Mack) to see what a mistake she made in leaving him. Ironically, after both of them lose everything they first thought was important in life, they come to the realization that all they really need is each other.

Marjorie goes uncredited again in this one, playing Mrs. Stephens.

Trivia: King of the Newsboys was filmed at the following California locations—George Lewis Mansion, Benedict Canyon, and Bel Air.

18. *Test Pilot* (1938)

Director: Victor Fleming
Producer: Louis D. Lighton
Screenplay: Frank Wead (story), Howard Hawks, Vincent Lawrence, John Lee Mahin and Waldemar Young
Cinematographer: Ray June
Studio: MGM
Running time: 118 minutes
Black and White
Genre: Drama/Romance
Release dates: April 16, 1938 (premiere, New York City); April 22, 1938 (nationwide)
Awards and nominations: 1938 Academy Awards, Nominated, Best Film Editing, Tom Feld; Nominated, Best Picture, Louis D. Lighton; Nominated, Best Writing Original Story, Frank Wead.

Cast

Clark Gable	Jim Lane
Myrna Loy	Ann Barton
Spencer Tracy	Gunner Morris
Lionel Barrymore	Howard B. Drake
Samuel S. Hinds	General Ross
Marjorie Main	**Landlady**
Ted Pearson	Joe
Gloria Holden	Mrs. Benson
Louis Jean Heydt	Benson
Virginia Grey	Sarah
Priscilla Lawson	Mable
Claudia Coleman	Mrs. Barton
Arthur Aylesworth	Frank Barton

In an all-star cast, Clark Gable stars as Jim Lane, a test pilot who's married to the ever-nervous and insecure Ann (Myrna Loy). Her moments of angst are heart-wrenching as she watches her husband walk out the door on another mission, not knowing if he'll make it back alive.

Gunner's (Spencer Tracy) biggest job as devoted mechanic is to keep his flying buddy sober; so when Gunner is killed after Jim sends the plane into a tail-spin whilst testing it at 30,000 feet, Jim is understandably shaken to the bone. Jim never goes up again; instead he stays grounded, instructing future army pilots on how to fly in battle.

Marjorie plays the landlady whom Jim sweet-talks into not demanding rent in advance.

Trivia: Spencer Tracy picked up his second Best Actor Oscar the same year (1938) for his portrayal of the real-life Father Edward J. Flanagan in *Boys Town* (1938).

Clark Gable may have been known as "the King of Hollywood," but a closer inspection of his birth certificate reveals that he was mistakenly listed as a female!

Spencer Tracy grew increasingly hostile toward Clark Gable throughout the production. As filming progressed, Tracy began to realize that he was playing second fiddle in a "Gable Picture," and he didn't like it one little bit. So he decided to take the one pivotal scene that he did have—his death scene—and make it memorable. Gable remarked that Tracy died the slowest, most lingering death in history.

According to the Turner Classic Movies (TCM) website, while cradling Tracy's head during one particular take, Gable finally lost patience. He dropped Tracy's head to the ground and shouted, "Die, goddamnit, Spence! I wish to Christ you would!" Unfortunately, that take didn't make it into the final cut, but it surely would have made the scene memorable (and after all, that was Spencer Tracy's plan to begin with).

Poster tagline: "They're yours... in a heart-walloping love story!"

19. *Three Comrades* (1938)

Director: Frank Borzage
Producer: Joseph L. Mankiewicz
Screenplay: F. Scott Fitzgerald, Edward E. Paramore Jr. and Erich Maria Remarque (novel)
Cinematographer: Joseph Ruttenberg
Studio: MGM
Running time: 100 minutes
Black and White
Genre: Drama
Release dates: June 2, 1938 (premiere, New York City); June 3, 1938 (nationwide)
Awards and nominations: 1939 Academy Awards, Nominated, Best Actress in a Leading Role, Margaret Sullivan. 1939 New York Film Critics Circle Awards, Won, Best Actress in a Leading Role, Margaret Sullivan.

Cast

Robert Taylor	Erich Lohkamp
Margaret Sullivan	Patricia "Pat" Hollmann
Franchot Tone	Otto Koster
Robert Young	Gottfried Lenz
Guy Kibbee	Alfons
Lionel Atwill	Franz Breuer
Henry Hull	Dr. Heinrich Becker
Charley Grapewin	Local Doctor
Monty Woolley	Dr. Jaffe
Marjorie Main	**Old Woman near Phone (uncredited)**
Phillip Terry	Young Soldier (uncredited)

This is a bleak WWI love story surrounding Pat (Margaret Sullivan) and three young soldiers, all friends, played by Robert Taylor, Franchot Tone and Robert Young. All three men are desperately in love with Pat; however, her future is laid out for her after discovering she has contracted tuberculosis. Despite her bleak prognosis, she marries Erich (Robert Taylor); but after Gottfried (Robert Young) is killed in a street brawl, Pat is so grief stricken that she gives in to her illness and dies.

Trivia: Production was held up many times due to Margaret Sullivan's superstition about not working until it had rained.

Leading man Robert Taylor was one of the longest contracted players tied to the same studio, ever. He was with MGM for over twenty years.

Two of Joan Crawford's real-life husbands are in this film — Franchot Tone as "Otto" in a lead role, and Phillip Terry (uncredited) as a young soldier,.

Charley Grapewin, who played the local doctor in this film, would go on to play the most noted role of his 100-film career the following year — Dorothy's gentle Uncle Henry in *The Wizard of Oz* (1939).

Poster taglines: "Torn from a million souls." "A Tribute to Live That You'll Carry Through Life."

20. *Romance of the Limberlost* (1938)

Director: William Nigh
Screenplay: Marion Orth
Cinematographer: Gilbert Warrenton
Studio: Monogram Pictures
Running time: 75 minutes
Black and White
Genre: Drama
Release date: June 16, 1938

CAST

Jean Parker	Laurie
Eric Linden	Wayne
Marjorie Main	**Nora**
Edward Pawley	Corson
Betty Blythe	Mrs. Parker
Sarah Padden	Sarah
George Cleveland	Nathan
Hollis Jewell	Chris
Guy Usher	Judge
Jean O'Neill	Ruth
Budd Buster	Fair Barker
William Gould	Lawyer
Harry Harvey	Jones
Jack Kennedy	Abner

This is a romantic tale of a small-town girl (Jean Parker) who falls in love with a rookie lawyer (Eric Linden). After defending an innocent suspect for killing her intended husband (a pre-arranged marriage organized by her pushy aunt), the neophyte barrister wins his first case—and gets the girl as a bonus!

Marjorie plays the Aunt of Jean Parker's character, and is nothing short of superb in a difficult, unsympathetic role.

Trivia: Little is known about this film. Its status is officially labeled as "lost"—meaning no prints are currently known to exist.

It was based on the novel *Girl of the Limberlost* by Gene Stratton Porter.

21. *Prison Farm* (1938)

Director: Louis King
Producers: William LeBaron and Stuart Walker
Screenplay: Stuart Anthony, Eddie Welch, Robert Yost and Edwin V. Westrate (story)
Cinematographer: Harry Fischbeck
Studio: Paramount Pictures
Running time: 67 minutes
Black and White
Genre: Drama
Release date: June 17, 1938

CAST

Shirley Ross	Jean Forest
Lloyd Nolan	Larry Harrison
John Howard	Dr. Roi Conrad
J. Carrol Naish	Senior Guard Noel Haskins
Porter Hall	Fran Supt. Chiston R. Bradby
Anna Q. Nilsson	Barricks Matron Ames
Esther Dale	Cora Waxley
May Boley	"Shifty" Sue
Marjorie Main	**Chief Matron Brand**
John Hart	"Texas" Jack
Diane Wood	Prisoner Dolly
Jimmy Conlin	Dave, the Grocer
Mae Busch	Prisoner Trixie
Blanche Rose	Laundry Trustee
Ruth Warren	Prisoner Josie
Robert Brister	Joe Easy
Virginia Dabney	Prisoner Maisie
Dick Elliott	The Glenby Judge
William Holden	Prisoner

When a young woman falls in love with a prisoner, she gets herself arrested and ends up in prison herself.

Marjorie plays Chief Matron Brand, the head of the prison farm where Jean (Shirley Ross) and Larry (Lloyd Nolan) are sent.

Trivia: Prison Farm was 20-year-old William Holden's first film. He plays a prisoner. Silent film stars Anna Q. Nilsson and Mae Busch find their voices in this film; both have prominent roles.

22. *Little Tough Guy* (1938)

Director: Harold Young
Producer: Ken Goldsmith
Screenplay: Gilson Brown and Brenda Weisberg (story)
Cinematographer: Elwood Bredell
Studio: Universal
Running time: 86 minutes
Black and White
Genre: Crime/Drama
Release date: July 22, 1938

Cast

Robert Wilcox	Paul Wilson
Helen Parrish	Kay Boylan
Marjorie Main	**Mrs. Boylan**
Jackie Searl	Cyril Gerrard
Peggy Stewart	Rita Belle
Helen MacKellar	Mrs. Wanamaker
Edward Pawley	Mr. Gerard (as Ed Pawley)
Olin Howlin	Baxter (as Olin Howland)
Pat C. Flick	Peddler
Billy Halop	Johnny Boylan
Huntz Hall	Pig
Gabriel Dell	String
Bernard Punsly	Ape
Hal E. Chester	Dopey (as Hally Chester)
David Gorcey	Sniper

The first of the low-budget Universal "Dead End Kids" series, *Little Tough Guy* tells the story of Johnny Boylan (Billy Halop), who gets himself into all sorts of trouble by joining a street gang to provide for his family.

When a major crime is planned, Johnny goes along for the ride; however, the law catches up with the kids, and the all-too-familiar message that "crime doesn't pay" brings the movie to a ho-hum end.

Marjorie plays Mrs. Boylan, the brash mother of Billy Hallop's character, Johnny.

23. *Under the Big Top* (1938)

Director: Karl Brown
Producer: William T. Lackey
Screenplay: Llewellyn Hughes (story) and Marion Orth
Cinematographer: Gilbert Warrenton
Studio: Monogram Pictures
Running time: 64 minutes
Black and White
Genre: Drama/Romance
Release date: August 31, 1938

Cast

Anne Nagel	Penny
Jack La Rue	Ricardo
Marjorie Main	**Sara**
Grant Richards	Pablo
George Cleveland	Joe
Herbert Rawlinson	Herman
Rolfe Sedan	Pierre
Betty Compson	Marie
Harry Harvey	McCarthy
Charlene Wyatt	Penny (as a child)
Speed Hansen	Marty

This low-budget entry revolves around a predictable love triangle, this time based at the circus. A successful trapeze trio consisting of two men and a woman is on the brink of collapse when both men fall (not literally) for their female colleague.

Marjorie plays Sara, the owner of the shady circus.

Trivia: The film's working title was *The Circus Comes to Town.*

Poster tagline: "Tense drama on the trapeze 100 ft. above the sawdust... and only a split second to make a decision that meant death!"

24. *Too Hot to Handle* (1938)

Director: Jack Conway
Producer: Lawrence Weingarten
Screenplay: Len Hammond, John Lee Mahin, Laurence Stallings and Buster Keaton (uncredited)
Cinematographer: Harold Rosson
Studio: MGM
Running time: 103 minutes
Black and White
Genre: Comedy/Adventure/Romance
Release date: September 16, 1938

Cast

Clark Gable	Chris Hunter
Myrna Loy	Alma Harding
Walter Pidgeon	W.O. "Bill" Dennis
Walter Connolly	Arthur "Gabby" MacArthur, Union Newsreel
Leo Carrillo	Joselito, Hunter's Soundman
Johnny Hines	Parsons, Dennis Henchman
Virginia Weidler	Hulda Harding, Alma's Niece
Betty Ross Clarke	Mrs. Harry Harding
Henry Kolker	Pearly Todd, Atlas Newsreel
Marjorie Main	**Kitty Wayne**

This comedy adventure sets Clark Gable and Myrna Loy on an adventurous trek through the jungles of South America. On paper it promises enough good banter to keep the viewer interested; however, both stars look less than interested here. The highlight of the film is seeing Clark Gable dressed in a chicken suit—only one year before he played the suave Rhett Butler in *Gone with the Wind* (1939).

Marjorie plays Miss Wayne, secretary to Walter Connolly's character, Arthur "Gabby" MacArthur. Between takes on the film, Gable would playfully flirt with Marjorie.

Trivia: The opening scene involving a fake bombing raid was the idea of legendary comic Buster Keaton. He worked as a freelance gagman for the studio, and was the brains behind many of MGM's big stunt scenes and physical comedy gags.

25. *There Goes My Heart* (1938)

Director: Norman Z. McLeod
Producer: Hal Roach
Screenplay: Jack Jevne, Eddie Moran and Ed Sullivan (story)
Cinematographer: Norbert Brodine
Studio: United Artists / Hal Roach Studios
Running time: 84 minutes
Black and White
Genre: Comedy

Release dates: September 27, 1938 (premiere); October 14, 1938 (nationwide)
Awards and nominations: 1939 Academy Awards, Nominated, Best Musical Scoring, Marvin Hatley.

CAST

Fredric March	Bill Spencer
Virginia Bruce	Joan Butterfield
Patsy Kelly	Peggy O'Brien
Alan Mowbray	Penny E. Pennypepper
Nancy Carroll	Dorothy Moore
Eugene Pallette	Stevens
Claude Gillingwater	Cyrus Butterfield
Greta Granstedt	Thelda (the Swedish maid)
Etienne Girardot	Hinkley (the secretary)
Arthur Lake	Flash
Robert Armstrong	Det. O'Brien
Irving Bacon	Dobbs
Irving Pichel	Mr. Gorman
Syd Saylor	Robinson
Marjorie Main	**Irate customer**
Harry Langdon	Minister (uncredited)

It's a story about a rich girl who desperately wants a taste of the real world. She takes a job as a shopgirl in her grandfather's department store, hoping to find love and normalcy all at the same time.

Marjorie plays a flustered customer.

Trivia: Comedian Harry Langdon is seen briefly toward the end of the film, as a minister. It was his first performance in six years; his minor part goes uncredited.

Ed Sullivan, America's favorite variety show host, wrote the original story for the screen.

26. *Girls' School* (1938)

Director: John Brahm
Producer: Wallace MacDonald
Screenplay: Richard Sherman and Tess Slesinger (story)
Cinematographer: Franz Planer
Studio: Columbia Pictures
Running time: 71 minutes
Black and White
Genre: Comedy
Release dates: September 27, 1938 (premiere); September 30, 1938 (nationwide)
Awards and nominations: 1939 Academy Awards, Nominated, Best Musical Scoring, Morris Stoloff and Gregory Stone.

CAST

Anne Shirley	Natalie Freeman
Nan Grey	Linda Simpson
Ralph Bellamy	Michael Hendragin
Dorothy Moore	Betty Fleet
Gloria Holden	Miss Laurel
Marjorie Main	**Miss Armstrong**
Margaret Tallichet	Gwennie
Peggy Moran	Myra
Kenneth Howell	Edgar
Noah Beery Jr.	George
Cecil Cunningham	Miss Brewster
Pierre Watkin	Mr. Simpson
Doris Kenyon	Mrs. Simpson
Heather Thatcher	Miss Bracket
Virginia Howell	Miss MacBeth

Here's another 1930s film with a message, this time directed at young female viewers. When a student at a private all-girls school stays out all night, the rumors and gossip start, and the hall monitor is blamed and targeted as the tattletale who turned her in. The rest of the film is about her trying to redeem herself in the eyes of her peers.

Marjorie plays a prissy teacher, Miss Armstrong.

Trivia: The film's working title was *The Romantic Age.*

27. *Lucky Night* (1939)

Director: Norman Taurog
Producer: Louis D. Lighton
Screenplay: Oliver Claxton (story), Grover Jones and Vincent Lawrence
Cinematographer: Ray June
Studio: MGM
Running time: 82 minutes
Black and White
Genre: Drama/Comedy
Production dates: January 16, 1939–March 4, 1939
Release dates: May 4, 1939 (premiere New York City); May 5, 1939 (nationwide)

Cast

Myrna Loy	Cora Jordan Overton
Robert Taylor	William "Bill" Overton
Joseph Allen	Joe Hilton
Henry O'Neill	H. Calvin Jordan, Cora's Dad
Douglas Fowley	George, Bill's "Friend"
Bernard Nedell	"Dusty" Sawyer
Charles Lane	Mr. Carpenter, Paint Store Owner
Bernadene Hayes	Blondie, Clerk at Carpenters
Gladys Blake	Blackie, Clerk at Carpenters
Marjorie Main	**Mrs. Briggs, the Landlady**
Edward Gargan	Policeman in Park
Irving Bacon	Bus Conductor
Oscar O'Shea	Police Lieutenant Murphy

Another rich girl marries a no-good loser, as Myrna Loy stars as the heiress "Cora," who marries compulsive gambler Robert Taylor (aka "Bill") during a drunken night out on the town. Despite its popular male and female leads, *Lucky Night* bombed at the box office.

Marjorie plays the landlady, Mrs. Briggs, who helps the couple find an apartment to rent.

28. *They Shall Have Music* (1939)

Director: Archie Mayo
Producers: Samuel Goldwyn and Robert Riskin
Screenplay: Charles L. Clifford (novel), John Howard Lawson, Robert Presnell Sr., Anthony Veiller and Irmgard von Cube (story)
Cinematographer: Gregg Toland
Studio: Samuel Goldwyn Company / United Artists
Running time: 105 minutes
Black and White
Genre: Musical/Drama/Family
Release date: June 28, 1939
Awards and nominations: 1940 Academy Awards, Nominated,

Best Musical Scoring, Alfred Newman.

CAST

Jascha Heifetz	Himself
Joel McCrea	Peter McCarthy
Walter Brennan	Professor Lawson
Andrea Leeds	Ann Lawson
Gene Reynolds	Frankie
Terry Kilburn	Limey
Tommy Kelly	Willie
Chuck Stubbs	Fever
Walter Tetley	Rocks
Gale Sherwood	Betty (as Jacqueline Nash)
Mary Ruth	Suzy
Arthur Hohl	Miller
Marjorie Main	**Mrs. Miller**

Frankie (Gene Reynolds) is a young street hustler who happens to find two tickets to a Jascha Heifetz concert. He attends the concert himself, and the famed violinist's live performance inspires him to go back to learning the instrument he once loved. After running away from home, he ends up on the steps of a music school for underprivileged children, where he is taken in by Professor Lawson (Walter Brennen). Frankie thrives, but his new home is in jeopardy when diminishing funds threaten to close the school for good. Frankie leads the other students in a fund raising effort to save the school, and they just happen to bump into Heifetz in the process. The children plead with the violin master to play at a school concert to raise money, and he subsequently agrees to support the ailing school from that moment on.

Marjorie plays the mother of a band member.

Trivia: In the scene featuring a newspaper story about Heifetz' stolen violin, the missing instrument is called a Stradivarius. Despite Heifetz's use of a Guarnarius, both in the film and in real life, the director decided that the greater majority of the public knew only of the famous Stradivarius violin — hence the name change.

Watch for the restless kids in the orchestra — they are often caught looking directly into the camera, or eyeing it with a sideways glance.

They Shall Have Music is otherwise known as *Melody of Youth* (U.K.) and *Ragged Angels* (working title).

29. *The Angels Wash Their Faces* (1939)

Director: Ray Enright
Producers: Max Siegel (associate producer), Hal B. Wallis (executive producer)
Screenplay: Jonathan Finn (treatment), Michael Fessier, Niven Busch and Robert Buckner
Cinematographer: Arthur L. Todd
Studio: Warner Brothers
Running time: 86 minutes
Black and White
Genre: Drama
Production dates: March 13, 1939–April 15, 1939
Release date: August 26, 1939

CAST

Ann Sheridan	Joy Ryan
Billy Halop	William R. "Billy" Shafter
Bernard Punsly	Luke "Sleepy" Arkelian (as Bernard Punsley)
Leo Gorcey	Leo "Mousy" Finnegan
Huntz Hall	Huntz Garman

Gabriel Dell	Luigi Petaren
Bobby Jordan	Bernie Smith
Ronald Reagan	Deputy Dist. Atty. Patrick "Pat" Remson
Bonita Granville	Peggy Finnegan
Frankie Thomas	Gabe Ryan
Henry O'Neill	Dist. Atty. A.H. Remson
Eduardo Ciannelli	Alfred Martino
Margaret Hamilton	Miss Hannaberry
Marjorie Main	**Mrs. Arkelian**

Another one of the "Dead End Kids" films, *The Angels Wash Their Faces* tells the story of a young man just released from reform school who moves to a new neighborhood with his sister Joy (Ann Sheridan), intent on starting a new life.

When he gets involved with the local mob boss, he's soon set up for arson and murder, crimes that he didn't commit. Now he has to prove his innocence to the police — not an easy task, given his criminal past. This is where the "Dead End Kids" save the day, with the help of the District Attorney and his son Pat, played by future U.S President Ronald Reagan. A subplot involving the blossoming romance between Joy and Pat is secondary to the usual "Dead End Kids" plot line.

This was Marjorie's last role in a "Dead End Kids" film.

Trivia: The Angels Wash Their Faces was the sequel to the James Cagney classic *Angels with Dirty Faces* (1938), released one year before.

Variety (October 6, 1939) said, "Marjorie Main does a standout performance bit as the mother of a crippled boy who dies in a fire framed by crooked politicians."

30. *The Women* (1939)

Director: George Cukor
Producer: Hunt Stromberg
Screenplay: Clare Booth (play), Anita Loos, Jane Murfin, F. Scott Fitzgerald (uncredited) and Donald Ogden Stewart (uncredited)
Cinematographers: Oliver T. Marsh and Joseph Ruttenberg
Studio: MGM
Running time: 133 minutes
Black and White
Genre: Comedy/Drama
Production dates: April 25, 1939–July 7, 1939
Release dates: September 1, 1939; September 5, 1947 (re-release)

Cast

Norma Shearer	Mrs. Stephen Haines (Mary)
Joan Crawford	Crystal Allen
Rosalind Russell	Mrs. Howard Fowler (Sylvia)
Mary Boland	The Countess DeLave (Flora)
Paulette Goddard	Miriam Aarons
Phyllis Povah	Mrs. Phelps Potter (Edith)
Joan Fontaine	Mrs. John Day (Peggy)
Virginia Weidler	Little Mary Haines
Lucile Watson	Mrs. Moorehead
Marjorie Main	**Lucy**
Virginia Grey	Pat (perfume counter clerk)
Ruth Hussey	Miss Watts (Stephen's secretary)
Muriel Hutchison	Jane (Mary's maid)
Hedda Hopper	Dolly Dupuyster

Lucy (Marjorie Main) runs a Reno dude ranch where scorned women gather to await their quickie divorces. When the likes of Mary (Norma Shearer), Crystal (Joan Crawford), Sylvia (Rosalind Russell), "the Countess" (Mary Boland), Miriam (Paulette Goddard) and Peggy (Joan Fontaine) all show up at the same time, the claws come out when "the women" find out that husband swapping has been on the agenda for some time.

Memorable quote: "If the ocean was whiskey, and I was a duck, I'd dive to the bottom, and never come up!"—Marjorie as Lucy in *The Women.*

Trivia: Despite the subject matter (men), all 135 roles in *The Women* are played by women. Director George Cukor explains: "Everything was female. The books in the library were all by female authors. The photographs and the subjects were all female. Even the animals, the monkeys, the dogs, the horses, were female. I'm not sure the audience were aware of that, but there wasn't a single male represented in the entire film, although nine-tenths of the dialogue centered around them."

Rosalind Russell's ferocious bite in the fight scene was very real—so much so that it left a permanent scar on her co-star, Paulette Goddard. Despite the mishap, they remained friends.

Poster taglines: "It's all about men!" "The year's mightiest cast in the hit play that tells on the women!" "135 women with men on their minds."

31. *Another Thin Man* (1939)

Director: W. S. Van Dyke
Producer: Hunt Stromberg
Screenplay: Dashiell Hammett (story), Frances Goodrich and Albert Hackett
Cinematographers: William H. Daniels, Oliver T. Marsh and John F. Seitz
Studio: MGM
Running time: 103 minutes
Black and White
Genre: Comedy/Mystery/Crime/Drama/Romance
Production dates: July 1939–August 1939
Release date: November 17, 1939

Cast

William Powell	Nick Charles
Myrna Loy	Nora Charles
Virginia Grey	Lois MacFay, aka Linda Mills
Otto Kruger	Assistant District Attorney Van Slack
C. Aubrey Smith	Colonel Burr MacFay
Ruth Hussey	Dorothy Waters, Charles' nanny
Nat Pendleton	Lieutenant Guild
Patric Knowles	Dudley Horn, Lois' fiancé
Tom Neal	Freddie Coleman, MacFay's secretary
Phyllis Gordon	Mrs. Isabella Bellam, MacFay's housekeeper
Sheldon Leonard	Phil Church
Don Costello	"Diamond Back" Vogel
Harry Bellaver	"Creeps" Binder
William A. Poulsen	Nickie Jr.
Muriel Hutchison	H. Culverton "Smitty" Smith
Abner Biberman	Dum-Dum, Church's Henchman
Marjorie Main	**Mrs. Dolley, Landlady at the Chesterfield Apartments**

Nick (William Powell) and Nora (Myrna Loy) are back in another installment, the third, in the popular "Thin Man" series. The husband-and-wife detective team take on another murder mystery, with a little wit and humor thrown in for good measure.

Marjorie plays Mrs. Dolley, the nosy Landlady.

Trivia: The film's working title was *Return of the Thin Man.*

Another Thin Man (1939) is the third film in a series of six: *The Thin Man* (1934), *After The Thin Man* (1936), *Another Thin Man* (1939), *Shadow of the Thin Man* (1941), *The Thin Man Goes Home* (1945) and, lastly, *Song of the Thin Man* (1947).

Watch for the scene in which Harry Bellaver (Creeps) first meets up with Nick and Nora; he is clearly wearing suspenders. However, when he walks into the nursery to look at the baby, they've miraculously disappeared.

Poster taglines: "It's a blessed event." "Their Merriest Hit! Mr. and Mrs. Thin Man Have a B-A-B-Y!"

32. *Two Thoroughbreds* (1939)

Director: Jack Hively
Producer: Cliff Reid
Screenplay: Jerry Cady and Joseph Fields (story)
Cinematographer: Frank Redman
Studio: RKO Radio Pictures
Filming locations: Sedona, Arizona
Running time: 62 minutes
Black and White
Genre: Drama/Family
Release date: December 8, 1939

Cast

Jimmy Lydon	David Carey
Joan Leslie	Wendy Conway (credited as Joan Brodel)
Arthur Hohl	Thaddeus Carey
J.M. Kerrigan	Jack Lenihan
Marjorie Main	**Hildegarde Carey**
Selmer Jackson	Bill Conway
Spencer Charters	Doc Purdy
Paul Fix	Stablemaster
Bob Perry	Henchman
Al Ferguson	Rancer
Frank Darien	Beal, the mailman

In this surprisingly well made B movie (of B+ proportions), David (Jimmy Lydon) is a teenage orphan living with his nasty and abusive Aunt (Marjorie Main) and Uncle (Arthur Hohl). When the foal of a stolen brood mare finds its way to their farm, David convinces his Uncle to keep the colt in the hope that the rightful owner will offer a reward for its return. By the time the owners of the young horse are found, David has grown so attached to the animal that he can't bear to part with it.

Trivia: A fourteen-year-old Joan Leslie is billed under her real name of "Joan Brodel"; three years after this role, at the ripe old age of seventeen, she was to play the wife of James Cagney in the classic *Yankee Doodle Dandy* (1942).

33. *I Take This Woman* (1940)

Director: W.S. Van Dyke (final version)
Producers: Bernard H. Hyman, Louis B. Mayer, Lawrence Weingarten (all uncredited)
Screenplay: Charles MacArthur (story), James Kevin McGuiness and Ben Hecht
Cinematographer: Harold Rosson
Studio: MGM
Running time: 98 minutes
Black and White
Genre: Drama
Production dates: October 18, 1938–November 1938; November 7, 1938–January 1939; December 4, 1939–December 15, 1939
Release date: February 2, 1940
Budget: $700,000

CAST

Spencer Tracy	Dr. Karl Decker
Hedy Lamarr	Georgi Gragore
Verree Teasdale	Madame "Cesca" Marcesca
Kent Taylor	Phil Mayberry
Laraine Day	Linda Rodgers
Mona Barrie	Sandra Mayberry
Jack Carson	Joe, Man Yelling for Decker in Subway
Paul Cavanagh	Bill Rodgers
Louis Calhern	Dr. Martin Sumner Duveen
Frances Drake	Lola Estermont
Marjorie Main	**Gertie**
George E. Stone	Sid, the Taxi Driver
Willie Best	Sambo, the Clinic Attendant
Don Castle	Dr. Ted Fenton

When Georgi (Hedy Lamarr) attempts suicide because of a failed past love, her husband, Dr. Karl Decker (Spencer Tracy), does all that he can to ignite their dying romance. Thinking that financial security will make his wife happy, Dr. Decker sets out to become a doctor to the wealthy, and in turn abandons his modest medical practice administering to the poor, something that he truly loved to do.

Marjorie plays the clinic nurse, Gertie.

Trivia: When original director Josef Von Sternberg quit the film because of "artistic differences," Frank Borzage took over the plagued production, only to have it wrested from him and then shelved by the studio for almost a year. W.S. Van Dyke hoped that it would be third time lucky when he stepped in to save the troubled film. Under his direction, the film was almost entirely re-shot, with many of the original cast members being replaced. Hal Le Suer, brother of Joan Crawford, had his scenes deleted after the original version was re-worked. Walter Pidgeon's performance was left on the cutting room floor, too. Marjorie, however, was brought back to re-shoot her scenes as Gertie.

34. *Women Without Names* (1940)

Director: Robert Florey
Screenplay: Ernest Booth (play), William R. Lipman and Horace McCoy
Cinematographer: Charles Lang
Studio: Paramount Pictures
Running time: 62 minutes
Black and White
Genre: Drama
Release date: March 15, 1940

CAST

Ellen Drew	Joyce King
Robert Paige	Fred MacNeil
Judith Barrett	Peggy Athens
John Miljan	John Marlin, Asst. Dist. Atty.
Fay Helm	Millie
John McGuire	Walter Ferris
Louise Beavers	Ivory
James Seay	O'Grane
Esther Dale	Head Matron Ingles
Marjorie Main	**Mrs. Lowery**
Audrey Maynard	Maggie
Kitty Kelly	Countess
Virginia Dabney	Ruffles
Helen Lynch	Susie
Mae Busch	Rose

This is an unusual B-grade Paramount feature in that it features the bad guys getting away with murder—literally! As Joyce (Ellen Drew) tries to get her life in order after a tumultuous marriage to a former criminal, she meets Fred (Robert Paige), a construction engineer, and they fall in love and marry. On returning from their honeymoon, they find that her former husband (John McGuire) has broken into the house, along with girlfriend Judith (Peggy Athens).

Just prior to the newlyweds returning home, Detective Reardon (Thomas E. Jackson) had cornered the unsavory pair of housebreakers and was shot for his troubles. When Joyce and Fred enter the house, they're welcomed home by the body of the dead detective, and are instantly accused of the murder. Corrupt Assistant District Attorney John Marlin (John Miljan) sets out to frame the newlyweds to better position himself for a promotion. He succeeds, the bad guys win, and Fred is sentenced to death, while Joyce receives life in prison.

Marjorie plays the prison matron, Mrs. Lowery.

Poster tagline: "Public Enemies in Skirts!"

35. *Dark Command* (1940)

Director: Raoul Walsh
Producer: Sol C. Siegel (associate producer)
Screenplay: W. R. Burnett (novel), Jan Fortune (adaptation), F. Hugh Herbert, Lionel Houser and Grover Jones
Cinematographer: Jack Marta
Studio: Republic Pictures
Filming locations: Placerita Ranch, Newhall, California; Sherwood Forest, California
Running time: 94 minutes
Black and White
Genre: Romance/Western
Budget: $1 million
Production dates: November 29, 1939–December 23, 1939
Release dates: April 4, 1940 (Lawrence, Kansas); April 15, 1940 (nationwide)
Awards and nominations: 1941 Oscar: Nominated, Best Art Direction, John Victor Mackay; Nominated, Best Music, Original Score, Victor Young.

CAST

Claire Trevor	Miss Mary McCloud
John Wayne	Bob "Shortcut" Seton
Walter Pidgeon	William "Will" Cantrell
Roy Rogers	Fletcher "Fletch" McCloud

George "Gabby" Hayes	Andrew "Doc" Grunch (as George Hayes)
Porter Hall	Angus McCloud
Marjorie Main	**Mrs. Cantrell, aka Mrs. Adams**
Raymond Walburn	Judge Buckner
Joe Sawyer	Bushropp, Guerrilla (as Joseph Sawyer)
Helen MacKellar	Mrs. Hale

When Bob Seton (John Wayne) becomes the Federal Marshall of Kansas, his losing opponent, William Cantrell (Walter Pidgeon), seeks revenge by luring away his girl, Mary (Claire Trevor). After she accepts Cantrell's proposal of marriage, the rivalry between the two men really heats up. Eventually, true love wins out after Cantrell is killed, making way for Bob to take care of his widow, and rekindle their romance.

Marjorie plays Cantrell's mother, and pulls off a memorable deathbed scene, earning rave reviews. In fact, her performance was so good that her being overlooked for a Best Supporting Actress Oscar nomination sent shockwaves through Hollywood.

Trivia: As a novelty, the film premiered in Lawrence, Kansas, because the town was featured heavily throughout the film.

36. *Turnabout* (1940)

Director: Hal Roach
Producer: Hal Roach
Screenplay: Berne Giler, Rian James, John McClain, Mickell Novack and Thorne Smith (novel)
Cinematographer: Norbert Brodine
Studio: Hal Roach Studios
Running time: 83 minutes
Black and White
Genre: Comedy
Release dates: May 17, 1940

Cast

Adolphe Menjou	Phil Manning
Carole Landis	Sally Willows
John Hubbard	Tim Willows
William Gargan	Joel Clare
Verree Teasdale	Laura Bannister
Mary Astor	Marion Manning
Donald Meek	Henry
Joyce Compton	Irene Clare
Franklin Pangborn	Mr. Pingboom
Marjorie Main	**Nora**
Berton Churchill	Julian Marlowe
Margaret Roach	Dixie Gale
Ray Turner	Mose

Without a doubt, that special Hal Roach touch made this film better than it would have been under anyone else's direction. When Tim (John Hubbard) and Sally (Carole Landis) can't stop fighting, their angry words to a statue of Buddha has magical consequences. Suddenly, they've switched bodies. Although many of the gags are now dated, this "Freaky Friday"–type story is still worthy of a laugh or two.

Marjorie plays Nora, the cook, who acts as a go-between for the confused couple.

Hal Roach was so impressed with Marjorie's performance in this film that he began to draw up a long-term contract for her. But Louis B. Mayer beat him to it. Marjorie signed a seven-year contract with MGM, and when it expired she re-signed for another seven years.

Trivia: The part of "Dixie Gale" was played by Margaret Roach, Director Hal Roach's daughter.

37. *Susan and God* (1940)

Director: George Cukor
Producer: Hunt Stromberg
Screenplay: Rachel Crothers (play) and Anita Loos
Cinematographer: Robert Planck
Studio: MGM
Running time: 117 minutes
Black and White
Genre: Drama/Comedy
Release date: June 7, 1940

Cast

Joan Crawford	Susan Trexel
Fredric March	Barrie Trexel
Ruth Hussey	Charlotte "Charl"
John Carroll	Clyde Rochester
Rita Hayworth	Leonora "Lee" Hutchins
Nigel Bruce	Mr. "Hutchie" Hutchins
Bruce Cabot	Michael "Mike" O'Hara
Rose Hobart	Irene Burroughs
Constance Collier	Lady Millicent "Millie" Wigstaff
Rita Quigley	Blossom "Bloss" Trexel
Gloria DeHaven	Enid
Richard Crane	Bob Kent (as Richard O. Crane)
Norma Mitchell	Hazel Paige
Marjorie Main	**Mary Maloney**
Aldrich Bowker	Patrick "Pat" Maloney

Susan Trexal (Joan Crawford) has just come back from a European vacation with more than souvenirs and holiday snap shots—she's undergone a religious transformation. She's found God. Neglecting her husband Barrie (Fredric March) and daughter Blossom (Rita Quigley) for her newfound religion, she is unaware that all her family really want is a wife and mother. It's not until Charlotte's (Ruth Hussey) unselfish act of love that Susan finally realizes what she really has in front of her — a family.

Marjorie has a small role as the gardener's wife, Mary.

Trivia: This production was another Norma Shearer reject swiftly and successfully taken by Joan Crawford. Despite being thirty-eight years old at the time, a vain Shearer refused to play a character old enough to be the mother of a fourteen-year-old girl. Joan Crawford jumped at the chance, giving one of her finer performances as the likable, albeit self-serving Susan Trexal.

Gertrude Lawrence played the title role of "Susan" in the stage production. After opening in New York City on October 7, 1937, it ran for 288 performances.

38. *The Captain Is a Lady* (1940)

Director: Robert B. Sinclair
Producer: Frederick Stephani
Screenplay: Henry Clark, Rachel Crothers (play) and Louise Forsslund (novel)
Cinematographer: Leonard Smith
Studio: MGM
Production dates: April 18, 1940–May 9, 1940
Running time: 65 minutes
Black and White
Genre: Comedy
Release date: June 21, 1940

Cast

Charles Coburn	Captain Abe Peabody
Beulah Bondi	Angie Peabody

Virginia Grey	Mary Peabody
Helen Broderick	Nancy Crocker
Billie Burke	Blossy Stort
Dan Dailey	Perth Nickerson (as Dan Dailey Jr.)
Helen Westley	Abigail Morrow
Cecil Cunningham	Mrs. Jane Homans
Marjorie Main	**Sarah May Willett**
Clem Bevans	Samuel Darby
Francis Pierlot	Roger Bartlett
Tom Fadden	Pucey Kintner

When Captain Peabody (Charles Coburn) loses his house because of a bad investment, he and his wife must resort to life in a retirement home. Since the home caters to women only, the couple have to accept that they'll now be living apart. But, after their emotional goodbye, the residents of the home vote to allow the couple to move in together, and this is where the laughs begin. Captain Peabody is the thorn amongst the roses, and when his crusty buddies start referring to him as "Old Lady," he sets out to prove his manhood.

Marjorie plays Sarah, and pokes her nose into a few scenes as the cook and housekeeper.

Trivia: This was based on the novel and play *Old Lady 31.*

Beulah Bondi, who portrayed "Angie Peabody" in this film, died at the age of 92 as a result of tripping over her cat.

39. *Wyoming* (1940)

Director: Richard Thorpe
Producer: Milton Bren
Screenplay: Jack Jevne (story and screenplay) and Hugo Butler
Cinematographer: Clyde DeVinna
Studio: MGM
Black and White
Production dates: June 1940–July 29, 1940
Filming locations: Jackson Hole, Wyoming; Teton Range, Wyoming
Running time: 88 minutes
Genre: Western
Release date: September 13, 1940

Cast

Wallace Beery	"Reb" Harkness
Leo Carrillo	Pete Marillo
Ann Rutherford	Lucy Kincaid
Lee Bowman	Sergeant Connelly
Joseph Calleia	John Buckley
Bobs Watson	Jimmy Kincaid
Paul Kelly	General George Armstrong Custer
Henry Travers	Sheriff
Marjorie Main	**Mehitabel**

Reb (Wallace Beery) is an outlaw, a liar, and on the run from the Army. He makes his way to Wyoming, where General Custer (yes, *the* General Custer) and his cavalry of two chase him down.

Marjorie plays the loudmouthed blacksmith who sets her sights on winning Beery's affections. Her performance was so good that reviewers noted that she had done the impossible — she had stolen the spotlight from Beery. His bruised ego was the probable cause of his bitter treatment of Marjorie in their future productions. It was this film that prompted MGM to offer Marjorie a seven-year contract.

Trivia: Wyoming was released as *The Bad Man of Wyoming* in the U.K.

40. *The Wild Man of Borneo* (1941)

Director: Robert B. Sinclair
Producer: Joseph L. Mankiewicz
Screenplay: Marc Connelly (play), Herman J. Mankiewicz (play), Waldo Salt (screenplay) and John McClain (screenplay)
Cinematographer: Oliver T. Marsh
Studio: MGM
Production dates: October 1940–November 1940
Running time: 78 minutes
Black and White
Genre: Comedy
Release date: January 24, 1941

Cast

Frank Morgan	J. Daniel "Dan" Thompson
Mary Howard	Mary Thompson
Billie Burke	Bernice Marshall, Boardinghouse Keeper
Donald Meek	Professor Charles W. Birdo
Marjorie Main	**Irma, the Cook**
Connie Gilchrist	Mrs. Evelyn Diamond
Bonita Granville	Francine "Frankie" Diamond
Dan Dailey	Ed LeMotte (as Dan Dailey Jr.)
Andrew Tombes	"Doc" Dunbar
Walter Catlett	"Doc" Skelby
Joseph J. Greene	Mr. Robert Emmett Ferderber, Private Detective
Phil Silvers	Murdock, Sideshow Barker

In this entertaining comedy, con man Dan Thomson (Frank Morgan) moves into a New York boarding house for actors, and attempts to build a relationship with the daughter he hardly knows, played by Mary Howard. Although a man of good heart, Dan is less than enthusiastic about work; but in order to impress his daughter and his fellow boarders, he convinces them all that he's an actor in the "legitimate theater." In reality, he's just a traveling medicine man.

Marjorie plays the robust cook in Billie Burke's boarding house.

41. *The Trial of Mary Dugan* (1941)

Director: Norman Z. McLeod
Producer: Edwin H. Knopf
Screenplay: Bayard Veiller (play)
Cinematographer: George J. Folsey
Studio: MGM
Running time: 87 minutes
Black and White
Genre: Drama
Release date: February 14, 1941

Cast

Laraine Day	Mary Dugan
Robert Young	Jimmy Blake
Tom Conway	Edgar Wayne
Frieda Inescort	Mrs. Wayne
Henry O'Neill	Galway
John Litel	Mr. West
Marsha Hunt	Agatha Hall
Sara Haden	Miss Matthews
Marjorie Main	**Mrs. Collins**
Nora Perry	Sally
Alma Kruger	Dr. Saunders
Pierre Watkin	Judge Nash
Addison Richards	Captain Price
Francis Pierlot	John Masters

A splash of romance did nothing to make this poorly written courtroom drama into a watchable, enjoyable film. As Mary (Laraine Day) anxiously awaits release from reformatory, her sentence is increased after she throws ink over a teacher. Not content with seeing it through, she plans to escape to Los Angeles where she intends to meet up with her criminal father. His untimely death in a car accident puts an end to their reunion. She finds work at the company of the man who was driving the car that killed her father, and falls in love with company attorney George Blake (Robert Young).

All seems fine until George takes a job overseas and asks Mary to join him as his wife. After realizing that her application for a passport will reveal her shady past, Mary (Laraine Day) ends their romance rather than come clean.

The story takes a bizarre turn at this point. George goes to Chile, and the next we see of him is on his return to the United States when he is greeted with a newspaper headline stating that Mary is on trial for the slaying of her boss. George takes over her case, and makes it his prime objective to find the real killer and win back the woman he's always loved.

This is the film in which Marjorie (playing the landlady) assumes the position of the corpse on the courtroom floor. Her brief performance earned her rave reviews.

Trivia: This was a remake of the 1929 film of the same name, with Norma Shearer, Lewis Stone and H. B. Warner in the lead roles.

Tom Conway, who portrayed "Edar Wayne" in this film, was the real-life brother of fellow actor George Sanders.

42. *Barnacle Bill* (1941)

Director: Richard Thorpe
Producer: Milton Bren
Screenplay: Jack Jevne (story and screenplay) and Hugo Butler
Cinematographer: Clyde DeVinna
Studio: MGM
Running time: 90 minutes
Black and White
Genre: Drama/Comedy
Release date: April 7, 1941

Cast

Wallace Beery	Bill Johansen
Marjorie Main	**Marge Cavendish**
Leo Carrillo	Pico Rodriguez
Virginia Weidler	Virginia Johansen
Donald Meek	"Pop" Cavendish
Barton MacLane	John Kelly
Connie Gilchrist	Mamie
Sara Haden	Aunt Letty
William Edmunds	Joe Petillo

Perhaps the funniest scene from this film is Marjorie's attempt to sing in tune with the rest of the congregation at a church service.

Marjorie plays Martha, a spinster who makes it her business to drag bankrupt fishing boat owner Bill (Wallace Beery) to the altar. He sees her romantic advances as an opportunity to swindle enough money from her to buy a new fishing boat, which he does—but it all comes at a price.

Trivia: The New York Times (July 25, 1941) fueled Beery's jealousy of his now-regular female counterpart by saying, "Wallace Beery has found the perfect foil in Marjorie Main, all right. And, perhaps more than either he or his Metro bosses bargained for, a competitor who comes close to stealing some of his best scenes in the film."

The *Hollywood Reporter* (June 30, 1941) said, "Miss Main is excellent. Her moments of coyness, her singing scene in church and a scene with Beery flattering her into helping him buy a larger boat, in which he plans to leave her for the South Seas, are exceptionally well acted and directed."

Variety (June 30, 1941) wrote, "Miss Main hits full stride as the blowsy, raucous waterfront business woman."

The fishing schooner used in *Barnacle Bill* was also seen in *Captain Courageous* (1937). To cut costs, some of the sea footage from the earlier film was used here (an added advantage to using the same boat).

43. *A Woman's Face* (1941)

Director: George Cukor
Producer: Victor Saville
Screenplay: Francie De Croisset (play), Donald Ogden Stewart and Elliot Paul
Cinematographer: Robert Planck
Studio: MGM
Black and White
Filming locations: Sun Valley, Idaho (snow scenes)
Production dates: January 23, 1941–March 29, 1941
Running time: 106 minutes
Genre: Thriller/Drama
Release dates: May 15, 1941 (premiere, New York City, N.Y.); May 23, 1941 (nationwide)

Cast

Joan Crawford	Anna Holm, aka Ingrid Paulson
Melvyn Douglas	Dr. Gustaf Segert
Conrad Veidt	Torsten Barring
Osa Massen	Vera Segert
Reginald Owen	Bernard Dalvik
Albert Bassermann	Consul Magnus Barring
Marjorie Main	**Emma Kristiansdotter**
Donald Meek	Herman Rundvik

When Anna (Joan Crawford) undergoes plastic surgery to remove the unsightly scar from her face, she is torn between returning to her old, evil ways or starting afresh with a new face and new attitude. Once again, Cukor pulls every drop of melodrama from his story, and as a result, it's solid, edge-of-your-seat entertainment.

Marjorie plays the role of the matronly German housekeeper Emma. In this film the familiar Marjorie character that we're all accustomed to has all but disappeared. Her fly-away hair has been tamed and is pulled harshly back from her face; she wears glasses and dull clothing; and her mid-western twang is masterfully transformed into a strong German dialect.

Trivia: Melvyn Douglas, who portrays "Dr. Gustaf Segert" in this film, is one of the few actors ever to win an Oscar, an Emmy and a Tony award. His granddaughter, Illeana Douglas, is also an actor.

Poster taglines: "They called her a scar-faced she-devil." "Whatever I am... men made me!"

44. *The Shepherd of the Hills* (1941)

Director: Henry Hathaway
Producer: Jack Moss
Screenplay: Stuart Anthony, Grover Jones and Harold Bell Wright (novel)
Cinematographers: W. Howard Greene and Charles Lang Jr.
Studio: Paramount Pictures
Filming locations: Big Bear Lake and Cedar Lake, Big Bear Valley, San Bernardino National Forest, California
Running time: 98 minutes
Color (Technicolor)
Genre: Drama
Release date: July 18, 1941

Cast

John Wayne	Young Matt
Betty Field	Sammy Lane
Harry Carey	Daniel Howitt
Beulah Bondi	Aunt Mollie
James Barton	Old Matt
Samuel S. Hinds	Andy Beeler
Marjorie Main	Granny Becky
Ward Bond	Wash Gibbs
Marc Lawrence	Pete
John Qualen	Coot Royal
Fuzzy Knight	Mr. Palestrom
Tom Fadden	Jim Lane
Olin Howlin	Corky (as Olin Howland)
Dorothy Adams	Elvy
Virita Campbell	Baby

Marjorie went to Paramount for this little known John Wayne film about a group of outcast moonshiners living in the Ozarks. Marjorie gives a moving performance as Granny Becky. The scene in which she regains her sight and identifies Daniel Howitt (Harry Carey) as Young Matt's (John Wayne) father is undoubtedly the most understated, most underrated dramatic performance of her career.

Trivia: This 1941 version was a remake of two earlier films of the same name, *The Shepherd of the Hills* (1919) and *The Shepherd of the Hills* (1927). Interestingly, two remakes of this 1941 version were subsequently made, one for television in 1960, the other as a theatrical release in 1963.

Ward Bond and John Wayne were lifelong friends. On a hunting trip, Wayne accidentally shot his friend, superficially; so as an inside joke, Bond left him his favorite shotgun in his will.

On the day of his death (November 5, 1960), Bond had an appointment to meet with singer Johnny Horton to sign a contract for his upcoming appearance on the television series *Wagon Train*. However, tragedy struck twice within twenty-four hours, and they both failed to make the meeting. Johnny Horton was killed instantly when his car was hit by a drunk driver; and Ward Bond died in his hotel room, the result of a heart attack, the very same day. Ward Bond was 57 years old.

45. *Honky Tonk* (1941)

Director: Jack Conway
Producer: Pandro S. Berman
Screenplay: Marguerite Roberts, John Sanford and Annalee Whitmore (uncredited)
Cinematographers: Harold Rosson and William H. Daniels (uncredited)
Studio: MGM
Genre: Western/Comedy
Production dates: June 1941–August 1941

Running time: 105 minutes
Black and White
Release date: October 1, 1941

CAST

Clark Gable	"Candy" Johnson
Lana Turner	Elizabeth Cotton
Frank Morgan	Judge Cotton
Claire Trevor	"Gold Dust" Nelson
Marjorie Main	**Mrs. Varner**
Albert Dekker	Brazos Hearn
Henry O'Neill	Daniel Wells
Chill Wills	The Sniper
Veda Ann Borg	Pearl
Douglas Wood	Gov. Wilson
Betty Blythe	Mrs. Wilson
Harry Worth	Harry Gates
Lew Harvey	Blackie

"Sweater Girl," Lana Turner and "the King of Hollywood," Clark Gable team up for the first time in this comedic western romance. Candy (Clark Gable) is the gambling, no-good manipulator, while Elizabeth (Lana Turner) is the beautiful girl caught up in an ugly situation. Watch the sparks— and the bullets—fly as they fall in love.

Marjorie plays Mrs. Varner, the boarding house owner who sets out to reform the gambling townspeople, all in the name of good clean living. She reluctantly accepts a donation from Candy to help build a church for the town, but she knows full well that the money he gave to rehabilitate the townspeople from their sins was funded by the sin itself.

Trivia: A 1974 tele-movie remake of the same name starred Richard Crenna and Stella Stevens.

Variety (September 15, 1941) said, "Marjorie Main gets top acting honors among the featured players."

46. *The Bugle Sounds* (1941)

Director: S. Sylvan Simon
Producer: J. Walter Ruben
Screenplay: Cyrul Hume, Lawrence Kimble
Cinematographer: Clyde DeVinna
Studio: MGM
Filming locations: Fort Ord, California
Running time: 101 minutes
Black and White
Genre: Drama/War
Release dates: December 17, 1941 (premiere); January 2, 1942 (nationwide)

CAST

Wallace Beery	"Hap" Doan
Marjorie Main	**Susie**
Lewis Stone	Col. Jack Lawton
George Bancroft	Russell
Henry O'Neill	Lt. Col. Harry Seton
Donna Reed	Sally Hanson
Chill Wills	Sgt. Larry Dillon
William Lundigan	Joe Hanson
Tom Dugan	Sgt. Strong
Guinn "Big Boy" William	Sgt. Krims
Ernest Whitman	Cartaret
Roman Bohnen	Leech
Jerome Cowan	Nichols
Arthur Space	Hank
Jonathan Hale	Brigadier General

This was Marjorie's last picture for the year 1941, and once again she co-starred with Wallace Beery. It was not their strongest film together, yet it did well enough for the studio to start prepping another script for the pair.

Trivia: The film's working title was *Steel Cavalry.*

47. *We Were Dancing* (1942)

Director: Robert Z. Leonard
Producers: Orville O. Dull and Robert Z. Leonard
Screenplay: Lenore J. Coffee (uncredited), Noel Coward (play), George Froeschel, Hans Rameau and Claudine West
Cinematographer: Robert Planck
Studio: MGM
Running time: 95 minutes
Black and White
Genre: Comedy
Release date: March 1942

Cast

Norma Shearer	Victoria Anastasia "Vicki" Wilomirska
Melvyn Douglas	Nicholas Eugen August Wolfgang "Nikki" Prax
Gail Patrick	Linda Wayne
Lee Bowman	Hubert Tyler
Marjorie Main	**Judge Sidney Hawkes**
Reginald Owen	Major Berty Tyler-Blane
Alan Mowbray	Grand Duke Basil
Florence Bates	Mrs. Elsa Vanderlip
Heather Thatcher	Mrs. Tyler-Blane
Connie Gilchrist	Olive Ransome
Nella Walker	Mrs. Janet Bentley
Florence Shirley	Mrs. Charteris
Russell Hicks	Mr. Bryce-Carew
Norma Varden	Mrs. Bryce-Carew

Based on Noel Coward's play *Tonight at Eight*, this film adaptation proved a poor remake of the original story, and the critics were not kind. It was to be Norma Shearer's second-to-last appearance before her early retirement at age forty. One critic commented that her performance was "as sparkling as flat champagne." Marjorie plays the busybody courtroom judge who takes great satisfaction from seeing the society couple squirm as they air their dirty laundry during their divorce proceedings.

Trivia: Norma Shearer's nervous condition after the death of her beloved husband, studio head Irving Thalberg, did nothing to help her career. In fact, she was so used to his guidance in choosing the appropriate roles for her to play, his death was more than just a personal loss for her — it almost ended her career. To think that she turned down the role of Kay Miniver in *Mrs. Miniver* (1942) in favor of this flop just points out her poor personal judgment. Of course, Greer Garson went on to play Mrs. Miniver, with her brilliant performance earning her an Academy Award for Best Actress. Both Ava Gardner and Leatrice Joy Gilbert have uncredited bit parts in *We Were Dancing*.

48. *The Affairs of Martha* (1942)

Director: Jules Dassin
Producer: Irving Starr
Screenplay: Lee Gold and Isobel Lennart
Cinematographer: Charles Lawton Jr.
Studio: MGM
Running time: 66 minutes
Black and White
Genre: Comedy
Release date: June 21, 1942

Cast

Marsha Hunt	Martha Linddstrom
Richard Carlson	Jeff Sommerfield
Marjorie Main	**Mrs. McKessic**

Virginia Weidler	Mirand Sommerfield
Spring Byington	Sophia Sommerfield
Allyn Joslyn	Joel Archer
Frances Drake	Sylvia Norwood
Barry Nelson	Danny O'Brien
Melville Cooper	Dr. Clarence Sommerfield
Inez Cooper	Mrs. Jacell
Sara Haden	Mrs. Justin I. Peacock
Margaret Hamilton	Guinevere
Ernest Truex	Llewellyn Castle

This film's mix of character actors make *The Affairs of Martha* more enjoyable than one lead player ever could have. The combination of Margaret Hamilton, Spring Byington and Marjorie is a delight to watch.

When a local newspaper runs a headline indicating that a maid from one of the society families of Rocky Bay, Long Island, is set to write an exposé on her employers, everyone everywhere becomes *very* nervous. When it's revealed that the domestic, Martha (Marsha Hunt), is actually writing a book on how much she *likes* the Sommerfield family, everyone breathes a sigh of relief. However, the tension leading up to what "skeletons" might be taken out of the closet makes for a lot of laughs.

Marjorie plays head cook and advice-giver to all.

Trivia: The Affairs of Martha was released as *Once Upon a Thursday* in the U.K.

49. *Jackass Mail* (1942)

Director: Norman Z. McLeod
Producer: John W. Considine Jr.
Screenplay: C. Gardner Sullivan (story) and Lawrence Hazard (screenplay)
Cinematographer: Clyde DeVinna
Studio: MGM
Filming locations: Iverson Ranch, Chatsworth, Los Angeles, California
Running time: 80 minutes
Black and White
Genre: Western
Release date: July 1, 1942

Cast

Wallace Beery	Marmaduke "Just" Baggott
Marjorie Main	**Clementine "Tiny" Tucker**
J. Carrol Naish	Signor O'Sullivan
Darryl Hickman	Tommie Gargan
William Haade	Red Gargan
Hobart Cavanaugh	Gospel Jones
Dick Curtis	Jim Swade
Joe Yule	Barky

Marjorie is a riot in this one. Her singing scenes within the line-up of can can dancers is worth the price of admission alone. But there's much more to it, and it's those elements that makes this an enjoyable, all-round film.

Told in flashback, the film opens on a view of a modern-day Baggott City. The camera zooms in on two statues in the town's square; they're the unlikely founders—Marmaduke "Just" Baggott and Clementine "Tiny" Tucker. The rest of the film tells the story of how the town came to honor the pair with such a monument.

As the owner of the Gold Camp gambling saloon, "Tiny" (Marjorie Main) can be seen kicking up her heels at night, while during the day she works as the town's postmistress. Crooked Marmaduke "Just" Baggott (Wallace Beery) is having no luck in robbing her mail line, so he hatches the somewhat desperate, albeit clever, plan to marry her instead.

However, his plan backfires. As soon as Clementine "Tiny" Tucker gets her hooks into him, she reforms him into an honest, non-drinking citizen. Whenever he shows signs of slipping back into his old ways, she's not adverse to hitting him over the head with one of her kitchen utensils.

Poster tagline: "Beery Does It Again! A New Thrill and Fun Hit!"

50. *Tish* (1942)

Director: S. Sylvan Simon
Producer: Orville O. Dull
Screenplay: Mary Roberts Rinehart (stories), Annalee Whitmore Jacoby (adaptation), Thomas Seller (adaptation) and Harry Ruskin (screenplay)
Cinematographer: Paul Vogel
Studio: MGM
Filming locations: Big Bear Lake, Big Bear Valley; San Bernardino National Forest, California; Lake Arrowhead, California
Production dates: April 22, 1942–May 19, 1942
Running time: 84 minutes
Black and White
Genre: Comedy/Drama
Release dates: September 17, 1942 (New York City, N.Y.); November 19, 1942 (Los Angeles, California)

Cast

Marjorie Main	**Miss Letitia "Tish" Carberry**
ZaSu Pitts	Aggie Pilkington (as ZaSu Pitts)
Aline MacMahon	Lizzie Wilkins
Susan Peters	Cora Edwards Bowzer
Lee Bowman	Charles "Charlie" Sands, Tish's Nephew
Guy Kibbee	Judge Horace Bowser
Virginia Grey	Katherine "Kit" Bowser Sands
Richard Quine	Theodore "Ted" Bowser

Letitia "Tish" Carberry (Marjorie) controls the lives and loves of all around her. Her two closest friends, Lizzie Wilkins (Aline MacMahon) and Aggie Pilkington (Zasu Pitts), like to stick their noses into other people's business, too. The three form a gossipy force to be reckoned with! All three veteran character actresses do a fine job of giving life to these meddling ladies (based on Mary Roberts Rinehart's characters from her popular series of books)on the big screen.

Despite its promising story line, and the honor of having her name appear above the title of the film, Marjorie was disappointed in the final results.

Poster tagline: "Mary Roberts Rinehart's Character! Comedy Surprise Hit of the Year!"

51. *Tennessee Johnson* (1943)

Director: William Dieterle
Producer: J. Walter Ruben
Screenplay: John L. Balderston, Milton Gunzburg (story), Alvin Meyers (story) and Wells Root
Cinematographer: Harold Rosson
Studio: MGM
Running time: 100 minutes
Black and White
Genre: Drama
Release date: January 12, 1943 (premiere, New York City, N.Y.)

Cast

Van Heflin	Andrew Johnson
Ruth Hussey	Eliza McCardle
Lionel Barrymore	Thaddeus Stevens
Marjorie Main	**Mrs. Fisher**
Regis Toomey	McDaniel
Montagu Love	Chief Justice Chase
Porter Hall	The Weasel
Charles Dingle	Senator Jim Waters
J. Edward Bromberg	Coke
Grant Withers	Mordecai Milligan
Alec Craig	Andrews
Morris Ankrum	Jefferson Davis
Sheldon Leonard	Atzerodt
Noah Beery	Sheriff Cass
Lloyd Corrigan	Mr. Secretary
Charles Trowbridge	Lansbury
Robert Warwick	Major Crooks

This a biopic of sorts is loosely based on the life and career of president Andrew Johnson (Van Heflin). Marjorie appears early in the film, as Mrs. Fisher, a pioneer woman whose lot in life is all about making the town she lives in sober, honest and just plain decent. A mid-war propaganda drama that did poorly at the box office, *Tennessee Johnson* was a heavy story in too heavy a time.

Trivia: The film was released as *The Man on America's Conscience* in the U.K.

52. *Heaven Can Wait* (1943)

Director: Ernst Lubitsch
Producer: Ernst Lubitsch
Screenplay: Leslie Bush-Fekete (play) and Samson Raphaelson (screenplay)
Cinematographer: Edward Cronjager
Studio: 20th Century-Fox
Running time: 112 minutes
Color (Technicolor)
Genre: Comedy/Romance
Release date: August 11, 1943
Awards and nominations: 1944 Academy Awards: Nominated, Best Cinematography, Color, Edward Cronjager; Nominated, Best Director, Ernst Lubitsch; Nominated, Best Picture, Ernst Lubitsch.

Cast

Gene Tierney	Martha Strabel/Van Cleve
Don Ameche	Henry Van Cleve
Charles Coburn	Hugo Van Cleve, Grandfather
Marjorie Main	**Martha's Mother**
Laird Cregar	His Excellency
Spring Byington	Bertha Van Cleve, Mother
Allyn Joslyn	Albert Van Cleve, Cousin
Eugene Pallette	E.F. Strabel, Martha's Father
Signe Hasso	Mademoiselle

Louis Calhern	Randolph Van Cleve, Father
Helene Reynolds	Peggy Nash, Showgirl
Aubrey Mather	James, Jack's Butler
Tod Andrews	Jack Van Cleve, Henry's Son (as Michael Ames)

Perpetual womanizer Henry Van Cleve (Don Ameche) has died and assumes (based on the way he's lived his life) that he'll be destined for hell. Throughout the rest of the film he reflects on his life with the Devil (Laird Creger), explaining why he thinks he is a worthy candidate to enter the gates of hell.

After hearing the story of Henry's lecherous life, the Devil concludes that Henry has brought joy to the lives of many women during his 70 years, thus giving him a green light to go onward and upward to the pearly gates of Heaven.

It is somewhat astounding that a character of Henry Van Cleve's low moralistic values can be looked upon with a sympathetic eye, but Lubitsch manages to give him just enough soul to make him likable, even lovable at times.

The three main elements—comedy, fantasy and romance—blend beautifully in this Eric Lubitsch masterpiece. Helped by the brilliance of Technicolor, *Heaven Can Wait* is nothing short of a visual feast.

For the first time in her career, Marjorie gets all dressed up as Martha's (Gene Tierney) mother.

Trivia: This was based on the play *Birthday* by Leslie Bush-Fekete.

Gene Tierney found out she was pregnant while making this film. After Gene contracted German Measles in her first trimester of pregnancy, however, her little girl, Daria, was born mentally and physically retarded. Daria Cassini (her father is fashion designer Oleg Cassini) has been institutionalized much of her life. The realization that her daughter was never going to be normal was one of the main factors in Gene Tierney's tragic spiral into years of mental illness.

In her autobiography, *Self Portrait*, Gene remembered a note that fellow actor and good friend Richard Widmark had sent her in the midst of her illness. She wrote, "The kindness of others made my return to work possible. Richard Widmark wrote a gentle, teasing note from Hollywood. In it he said, 'Hurry back, or there will be nothing left for us to play but Ma and Pa Kettle pictures!'"

Variety (July 21, 1943) said, "Eugene Pallette and Marjorie Main provide much amusement as the Kansas City meat packer and his wife, eternally fighting, rolling in riches, living in a great and gaudy palace, yet awkwardly bereft when their daughter permits herself to elope with the wrong Van Cleve—a black mark on their social aspirations."

Despite sharing the same title, *Heaven Can Wait* (1978), starring Warren Beatty, is not a remake of this film.

53. *Johnny Come Lately* (1943)

Director: William K. Howard
Producer: William Cagney
Screenplay: Louis Bromfield (novel) and John Van Druten
Cinematographer: Theodore Sparkuhl
Studio: United Artists/Cagney Productions
Running time: 97 minutes
Black and White
Genre: Drama
Release dates: September 3, 1943
Awards and nominations: 1944 Academy Awards, Nominated, Best Music,

Scoring of a Dramatic or Comedy Picture, Leigh Harline.

Cast

James Cagney	Tom Richards
Grace George	Vinnie McLeod
Marjorie Main	**"Gashouse" Mary McGovern**
Marjorie Lord	Jane
Hattie McDaniel	Aida
Edward McNamara	W.M. Dougherty
William Henry	Pete Dougherty (as Bill Henry)
Robert Barrat	Bill Swain
George Cleveland	Willie Ferguson
Margaret Hamilton	Myrtle Ferguson
Norman Willis	Dudley Hirsh
Lucien Littlefield	Blaker
Edwin Stanley	Winterbottom
Irving Bacon	Chief of Police
Tom Dugan	First Cop
Charles Irwin	Second Cop
John Sheehan	Third Cop
Clarence Muse	Butler
John "Skins" Miller	First Tramp (as John Miller)
Arthur Hunnicutt	Second Tramp
Victor Kilian	Tramp in Box Car

Cagney plays the familiar misfit with a heart of gold in this one, saving the small-town newspaper and making sure that the crooks pay for their crimes.

Marjorie plays the raucous "Gashouse" Mary McGovern. She gets the opportunity to step into some fancier costumes than her usual matronly characters generally allowed. Interestingly, both Marjorie and James Cagney considered *Johnny Come Lately* one of their all-time favorite films.

Trivia: Johnny Come Lately was based on the novel *McLeod's Folley* by Louis Bromfield.

William Cagney, producer of this film, was the real-life brother and manager of actor James Cagney.

Despite being nominated for an Academy Award for his original score on the film, composer Leigh Harline went without mention in the credits.

54. *Rationing* (1944)

Director: Willis Goldbeck
Producer: Orville O. Dull
Screenplay: Grant Garrett, William R. Lipman and Harry Ruskin
Cinematographer: Sidney Wagner
Studio: MGM
Running time: 93 minutes
Black and White
Genre: Comedy
Release date: March 24, 1944

Cast

Wallace Beery	Ben Barton
Marjorie Main	**Iris Tuttle**
Donald Meek	Wilfred Ball
Dorothy Morris	Dorothy Tuttle
How eeman	Cash Riddle
Connie Gilchrist	Mrs. Porter
Tommy Batten	Lance Barton
Gloria Dickson	Miss McCue
Henry O'Neill	Senator Edward White
Richard Hall	Teddy
Charles Halton	Ezra Weeks
Chill Wills	Bus driver
Carol Ann Beery	Carol Ann

Marjorie teams up with Wallace Beery again, this time playing Iris Tuttle, postmistress and one-woman ration board member amidst a time of war in the town of Tuttleton. Ben Barton (Wallace Beery), the town butcher, ends up leaving his store when the restrictions of rationing becomes too much for him.

But after arriving in Washington, intent on joining the military, he is asked to return to Tuttleton since the meat industry is once again a viable venture. He returns home, and even joins the rationing board alongside Iris (Marjorie). When Iris' daughter falls for Ben's son, the real sparks—and laughs—begin to fly!

Trivia: Wallace Beery's real-life daughter, Carol Ann Beery, plays her namesake, Carol Ann, in this film. She also played the character of Carol Ann in another Beery production, *China Seas* (1935). These two films comprised the extent of her short-lived acting career.

Marjorie takes her first onscreen nip of alcohol in this film, going against her strict studio contract clause that she would not be made to drink alcohol onscreen.

55. *Meet Me in St. Louis* (1944)

Director: Vincente Minnelli
Producer: Arthur Freed
Screenplay: Sally Benson (novel), Irving Brecher and Fred F. Finklehoffe
Cinematographer: George Folsey
Studio: MGM
Running time: 113 minutes
Color (Technicolor)
Genre: Musical/Family/Romance
Production dates: December 1, 1943–April 7, 1944
Release dates: November 28, 1944 (premiere, New York City, N.Y); January, 1945 (nationwide)
Awards and nominations: 1945 Academy Awards: Nominated, Best Cinematography (color), George J. Folsey; Nominated, Best Music, Original Song, Ralph Blane and Hugh Martin for "The Trolley Song"; Nominated, Best Music, Scoring of a Musical Picture, George E. Stoll; Nominated, Best Writing, Screenplay, Irving Brecher and Fred F. Finklehoffe.

Cast

Judy Garland	Esther Smith
Margaret O'Brien	"Tootie" Smith
Mary Astor	Mrs. Anna Smith
Lucille Bremer	Rose Smith
Leon Ames	Mr. Alonzo Smith
Tom Drake	John Truett
Marjorie Main	**Katie (the maid)**
Harry Davenport	Grandpa
June Lockhart	Lucille Ballard
Henry H. Daniels Jr.	Alonzo "Lon" Smith Jr.
Joan Carroll	Agnes Smith
Hugh Marlowe	Col. Darly
Robert Sully	Warren Sheffield
Chill Wills	Mr. Neelyl (the iceman)

In this upbeat musical revolving around the 1903 World's Fair, the audience is introduced to the Smith family, a bunch of characters who are about to be uprooted from their beloved St. Louis to move to New York as a result of Mr. Smith's (Leon Ames) job promotion.

Played by an all-star cast, the characters consisted of Mrs. Smith (Mary Astor), their son Alonzo (Henry H. Daniels Jr.) and their four daughters, Esther (Judy Garland), Rose (Lucille Bremer), Agnes (Joan Carroll) and their death obsessed youngest, "Tootie" (Margaret O'Brien). Eccentric Grandpa (Harry Davenport) and, of course, Katie (Marjorie), their acid-tongued maid, give the story that extra bit of zip when needed.

Meet Me in St. Louis is without question a perfect example of an MGM classic musical, offering a little comedy, a dash of romance, an impromptu song when the mood takes you, and a good old-fashioned story with family values to wrap up the package. Filmed in the middle of WWII, the whimsical feeling of *Meet Me in St. Louis* was the perfect "pick-me-up" for audiences the world over.

Memorable quote: "A lie's a lie, and dressed in white don't help it."—Marjorie as Katie in *Meet Me in St. Louis*

Trivia: The Smith family lived at 5135 Kensington Avenue, St. Louis, Missouri. Many families resided at that stately home over the years; however, it was torn down in December 1994.

At the time, the still-standing Hardy family street set (used in the popular Andy Hardy series) was going to be converted (at a cost of $58,275) and used for the Smith family. But director Vincente Minnelli had other ideas, and insisted that a new set be built (at an outlay of $208, 275). The entire set remained standing in all of its majestic glory until, sadly, it was torn down in 1970.

Other production costs included $86,616.67 for the screenplay (including early drafts and treatments dating back to 1942); $62,225 for the lower floor of the Smith home; $16,625 for the miniature of the exterior of the World's Fair; and $15,625 for the trolley depot, and $5,091 for the trolley tracks.

Meet Me in St. Louis sported a hefty budget of $1.7 million; however, worldwide ticket sales topped 7.5 million upon its first release. It was the second most successful film that MGM ever produced. The studio's number-one moneymaker was *Gone With The Wind* (1939).

Director Vincente Minnelli and lead actress Judy Garland met on the set, fell in love, and married on June 15, 1945. They divorced in 1951. Their daughter, Liza Minnelli, is a legend in her own right—no small achievement considering her famous parentage.

The period in which the film is set is 1903; and despite the famous "The Trolley Song" being a featured production number in the film, historically, trolleys didn't exist in St. Louis in 1903.

Judy Garland's flawless version of "Have Yourself a Merry Little Christmas" makes this film a holiday favorite. Her equally popular "The Trolley Song" rose to number one on the American hit parade, even before the film's Thanksgiving Day release.

The Academy of Motion Picture Arts and Sciences awarded Margaret O'Brien a special miniature Oscar in1945 for "Best Child Actress of the Year" for her portrayal of "Tootie" in *Meet Me in St. Louis.* Ironically, her co-star, Judy Garland, received the same juvenile Academy Award (1939) for her portrayal of Dorothy in *The Wizard of Oz* (1939).

In an odd coincidence, on the day of Judy Garland's death (June 22, 1969) a tornado touched down in Kansas. It's ironic, considering her most famous role was Dorothy Gale, the girl who dreams of a land of Oz after a Kansas tornado... *The Wizard of Oz* (1939) is considered one of the finest musicals in cinematic history. In fact, it often tops various "Best Films of All Time" lists.

Poster tagline: "M-G-M's glorious love story with music."

56. *Gentle Annie* (1944)

Director: Andrew Marton
Producer: Robert Sisk
Screenplay: Lawrence Hazard and MacKinlay Kantor (story)
Cinematographer: Charles Salerno Jr.
Studio: MGM
Running time: 80 minutes
Black and White
Genre: Western
Release date: December 20, 1944

Cast

James Craig	U.S. Marshal Lloyd Richland, posing as Rich Williams
Donna Reed	Mary Lingen
Marjorie Main	**Annie Goss**
Harry Morgan	Cottonwood Goss (as Henry Morgan)
Paul Langton	Violet Goss
Barton MacLane	Sheriff Tatum
John Philliber	Barrow
Morris Ankrum	Deputy Gansby
Noah Beery	Hansen (as Noah Beery Sr.)
Frank Darien	Jake

In this little known and vastly underrated MGM western weepie, Marjorie plays the title character, Annie, mother of train-robbing sons Violet (Paul Langton) and Cottonwood (Harry Morgan). With the help of saloon waitress Mary (Donna Reed), U.S Marshall Lloyd Richland (James Craig) comes to town intent on catching the no-good thieves.

Before the credits roll, Annie is killed, Violet is mortally wounded and Cottonwood is sent to prison for his crimes. The only happiness in this one comes from the and-they-lived-happily-ever-after relationship between Mary and the lawmaker, Lloyd Richland. *Gentle Annie* is a solid film featuring strong performances by all.

Trivia: The *Hollywood Reporter* (December 20, 1944) said, "As Gentle Annie, Marjorie Main gives a delightful characterization, one of her most outstanding performances, shading it beautifully and playing it in a more restrained manner than usual."

57. *Murder, He Says* (1945)

Director: George Marshall
Producer: E. D. Leshin (assoc. producer)
Screenplay: Lou Breslow and Jack Moffitt
Cinematographer: Theodor Sparkuhl
Studio: Paramount Pictures
Running time: 91 minutes
Black and White
Genre: Comedy

Cast

Fred MacMurray	Pete Marshall
Helen Walker	Claire Matthews
Marjorie Main	**Mamie Johnson**
Jean Heather	Elany Fleagle
Porter Hall	Mr. Johnson
Peter Whitney	Mert/Bert Fleagle
Mabel Paige	Grandma Fleagle
Barbara Pepper	Bonnie Fleagle
Walter Baldwin	Vic Hardy
James Flavin	Police Officer
Francis Ford	Lee
Si Jenks	80-Year-Old
Tom Fadden	Sheriff Murdock

When mild-mannered Pete Marshall (Fred MacMurray) sets out to find a missing co-worker, he gets more than he bargained for when he stumbles upon the nutty Fleagle family. As Pete gets himself deeper into the woodland areas of Kallikaw City, he runs into the matriarch of the clan, Mamie (Marjorie Main). As if her whipcrackin,' wisecrackin' ways aren't enough to contend with, Pete is introduced to the rest of the bunch, including her new husband, Mr. Johnson (Porter Hall), who has a thing for building coffins in the basement. Then there's the simpleton twin sons Mert and Bert, the childlike daughter Elany (Jean Heather), and, of course, Granny (Mabel Paige).

Shortly before she passes on, Granny gives Pete a cryptic clue to the secret hiding place of $70,000 in stolen cash. When the rest of the Fleagles find out Granny confided in Pete, he's held against his will, shot at, chased relentlessly and beaten in an attempt to extract the clues to the stolen stash of cash.

As the bumbling Pete becomes more and more involved with the crazy brood, the laughs are endless and hearty. Luckily for Pete, his efforts are rewarded with a dose of romance from a beautiful girl on a mission to clear her father's name. The final scene in the barn treats the audience to some of the funniest moments of the entire film.

Marjorie gives the best pre–Ma Kettle performance of her career here. In fact, her character, Mamie, in *Murder He Says* is not unlike a sardonic Ma Kettle in many ways. Mamie could easily pass as Ma's evil twin!

Poster tagline: "A romantic comedy about two ordinary people...and one oddball family."

58. *The Harvey Girls* (1946)

Director: George Sidney
Producer: Arthur Freed
Screenplay: Samuel Hopkins Adams (novel), Edmund Beloin, Harry Crane, Nathaniel Curtis, Eleanore Griffin (story), James O'Hanlon, William Rankin (story), Sampson Raphaelson and Kay Van Riper (additional dialogue)
Cinematographer: George J. Folsey
Studio: MGM
Production dates: January 12, 1945–June 4, 1945
Filming locations: Iverson Ranch, Chatsworth, California; Monument Valley, Utah
Running time: 102 minutes
Color (Technicolor)
Genre: Musical/Western
Release date: January 18, 1946
Awards and nominations: 1947 Academy Awards: Won, Best Music, Original Song, Harry Warren (music), Johnny Mercer (lyrics), for the song "On the Atchison, Topeka and Santa Fe"; Nominated, Best Music, Scoring of a Musical Picture, Lennie Hayton.

Cast

Judy Garland	Susan Bradley
John Hodiak	Ned Trent
Ray Bolger	Chris Maule
Preston Foster	Judge Sam Purvis
Virginia O'Brien	Alma
Angela Lansbury	Em
Marjorie Main	**Sonora Cassidy**
Chill Wills	H. H. Hartsey
Kenny Baker	Terry O'Halloran
Selena Royle	Miss Bliss
Cyd Charisse	Deborah

Ruth Brady	Ethel
Catherine McLeod	Louise
Jack Lambert	Marty Peters
Edward Earle	Jed Adams
William "Bill" Phillips	Buck (cowboy #1)
Norman Leavitt	Cowboy #2
Morris Ankrum	Rev. Claggett
Ben Carter	John Henry
Mitchell Lewis	Sandy
Stephen McNally	Golddust McClean (as Horace McNally)
Bill Hale	Big Joe
Ray Teal	Conductor
Vernon Dent	Engineer
Jim Toney	Muleskinner

The Harvey Girls was one of the top grossing films of 1946, and it's not surprising. The feel-good story line and upbeat musical numbers still have the ability to make modern audiences smile. The ensemble cast singing the Oscar winning "On the Atchison, Topeka and Santa Fe" for close to ten minutes is one of the highlights of the film.

The story of *The Harvey Girls* is loosely based on factual events. Back in the late 1880s Fred Harvey was a real guy who made a landmark deal with the Atchison, Topeka and Santa Fe (hence the name of the main song) railway to open a chain of roadhouses along their line to feed and house his hungry, weary travelers. A chain of "Harvey Houses," as they were known, were opened, and the wholesome waitresses who served there were aptly named "the Harvey Girls." Historically, that's as far as the truth takes us on film. The rest of the story is Hollywood fanfare at its finest—just good old-fashioned family entertainment.

In reality, the moralistic "Harvey Houses" were initially set up to rival the roughhouse saloons so prevalent throughout the Old West. The good girls would work on one side of the street as a "Harvey Girl," and the bad girls would work on the other side of the street as a "Call Girl." These diverse lifestyle choices are highlighted in the film.

Naive Susan Bradley (Judy Garland) boards a train to Sandrock, New Mexico, intent on becoming a mail order bride. On her way she meets a group of girls who are all waitresses-in-training for the new "Harvey House" restaurant. Upon arriving at her destination, Susan meets her wild-looking husband-to-be (Chill Wills), and, after realizing her mistake, backs out of the proposed marriage to become a "Harvey Girl" instead.

Despite the strong ensemble cast, this is most definitely a Judy Garland film. There's nothing wrong with that, but her co-stars were far too talented to be pushed into the background. Garland is superb, but as the film progresses you will find yourself hoping to see more of the supporting characters. Unfortunately, the film ends before that can happen.

Marjorie plays Sonora Cassidy, the recruiter and trainer of the new waitresses. She's also featured in a few of the group musical numbers.

Trivia: The Budget for *The Harvey Girls* was $2.5 million. The film doubled its outlay in ticket sales, returning a little over five million dollars to the studio.

Virginia O'Brien completely disappears from the film after singing her "The Wild Wild West" number; this was due to her advancing pregnancy. The wardrobe department were beyond disguising her expanding belly with clever costume designs and strategically placed props, so she was forced to leave the production altogether.

Incredibly, Judy Garland did her scenes in one take for the lengthy "On the Atchison, Topeka and Santa Fe" number. In theaters, the lengthy song and dance number received rousing cheers from audiences everywhere.

The Harvey Girls featured the first on-screen reunion of Judy Garland and Ray Bolger since *The Wizard of Oz* (1939).

Director George Sidney was the founder of the animation studio Hanna-Barbera Productions (1944). It was his idea to have Gene Kelly dance with cartoons in *Anchors Aweigh* (1945), a film that he also directed. Gene Kelly's dance number with "Jerry the Mouse" is referenced in Hollywood documentaries as an innovative moment in film history.

An unheard-of nine writers collaborated on this project. The script was shelved for many years, rewritten, shelved again, rewritten again, and so forth. Each time MGM decided to make it, they'd give the script to a new writer to polish. By the time it began production, an ensemble list of writers had to be credited for their involvement.

Joan Crawford was offered a role in *The Harvey Girls*, but she turned it down in favor of going to Warners to make a film about another waitress, *Mildred Pierce* (1945). It was a good choice, as the role won her an Academy Award for Best Actress.

In David Shipman's book *Judy Garland: The Secret Life of an American Legend*, Judy Garland remembered back to her less-than-pleasant experience on *The Harvey Girls*. "I was a nervous wreck," she said. "I was jumpy and irritable from sleeping too little. I couldn't take the tension at the studio. Everything at MGM was competition. Everyday I went to work with tears in my eyes. Work gave me no pleasure. The studio had become a haunted house for me. It was all I could do to keep from screaming every time the director looked at me."

59. *Bad Bascomb* (1946)

Director: S. Sylvan Simon
Producer: Orville O. Dull
Screenplay: D. A. Loxley (story), William Lipman and Grant Garett
Cinematographer: Charles Schoenbaum
Studio: MGM
Filming locations: Grand Teton Nation Park, Moose, Wyoming
Running time: 112 minutes
Black and White
Genre: Western
Release date: November 1946

Cast

Wallace Beery	Zed Bascomb
Margaret O'Brien	Emmy
Marjorie Main	**Abbey Hanks**
J. Carrol Naish	Bart Yancy
Frances Rafferty	Dora McCabe
Marshall Thompson	Jimmy Holden
Russell Simpson	Elijah Walker
Warner Anderson	Luther Mason
Donald Curtis	John Fulton
Connie Gilchrist	Annie Freemont
Sara Haden	Tillie Lovejoy
Renie Riano	Lucy Lovejoy
Jane Green	Hannah McCabe
Henry O'Neill	Gov. Winton of Wyoming
Frank Darien	Elder Moab McCabe

Marjorie plays Abey Hanks, the dominant grandmother to little orphaned Emmy (Margaret O'Brien). The unlikely pair are part of a Mormon wagon train heading to Utah with enough gold on board to build themselves a Mormon hospital.

In an attempt to outsmart the sheriff, outlaw Zed Bascomb (Wallace Beery) decides to seek refuge with the religious group. Just when he's tempted to rob the assemblage of their fortune, he becomes an unlikely hero, defending them from savage Indians and saving Emmy (Margaret O'Brien) from drowning after their wagon flips over during a dangerous river crossing.

It's a stereotypical pairing of both Marjorie and Wallace Beery. Marjorie plays the loud, boisterous role, while Beery plays the underhanded crook who's softened by the innocence of a child and ends up righting his wrongs by film's end.

60. *Undercurrent* (1946)

Director: Vincente Minnelli
Producer: Pandro S. Berman
Screenplay: Edward Chodorov, George Oppenheimer, Margeurite Roberts and Thelma Strabel (story)
Cinematographer: Karl Freund
Studio: MGM
Running time: 116 minutes
Black and White
Genre: Film-Noir/Thriller
Release date: November 28, 1946

Cast

Katharine Hepburn	Ann Hamilton
Robert Taylor	Alan Garroway
Robert Mitchum	Michael Garroway
Edmund Gwenn	Prof. "Dink" Hamilton
Marjorie Main	**Lucy**
Jayne Meadows	Sylvia Burton
Clinton Sundberg	Mr. Warmsley
Dan Tobin	Prof. Joseph Bangs
Kathryn Card	Mrs. Foster
Leigh Whipper	George
Charles Trowbridge	Justice Putnam
James Westerfield	Henry Gilson
Billy McClain	Uncle Ben (as Billy McLain)
Bess Flowers	Julia Donnegan
Sarah Edwards	Cora
Ellen Ross	Gwen
Betty Blythe	Saleslady
Milton Kibbee	Minister
Jean Adren	Mrs. Davenport
Forbes Murray	Sen. Edwards
Wheaton Chambers	Proprietor

Ann Hamilton's (Katharine Hepburn) excitement at becoming a newlywed is soon overshadowed by mounting evidence that her charming husband Alan (Robert Taylor) may be trying to kill her!

When Alan tells his new wife that his brother Michael (Robert Mitchum) is missing, Ann thinks the worst and suddenly realizes that she's slated to be her husband's next victim. She's right; but, luckily for her, Michael turns up just in time to save his sister-in-law from the deadly clutches of his psychotic brother.

Marjorie plays Lucy, the vocal housekeeper, a familiar role for her.

Trivia: The film's working title was *You Were There.*

61. *The Show-Off* (1946)

Director: Harry Beaumont
Producer: Albert Lewis
Screenplay: George Kelly (play) and George Wells
Cinematographer: Robert Planck
Studio: MGM
Production dates: February 13, 1946–March 1946 (with retakes shot June 11–14, 1946)
Running time: 83 minutes
Black and White
Genre: Comedy
Release date: December 1946

Cast

Red Skelton	J. Aubrey Piper
Marilyn Maxwell	Amy Fisher Piper
Marjorie Main	**Mrs. Fisher**
Virginia O'Brien	Hortense
Eddie "Rochester" Anderson	Eddie
George Cleveland	Pop Fisher
Leon Ames	Frank Harlin
Marshall Thompson	Joe Fisher
Jacqueline White	Clara Harlin
Wilson Wood	Horace Adems
Lila Leeds	Flo
Emory Parnell	Mr. Appelton

When Amy (Marilyn Maxwell) announces to her parents that she's going to marry pathological liar J. Aubrey Piper (Red Skelton), they are understandably shaken. The chain of events that follow is what makes the film funny. Skelton manages to maim a policeman, crash a friend's car, run up debts he can't afford, ruin his brother-in-law's business deal, and finally get evicted from his apartment. What's more, by film's end he's still the same "show off" that he was when the movie started.

This is a comedic dream for Skelton, who gets the opportunity to make silly faces and pull off crazy stunts throughout the entire film.

Marjorie plays his disapproving mother-in-law, Mrs. Fisher. It was her last performance for 1946.

Trivia: The original play, directed by the author, George Kelly, opened in New York City on February 5, 1924.

This particular production is based on three earlier film versions: *The Show Off* (1926), *Men Are Like That* (1930) and *The Show Off* (1934).

During the chase sequence, the street scenes were supposed to reflect Market Street, Philadelphia; however, the research department at MGM got their cities mixed up, running stock footage of Market Street, San Francisco, instead!

The completion of *The Show Off* (1946) meant that Marjorie had completed her contractual salary climb under the terms in her contract. Each year her salary would escalate until it reached its peak of $1,000 per week. To give you an idea of the bargain deal that MGM had made with her, her frequent co-star, Wallace Beery, received $15,000 per week, based on a thirteen-week year. Studio boss Louis B. Mayer was so intolerant of Beery's brash behavior he made special arrangements for him to work a minimum amount of time, and as quickly as possible.

62. *The Egg and I* (1947)

Director: Chester Erskine
Producer: Chester Erskine and Fred F. Finklehoffe
Screenplay: Betty MacDonald (novel), Chester Erskine and Fred F. Finklehoffe
Cinematographer: Milton Krasner
Studio: Universal International Pictures
Running time: 108 minutes
Black and White
Genre: Comedy/ Romance
Release dates: March 21, 1947 (premiere, Los Angeles); May 1947 (nationwide); July 3, 1954 (re-release)
Awards and nominations: 1948 Academy Awards, Nominated, Best Actress in a Supporting Role, Marjorie Main.

CAST

Claudette Colbert	Betty MacDonald
Fred MacMurray	Bob MacDonald
Marjorie Main	**Ma Kettle**
Louise Allbritton	Harriett Putnam
Percy Kilbride	Pa Kettle
Richard Long	Tom Kettle
Billy House	Billy Reed
Ida Moore	Emily, the Old Lady
Donald MacBride	Mr. Henty
Samuel S. Hinds	Sheriff
Esther Dale	Birdie Hicks
Elisabeth Risdon	Betty's Mother
John Berkes	Geoduck
Victor Potel	Crowbar (as Vic Potel)
Fuzzy Knight	Cab Driver
Isabel O'Madigan	Mrs. Hicks' Mother

When new bride Betty MacDonald (Claudette Colbert) gives in to her husband Bob's (Fred MacMurray) romantic idea of owning a chicken farm, it doesn't take long for her to regret her decision.

After moving to a rundown house in the country, the MacDonalds' vows are tested to the limit as they attempt to fix up the place, raise chickens, and deal with Louise (Harriett Putnam), their flirtatious neighbor who only has eyes for Bob.

The introduction of Ma and Pa Kettle (their other neighbors) and their brood of thirteen feral children (they added two more for their subsequent solo series) was the springboard to the popular Ma and Pa Kettle films.

Memorable quote: "Can't fall down around here without landin' on the Hicks!"—Marjorie as Ma Kettle in *The Egg and I.*

Trivia: After the Kettles' debut appearance in *The Egg and I,* the overwhelming public demand to see more of the hillbilly clan spawned nine solo Ma and Pa Kettle films between 1949 and 1957. The films were so popular they single-handedly saved Universal International Pictures from bankruptcy!

The relatively low-budget *The Egg and I* put a hefty 5.5 million dollars into the studio bank account. It was a clean profit of 5.1 million, and with that return Universal was back in business.

Universal International paid Betty MacDonald $100,000 for the film rights to her best-selling book of the same name. In order to use her Ma and Pa Kettle characters in future films, they paid her an additional $10,000 per film.

Marjorie was known as a clean freak, and being the onscreen mother of thirteen (soon to be fifteen) children sent her into anti-germ overdrive. A UI production report (August 22, 1949) claims she'd say, "Open the doors, air out these sets, ya never do know what these kids are carryin'."

Throughout their careers, Fred MacMurray and Claudette Colbert starred in seven films together. Despite her charming performance as Betty MacDonald, Colbert made no secret of her dislike for *The Egg and I.* She never gave a direct reason, but perhaps it was because the Kettles shared her spotlight.

Daily Variety (24 March, 1947) said, "Top laugh-getters of the piece are indisputably Marjorie Main and Percy Kilbride in the main character roles of Ma and Pa Kettle. Both parts present constant temptation to burlesque and hamming. Miss Main and Kilbride resist the temptation and give an honest interpretation that simultaneously rouses the merriment and tugs at the heartstrings of the audience."

Hollywood Reporter (March 24, 1947) said, "Marjorie Main and Percy Kilbride are delightfully teamed as Ma and Pa Kettle."

63. *The Wistful Widow of Wagon Gap* (1947)

Director: Charles Barton
Producer: Robert Arthur
Screenplay: D. D. Beauchamp (story), William Bowers (story), John Grant, Robert Lees and Frederic I. Rinaldo
Cinematographer: Charles Van Enger
Studio: Universal International
Filming locations: Iverson's Flats, California
Running time: 78 minutes
Black and White
Genre: Comedy/Western
Release date: October 8, 1947

Cast

Bud Abbott	Duke Egan
Lou Costello	Chester Wooley
Marjorie Main	**Widow Hawkins**
Audrey Wilder	Juanita Hawkins (as Audrey Young)
George Cleveland	Judge Benbow
Gordon Jones	Jake Frame
William Ching	Jim Simpson
Peter M. Thompson	Phil (as Peter Thompson)
Bill Clauson	Matt Hawkins
Bill O'Leary	Billy Hawkins (as Billy O'Leary)
Pamela Wells	Sarah Hawkins
Jimmy Bates	Jefferson Hawkins
Paul Dunn	Lincoln Hawkins
Diane Florentine	Sally Hawkins
Rex Lease	Hank
Glenn Strange	Lefty
Edmund Cobb	Lem
Wade Crosby	Squint
Dewey Robinson	Miner
Murray Leonard	Bartender

This is more of a Costello and Main film than an Abbott and Costello film; however, Marjorie's role as the poor widow who needs taking care of after Lou accidentally shoots her husband is a welcome addition to the comedic pair. Lou's newfound confidence as he becomes sheriff of the town is especially satisfying. As chief lawman he finally gets to turn the tables on Abbott, bullying him with as much gusto as we're so used to seeing in reverse. Watch for the frog soup scene, it's one of the highlights of the film.

Trivia: Lou Costello's father passed away in the middle of the production, so to honor his memory, Costello insisted that he be credited as an associate producer. He got his wish — Sebastian Cristillo is listed as the associate producer on *The Wistful Widow of Wagon Gap*. The film was released as *The Wistful Widow* in the U.K.

64. *Feudin', Fussin' and A-Fightin'* (1948)

Director: George Sherman
Producer: Leonard Goldstein
Screenplay: D. D. Beauchamp
Cinematographer: Irving Glassberg
Studio: Universal International
Running time: 78 minutes
Black and White
Genre: Comedy
Release date: July 1948

CAST

Donald O'Connor	Wilbur McMurty
Marjorie Main	**Maribel Mathews**
Percy Kilbride	Billy Caswell
Penny Edwards	Libby Mathews
Joe Besser	Sharkey Dolan
Harry Shannon	Chauncey
Howland Chamberlain	Doc Overholt
Fred Kohler Jr.	Emory Tuttle
Edmund Cobb	Stage Driver
Joel Friedkin	Stage Passenger
I. Stanford Jolley	Guard
Alvin Hammer	Milton Wurtle

Hair tonic salesman Wilbur McMurty (Donald O'Connor) is kidnapped by a small town so he can run in their annual footrace. The chain of events that follow, including the spectacle of O'Connor dancing up walls—pre-*Singin' in the Rain (1952)*—makes for a very enjoyable film indeed.

Marjorie plays Maribel Matthews, mayor of the tiny town of Rimrock. It was her only film for the year. Percy Kilbride teams up with Marjorie for the first time since *The Egg and I* (1947) as her political assistant. Joe Besser does a wonderful job of playing the dim-witted sheriff.

Trivia: The film was shot under the working title of *The Wonderful Race at Rimrock.*

Variety (June 8, 1948) said, "'*Feudin,' Fussin' and A-Fightin'* packs the stuff from which comedy hits are made. The film is full of breezy slapstick with a multitude of laughs and offers Donald O'Connor, Marjorie Main and Percy Kilbride in sharp performances which will hit audiences right between the eyes. Picture is a smart package of comedy-making which will pay off handsomely."

65. *The Further Adventures of Ma and Pa Kettle* (1949)

Director: Charles Lamont
Producer: Leonard Goldstein
Screenplay: Al Lewis, Betty MacDonald (characters), Herbert Margolis and Louis Morheim
Cinematographer: Maury Gertsman
Studio: Universal International
Running time: 76 minutes
Black and White
Genre: Comedy
Release date: April 1, 1949

CAST

Marjorie Main	**Ma Kettle**
Percy Kilbride	Pa Kettle
Richard Long	Tom Kettle
Meg Randall	Kim Parker
Patricia Alphin	Secretary
Esther Dale	Mrs. Birdie Hicks
Barry Kelley	Mr. Victor Tomkins
Harry Antrim	Mayor Dwiggins

Isabel O'Madigan	Mrs. Hick's Mother
Ida Moore	Emily
Emory Parnell	Bill Reed
Boyd Davis	Mr. Simpson
O.Z. Whitehead	Mr. Billings
Ray Bennett	Sam Rogers
Alvin Hammer	Alvin
Lester Allen	Geoduck
Chief Yowlachie	Crowbar
Rex Lease	Sheriff

Well, it took the studio two years from the time the Kettles first appeared onscreen in the smash hit *The Egg and I* (1947) to get them into their own starring feature film, but it was certainly worth the wait. When Pa wins the grand prize in a tobacco slogan contest, Ma, Pa and fourteen of their fifteen rowdy children (eldest boy Tom is away at college) move from their rundown shack to an upmarket house full of modern conveniences. The audience can't help but fall in love with Pa as he tries desperately to cope with all the buttons, levers and appliances that are installed to make his life easier. This is one of the best Kettle films in the nine-film series.

Trivia: More widely known as *The Further Adventures of Ma and Pa Kettle,* the film's original title was simply *Ma and Pa Kettle.*

According to a UI production report (February 2, 1949), Charles Lamont was directing a scene in *The Further Adventures of Ma and Pa Kettle* which required Percy Kilbride to pick Marjorie up and carry her over the threshold of their new home. Percy tried manfully to pick "Ma" up, but his 125 pounds just couldn't take the weight of Marjorie's buxom frame. "Shucks," squealed Marjorie, "why don't we do it this way?" and she picked Percy up and carried him into their new house.

"That's funnier than the other way," agreed Lamont.

It took some convincing, but Percy finally allowed the scene to be left in the final cut of the film. As a result, it's one of the funnier visual sequences of the entire series.

Variety (March 3, 1949) said, "Ma and Pa Kettle is a field day for Marjorie Main and Percy Kilbride, playing the characters they created in '*The Egg and I.*' They have it all to themselves this time, and all plot deficiencies will be forgiven for the sake of roars that will pile up when Miss Main sets the table and when Kilbride turns his radio on and off by jumping on a chair. First in the projected sequel to '*The Egg*' calls for a long string of 'em."

Poster tagline: "The Hilarious sequel to '*The Egg And I.*'"

66. *Big Jack* (1949)

Director: Richard Thorpe
Producer: Gottfried Reinhardt
Screenplay: Marvin Borowsky, Osso Van Eyss, Gene Fowler, Ben Hecht (uncredited) and Robert Thoeren
Cinematographer: Robert Surtees
Studio: MGM
Running time: 85 minutes
Black and White
Genre: Western
Release date: April 12, 1949

Cast

Wallace Beery	Big Jack Horner
Richard Conte	Doctor Alexander Meade
Marjorie Main	**Flapjack Kate**
Edward Arnold	Mayor Mahoney

Vanessa Brown	Patricia Mahoney
Clinton Sundberg	C. Petronius Smith
Charles Dingle	Mathias Taylor
Clem Bevans	Saltlick Joe
Jack Lambert	Bud Valentine
Will Wright	Will Farnsworth
William "Bill" Phillips	Toddy
Syd Saylor	Pokey

Marjorie plays the less-than-feminine, pipe-smokin' FlapJack Kate, who once again ties the knot with Wallace Beery. It was an all-too-familiar story line, reworked to death; and it was that one element that made for a bleak end to one of the most successful male-female comedy teams in Hollywood history.

Big Jack marked the end of an era for Marjorie actually—in more ways than one, as it was the end for Wallace Beery, too. Despite the couples' off-screen differences, audiences loved their onscreen chemistry, and for that reason alone the studio continued to make them suffer through one production after the other. Unfortunately, it was a lackluster end to a long relationship, the poor box office takings only further enforcing the studio's decision to stop casting the pair together in future films. Beery was ill for most of the production, and his death shortly after its completion ended he and Marjorie's working relationship without the studio's prior decision to do so. In hindsight, it was a fitting finale for Beery. He worked until the very end, and he only stopped because he died, not because some big shot film studio no longer required his services.

67. *Ma and Pa Kettle Go to Town* (1950)

Director: Charles Lamont
Producer: Leonard Goldstein
Screenplay: Betty MacDonald (characters), Martin Ragaway and Leonard Stern
Cinematographer: Charles Van Enger
Studio: Universal International
Running time: 79 minutes
Black and White
Genre: Comedy
Release date: April 1, 1950

Cast

Marjorie Main	**Ma Kettle**
Percy Kilbride	Pa Kettle
Richard Long	Tom Kettle
Meg Randall	Kim Parker Kettle
Charles McGraw	Mike "Shotgun" Munger, aka Jones
Gregg Martell	Louie
Jim Backus	Joseph "Little Joe" Roger

This, the second film starring Ma and Pa Kettle as the lead characters, picks up where *The Further Adventure's of Ma and Pa Kettle* (1949) left off. The Kettles are still residing in their modern home, and Pa is still entering his competitions. This time Pa's winning entry is rewarded with an all-expenses-paid trip to New York City; only problem is, who's going to look after the kids? Just when Ma and Pa resign themselves to not going, Pa stumbles across Shotgun Mike (Charles McGraw), a bank robber on the run from the law, who learns of Pa's dilemma and offers to step in as babysitter (thinking his new job would be the perfect cover. Shotgun Mike, however, has yet to meet the Kettle kids, and soon learns that turning himself in to the law would have been far easier than playing Mary Poppins to the wild bunch of children who torture him endlessly while Ma and Pa are in the Big Apple.

Much of the film revolves around a simple brown bag containing $100,000 cash that Pa has been instructed to deliver to Shotgun Mike's equally crooked brother in New York City. Always one to look out for his neighbor, Pa willingly agrees to be the trusty delivery guy, all the time unaware of the bag's rich contents. Ma and Pa get caught up with all sorts of unsavory characters, bags are stolen, Pa gets thrown in jail, Ma receives a makeover, and, back home, the out of control Kettle kids torture Shotgun Mike until he begs to go to jail.

Trivia: Ma and Pa Kettle Go to Town was known simply as *Going to Town* in the U.K.

With the success of the Kettle films, Universal could now afford to take Ma and Pa off the studio lot and on location. Bound for New York City, Marjorie and Percy stayed in town long after filming had ceased in order to promote the film with personal appearances.

In a 1950 box-office booking guide, Fred G. Weppler of the Colonial Theater in Colfax, Illinois, reported on the response of *Ma and Pa Kettle Go to Town* in his theater: "For the first time in a year, I filled my house before the first show started. This picture established a new house record for me. Yes, the picture is corny but a natural for a small town. After this showing, I'm ready to give up all heavy dramas and play light comedies."

68. *Summer Stock* (1950)

Director: Charles Walters
Producer: Joe Pasternak
Screenplay: George Wells and Sy Gomberg (also story)
Cinematographer: Robert Planck
Studio: MGM
Filming locations: MGM Studios, Culver City, California
Running time: 108 minutes
Color (Technicolor)
Genre: Musical/Romance
Release date: August 31, 1950
Awards and nominations: 1951 Writers Guild of America, Nominated, Best Written American Musical, George Wells and Sy Gomberg.

Cast

Judy Garland	Jane Falbury
Gene Kelly	Joe D. Ross
Eddie Bracken	Orville Wingait
Gloria DeHaven	Abigail Falbury
Marjorie Main	**Esme**
Phil Silvers	Herb Blake
Ray Collins	Jasper G. Wingait
Nita Bieber	Sarah Higgins
Carleton Carpenter	Artie
Hans Conried	Harrison I. Keath

With Judy Garland singing and Gene Kelly dancing, could this film be bad? Nope! It is a brilliant visual and musical spectacle of MGM proportions, and highly underrated at that. *Summer Stock*, the last time that Gene Kelly and Judy Garland ever appeared together onscreen, was one hell of a goodbye to a pair that few people now remember as a solid on screen duo.

Jane (Judy Garland) is the owner of a barn that her enthusiastic, stage-obsessed sister Abigail (Gloria DeHaven) allows a gypsy stock company, headed up by Joe D. Ross (Gene Kelly), to use as a venue for their newest show, *Fall in Love*. Not happy about her sister's decision to allow strangers to put on a show in her barn, Jane eventually softens to the idea and even catches the acting, singing, and dancing bug herself. She soon takes over the show with her own show-stopping performances.

Marjorie pops up as the overly cautious chaperone Esme. As per usual, her character is called upon to cook, yell and play nursemaid.

Trivia: Summer Stock was known as *If You Feel Like Singing* in the U.K.

In rehearsals, the "Heavenly Music" number was performed by a trio; Gene Kelly, Phil Silvers and Judy Garland were all supposed to be in the scene. However, when Judy Garland failed to show up for work the day it was to be shot, they went ahead and did it without her. Gene Kelly was sympathetic to his co-star's problems, saying, "We loved Judy and we understood what she was going through, and I had every reason to be grateful for all the help she had given me."

Judy Garland was just weeks out of rehab when MGM offered her the lead role in *Summer Stock*. It was part of a master plan to get their star back to work and back on track, both personally and professionally. The shooting days had been shortened, and Judy's hours were all scheduled for the afternoon. By starting her at 1p.m., there was at least a chance of her turning up for work; but there were days when she literally couldn't lift her head off her pillow. Her years of uppers and downers had taken their toll on her physical and mental condition; ironically (and sadly), it was MGM and Judy's pushy stage mother who advised her to take the addictive drugs as a teen in order to keep her weight down.

In his book *Easy the Hard Way*, producer Joe Pasternak said, "The picture was costing the studio thousands of dollars in delays, and there was no point in carrying on. Naturally, we all tried our best to help Judy, but it was no use. I told [studio boss Louis B.] Mayer to cut his losses and forget about *Summer Stock*."

Surprisingly, Mayer, who was notoriously frugal with studio funds, was adamantly against Pasternak's suggestion. "Judy Garland," Mayer said sternly, "has made this studio a fortune in the good days and the least we can do is to give her one more chance. If you stop production now, it'll finish her." Perhaps Mayer felt a certain degree of guilt over Judy's declining condition.

Not only did director Charles Walters have a tough time getting his lead actress on set, it proved just as difficult keeping Judy on her feet when she *was* there. He explained the situation in Pasternak's book: "Gene took her left arm and I took her right. Between us we literally tried to keep her on her feet. It wasn't easy. Emotionally she was at her lowest ebb. Physically she was pretty unsure of herself as well. There were even times when we had to nail the scenery down and provide her with supports so she wouldn't fall over. Once, I remember she had to walk up a few steps and she couldn't do it. So I had to cheat the shot and shoot it from a different angle. The whole experience was a ghastly, hideous nightmare which, happily, is a blur in my memory."

Summer Stock was Judy Garland's very last MGM production. *Annie Get Your Gun* (1950) was supposed to be her final film for the studio, but after so many mishaps on *Summer Stock,* combined with her "unfit state" in the lead-up to *Annie*, the studio decided to cut her loose early. She became a part-time employee on full-time wages, and the studio grew tired of that arrangement. It proved a bitter end to a long and once enormously successful partnership.

Compared to how she looks in the rest of the film, Judy Garland is noticeably thinner in the scene involving the upbeat "Get Happy" number. The reason? It was shot several months after the completion of the film, and she had lost upwards of 20 pounds. It's a well known fact that Judy Garland suffered from yo-yoing weight her entire life.

Mickey Rooney was originally the first choice for the role that Gene Kelly eventually played; but Rooney's declining box office appeal, even when teamed with Judy Garland, made the studio reconsider their initial decision.

69. *Mrs. O'Malley and Mr. Malone* (1951)

Director: Norman Taurog
Producer: William H. Wright
Screenplay: William Bowers, Stuart Palmer (story) and Craig Rice (story)
Cinematographer: Ray June
Studio: MGM
Running time: 69 minutes
Black and White
Genre: Comedy/Mystery
Release date: February 22, 1951

Cast

Marjorie Main	**Harriet "Hattie" O'Malley**
James Whitmore	John J. Malone
Ann Dvorak	Connie Kepplar
Phyllis Kirk	Kay, Malone's Secretary
Fred Clark	Inspector Tim Marino
Dorothy Malone	Lola Gillway
Clinton Sundberg	Donald, Steve's accountant
Douglas Fowley	Steve Kepplar
Willard Waterman	Big Man from Compartment 208-A
Don Porter	Myron Brynk
Jack Bailey	The Game Show Host
Nancy Saunders	Joan, Hattie's Niece
Basil Tellou	The Greek Passenger, with beard
James Burke	The Train Conductor

MGM originally intended *Mrs. O'Malley and Mr. Malone* to be the launching point for a film series, but the lack of audience enthusiasm caused the studio to scrap the idea altogether. The strange thing is, it's not a bad movie. It's actually quite charming, so perhaps its lack of success came down to Marjorie being typecast as Ma Kettle. Audiences just didn't want to see her as another leading character at the same time that their lovable hillbilly matriarch was frolicking across the screen.

Marjorie plays Mrs. O'Malley, amateur sleuth to her professional partner, Mr. Malone (James Whitmore). Together they must solve a double murder aboard a train, and talk their way out of being the main suspects at the same time. Marjorie's solo performance of "Possum Up a Gum Stump" is a highlight of the film.

70. *Mr. Imperium* (1951)

Director: Don Hartman
Producer: Edwin H. Knopf
Screenplay: Don Hartman and Edwin H. Knopf (also play)
Cinematographer: George J. Folsey
Studio: MGM
Running time: 87 Minutes
Color (Technicolor)

Genre: Drama/Musical/Romance
Release date: March 2, 1951

CAST

Lana Turner	Fredda Barlo
Ezio Pinza	Mr. Imperium
Marjorie Main	**Mrs. Cabot**
Barry Sullivan	Paul Hunter
Cedric Hardwicke	Fernand (as Sir Cedric Hardwicke)
Debbie Reynolds	Gwen
Ann Codee	Anna Pelan

This simple romantic musical is about a romance revisited some twelve years after the initial love affair. Fredda (Lana Turner) is now a successful Hollywood actress, while her past love, Mr. Imperium (Ezio Pinza), is now an exiled King. The lovers reunite at the home of Mrs. Cabot (Marjorie) and her niece, Gwen (Debbie Reynolds).

Mr. Imperium was structured as a musical vehicle for opera star Ezio Pinza, but it proved an unsuccessful attempt by the studio to transform an opera star into a leading man. Nelson Eddy and Mario Lanza had that niche covered years before, and Pinza's career went nowhere. Lana Turner played Pinza's pretty prop to which he sang, and Marjorie, as usual, played the comedy relief part to perfection.

Trivia: Lana Turner was pregnant during the filming of *Mr. Imperium*. She was married to millionaire playboy Bob Topping at the time (one of her eventual seven husbands); however, it was an unhappy, abusive relationship. Lana miscarried, the marriage ended, *Mr. Imperium* flopped at the box office, and her next beau was gangster Johnny Stompanato. His eventual death at the hands of Lana's young daughter Cheryl was yet another Hollywood scandal that rocked Tinseltown.

In Debbie Reynolds' Autobiography, *Debbie: My Life*, she speaks fondly of Marjorie, her co-star and onscreen aunt in *Mr. Imperium*. She does, however, describe Marjorie as being "eccentric" and a "funny one," not to mention a clean freak. Debbie remembers Marjorie immediately reaching for a pair of long gloves and a face mask in between scenes, "to ward off the germs!" she'd say.

Debbie described other eccentricities. "Marjorie was an older woman," she wrote, "who, so it happened, had a real life bladder problem. She'd be saying her lines on camera and nature would call. Continuing on with her lines, as if it were part of the movie, she'd walk right off the set into her dressing room. You'd hear the toilet seat go up, the toilet seat go down, the flushing, and Marjorie was still saying her lines. Then she'd come right back on the set, as if we hadn't cut, and finish the scene."

Debbie maintained that Marjorie always knew her lines, word for word, with her only problem being her delicate bladder. To save on production time, and rather than wait for her to run back to the main building to relieve herself, the studio decided it was cheaper to install a bathroom in Marjorie's dressing room. She was the only star on the lot with that personal luxury.

In Debbie's autobiography she refers to Marjorie's husband as Horace. Now it's entirely possible that she just has his name wrong; however, it was not beyond Marjorie to refer to Dr. Krebs as Horace or Fred or Charlie — whatever name she could pluck out of thin air would do.

Marjorie was long widowed by the time *Mr. Imperium* went into production, and despite the name discrepancy, Dr. Krebs was still very much with her — in her mind, anyway. Debbie recalls the first time that she became aware of the existence of Marjorie's deceased husband. "I was sitting in a chair next to Marjorie one day when I heard her say, 'Horace [Dr. Krebs] this is a very warm day and I'm tired. Why don't you get me a glass of water.'"

Another time, Debbie walked past Marjorie at the studio commissary. There she was, seated at the lunch counter, and beside her was an empty stool. This was Horace's (Dr. Krebs) seat. Debbie overheard Marjorie's order.

"Say hello to Horace," she said to the waitress.

"Uh...hello, Horace," the waitress stammered.

Marjorie continued, "I'll have the ham and swiss on rye toast and Horace will have the egg salad."

Debbie concluded that she'd never met or worked with anyone who'd gone so over the edge. "Marjorie was Off. Her. Rocker!" Debbie said. "But, she could put on a costume and know her lines, and that was all that counted."

Poster tagline: "What a love affair between LANA TURNER and the famed former star of 'South Pacific' EZIO PINZA."

71. *Ma and Pa Kettle Back on the Farm* (1951)

Director: Edward Sedgwick
Producer: Leonard Goldstein
Screenplay: Betty MacDonald (characters) and Jack Henley
Cinematographer: Charles Van Enger
Studio: Universal International
Filming locations: Iverson Ranch, Chatsworth, Los Angeles
Running time: 80 minutes
Black and White
Genre: Comedy
Release date: May 10, 1951

Cast

Marjorie Main	**Ma Kettle**
Percy Kilbride	Pa Kettle
Richard Long	Tom Kettle
Meg Randall	Kim Parker Kettle
Ray Collins	Jonathan Parker
Barbara Brown	Elizabeth Parker
Emory Parnell	Billy Reed
Teddy Hart	Crowbar
Oliver Blake	Geoduck

The plot of this Kettle installment revolves around Ma and Pa becoming grandparents to the first child of their son Tom (Richard Long) and his wife Kim (Meg Randall). As the baby's arrival approaches, Ma and Pa get word that Kim's snobbish parents are coming to stay. Determined to make a good impression, Ma does her best to snap Pa into shape; but after no more than a day of Elizabeth Parker's (Barbara Brown) meddlesome ways, it's all Ma can do to stop from wringing her neck.

The birth of baby Kettle brings the tension to a head, as Elizabeth suggests that Ma's hygiene habits are less than satisfactory, and that her child rearing is even worse. When the new parents begin to side with their respective families in the feud, Kim takes the baby and leaves Tom, for good! It's now up to the Parkers and the Kettles to put their differences aside in order to save their children's marriage. The finale, featuring a whacky car chase, is one of the funniest scenes in the film.

Trivia: Marjorie scrapped a scene wherein a billy goat was to chase a nanny goat over a hill, with love on his mind. Marjorie said the scene was "too suggestive" for a Kettle production, so, at her request, the scene was cut from the final print.

During the production of this film, in February of 1951, Raymond H. Johnson, the inspiration for the Indian character Crowbar in the series, sued Betty MacDonald and Universal International for close to one million dollars, on the grounds that the Kettle films portrayed him in an unfavorable light. The courts saw the lawsuit for the moneymaking ploy that it was, and Betty MacDonald and Universal International won the case.

By this movie, the third in the nine-film series, Universal International had already used over thirty children to play members of the Kettle brood. Only three of the original fifteen kids remained in *Ma and Pa Kettle Back on the Farm*—Teddy Infuhr, Gene Persson and Diane Florentine. These three started off as the youngest of the Kettles, but in this film they're almost the oldest. A UI production report (August 29, 1949) quoted Percy as saying, "Darned kids grow like wild flowers. Ma and I stay jes' the same, then all of a sudden the brats are bigger than we are. You know, I don't know a single one of my kids by their real names." Close to seventy children were used during the nine-film run.

72. *The Law and the Lady* (1951)

Director: Edwin H. Knopf
Producer: Edwin H. Knopf
Screenplay: Frederick Lonsdale (play, *The Last of Mrs. Cheney*), Leonard Spigelgass and Karl Tunberg
Cinematographer: George J. Folsey
Studio: MGM
Running time: 104 minutes
Black and White
Genre: Comedy
Release date: August 15, 1951

Cast

Greer Garson	Jane Hoskins
Michael Wilding	Nigel Duxbury/Lord Henry Minden
Fernando Lamas	Juan Dinas
Marjorie Main	**Julia Wortin**
Hayden Rorke	Tracy Collans
Margalo Gillmore	Cora Caighn
Ralph Dumke	James Horace Caighn
Rhys Williams	Inspector McGraw
Phyllis Stanley	Lady Sybil Minden
Natalie Schafer	Pamela Pemberson

This simple, lighthearted comedy is often touted as the least favorite of the screen adaptations of the famous play *The Last of Mrs. Cheney*. Michael Wilding plays a con man who somehow convinces Greer Garson that traveling the world as "high class" jewel thieves can be fun. Marjorie gets the full MGM glamor treatment in this one. She ditches her dowdy Ma Kettle wardrobe in favor of fine clothes and jewelry in order to play the wealthy Mrs. Wortin, the couple's next victim. But the crooked pair underestimate their newest mark, and the laughs begin.

Trivia: Two earlier versions of the story were filmed—1929 and 1937—both called *The Last of Mrs. Cheney*. A 1960s German adaptation, entitled *Frau Cheneys Ende* (1961), is the most modern screen version based on the original play.

Marjorie often said this was her "fish out of water role." She felt no affinity for the character; and in hindsight, knowing this fact, her uneasiness shows in her performance.

73. *It's a Big Country* (1951)

Directors: Clarence Brown, Don Hartman, John Sturges, Richard Thorpe, Charles Vidor, Don Weis and William A. Wellman
Producer: Robert Sisk
Screenplay: Edgar Brooke (story, segment 1), Ray Chordes (segment 4), Claudia Cranston (segment 5), Helen Deutsch (segments 2, 3), Dorothy Kingsley (segment 7), Isobel Lennart (story, segment 4), William Ludwig (segment 1), John McNulty (story), Joseph Petracca (story), Allen Rivkin (story, segment 5), Dore Schary (segment 8), Lucille Schlossberg (segment 6) and George Wells (segment 8).
Cinematographers: John Alton, Ray June, William C. Mellor and Joseph Ruttenberg
Studio: MGM
Running time: 89 minutes
Black and White
Genre: Comedy/Drama
Release date: November 20, 1951

Cast

Ethel Barrymore	Mrs. Brian Patrick Riordan
Keefe Brasselle	Sgt. Maxie Klein
Gary Cooper	Texas
Nancy Davis	Miss Coleman
Van Johnson	Rev. Adam Burch
Gene Kelly	Icarus Xenophon
Janet Leigh	Rosa Szabo Xenophon
Marjorie Main	**Mrs. Wrenley**
Fredric March	Joe Esposito
George Murphy	Mr. Callaghan
William Powell	Professor
S.Z. Sakall	Stefan Szabo
Lewis Stone	Church sexton
James Whitmore	Mr. Stacey
Keenan Wynn	Michael Fisher
Leon Ames	Secret Service man

When Dore Schary took over the reins of MGM studios, his first order of business was to churn out a string of patriotic films with a message. *It's a Big Country* is just that, an eight-episode mini-series of sorts.

Marjorie appears in the episode entitled "Letter from a Soldier," as Mrs. Wrenley, the mother of a young soldier killed in the Korean war. This nine-minute installment can sometimes be seen as an individual short subject; the sentimental piece represents propaganda filmmaking at its best.

74. *The Belle of New York* (1952)

Director: Charles Walters
Producer: Arthur Freed
Screenplay: Hugh Morten (play), Chester Erskine, Robert O'Brien and Irving Elinson
Cinematographer: Robert Planck
Studio: MGM
Production dates: June 18, 1951–October 3, 1951
Running time: 82 minutes
Color (Technicolor)
Genre: Comedy/Musical/Romance
Release date: February 22, 1952

Cast

Fred Astaire	Charlie Hill
Vera-Ellen	Angela Bonfils
Marjorie Main	**Mrs. Phineas Hill**
Keenan Wynn	Max Ferris

Gale Robbins	Dixie "Deadshot" McCoy

Charlie Hill (Fred Astaire) is a rich playboy who romances Angela Bonfils (Vera Ellen) in the film that some have suggested is "the worst musical of all time." Since the film features an array of show-stopping dance numbers by Astaire, it's best to just sit down and watch it for these brief snippets rather than the overall intended story.

Marjorie plays Charlie's wealthy aunt, Mrs. Phineas Hill.

Trivia: With a production cost of a little over 2.5 million dollars, *The Belle of New York* lost almost half-a-million dollars by the time worldwide box office receipts came in.

Mae West was first choice to play Marjorie's character, Mrs. Phineas Hill, but she was too expensive.

In 1897 the original play version of *The Belle of New York* was the first American stage musical to open in London's West End.

An early version of the film was produced in 1919 as a silent drama. Marion Davies played the lead in *The Belle of New York* (1919).

Lead actor Fred Astaire had been offered this role in 1946, but had turned it down. The studio shelved the script until he either changed his mind or they could convince him to reconsider. It took six years for either one of those things to happen; however, the film's ho-hum audience appeal perhaps suggests that his initial reservations were indeed well-founded.

Poster tagline: "M.G.M's Gay TECHNICOLOR Musical!"

75. *Ma and Pa Kettle at the Fair* (1952)

Director: Charles Barton
Producer: Leonard Goldstein
Screenplay: John Grant, Jack Henley (story), Richard Morris, Martin Ragaway (story) and Leonard Stern (story)
Cinematographer: Maury Gertsman
Studio: Universal International
Running time: 78 minutes
Black and White
Genre: Comedy
Release date: July 11, 1952

Cast

Marjorie Main	**Ma Kettle**
Percy Kilbride	Pa Kettle
James Best	Marvin Johnson
Lori Nelson	Rosie Kettle
Esther Dale	Birdie Hicks
Emory Parnell	Billy Reed
Oliver Blake	Geoduck
Russell Simpson	Clem Johnson
Rex Lease	Sheriff
George Arglen	Willie Kettle (uncredited)
Margaret Brown	Ruth Kettle (uncredited)
Douglas Carter	Ticket Seller (uncredited)
Zachary Charles	Crowbar (uncredited)
Harry Cheshire	Preacher (uncredited)
Billy Clark	George Kettle (uncredited)
Edmund Cobb	Man (uncredited)
Ray Collins	Jonathan Parker (uncredited)
Harry Cording	Ed (uncredited)
Bob Donnelly	Clown (uncredited)
Frank Ferguson	Sam, the Jailer (uncredited)

William Gould	Judge (uncredited)
James Griffith	Medicine Man (uncredited)
James Guilfoyle	Birdie's Trainer (uncredited)
Harry Harvey	Chairman (uncredited)
Hallene Hill	Mrs. Hick's Mother (uncredited)
Teddy Infuhr	Benjamin Kettle (uncredited)
Gary Lee Jackson	Billy Kettle (uncredited)
Jackie Jackson	Henry Kettle (uncredited)
Sherry Jackson	Susie Kettle (uncredited)
Donna Leary	Sally Kettle (uncredited)
Jenny Linder	Sara Kettle (uncredited)
Frank McFarland	Judge (uncredited)
Claire Meade	Sarah (uncredited)
Beverly Mook	Eve Kettle (uncredited)
Eugene Persson	Teddy Kettle (uncredited)
Mel Pogue	Delivery Guy (uncredited)
Roy Regnier	Man (uncredited)
Ronnie Rondell Jr.	Dannie Kettle (uncredited)
Syd Saylor	Postman (uncredited)
Elana Schreiner	Nancy Kettle (uncredited)
Forrest Taylor	Horse Owner with Sheriff (uncredited)

When Ma enters the baking and jam-making contest at the annual county fair, she hopes to win first prize in order to pay for daughter Rosie's (Lori Nelson) college fees. In the meantime, Pa meanders around town and options fifty percent of Ma's future winnings in exchange for a broken-down horse.

After Ma is disqualified as the winner of the jam contest, her only hope of furthering her daughter's education is with her prize-winning bread. She wins first prize, but Pa's creditors soon swoop in to collect what's owed them for the nag. Still broke, and with the horse race being their last chance at winning a prize, Ma agrees to let Pa run the horse — with him as driver!

Of course, this is where trouble starts brewing. Both Ma and Pa are thrown in jail for race fixing; but in the end, the truth comes out, and the Kettles become unlikely heroes.

Memorable quotes: Ma Kettle: "Pa, I always seem to be scoldin' you." Pa Kettle: "I know, Ma. You do all the barkin,' but it's me that's always in the doghouse."

76. *Ma and Pa Kettle on Vacation* (1953)

Director: Charles Lamont
Producer: Leonard Goldstein
Screenplay: Jack Henley
Cinematographer: George Robinson
Studio: Universal International
Running time: 79 minutes
Black and White
Genre: Comedy
Release date: April 20, 1953

CAST

Marjorie Main	**Ma Kettle**
Percy Kilbride	Pa Kettle
Ray Collins	Jonathan Parker
Bodil Miller	Inez Kraft
Sig Ruman	Cryus Kraft
Barbara Brown	Elizabeth Parker
Ivan Triesault	Henri Dupre

Oliver Blake	Geoduck
Teddy Hart	Crowbar
Peter Brocco	Adolph Wade
George Arglen	Willie Kettle (uncredited)
Margaret Brown	Ruthie Kettle (uncredited)
Billy Clark	George Kettle (uncredited)
Andre D'Arcy	Apache Team (uncredited)
Jean De Briac	Chief Chantilly (uncredited)
Lawrence Dobkin	Farrell (uncredited)
John Eldredge	Masterson (uncredited)
Carli Elinor	Orchestra Leader (uncredited)
Jon Gardner	Benjamin Kettle (uncredited)
Harold Goodwin	Harriman (uncredited)
Sam Harris	Plane Passenger (uncredited)
Rosario Imperio	Apache Team (uncredited)
Gary Lee Jackson	Billy Kettle (uncredited)
Jackie Jackson	Henry Kettle (uncredited)
Sherry Jackson	Susie Kettle (uncredited)
Alice Kelley	Stewardess (uncredited)
Jack Kruschen	Jacques Arnien (uncredited)
Donna Leary	Sally Kettle (uncredited)
Eddie Le Baron	Wine Steward (uncredited)
Jenny Linder	Sara Kettle (uncredited)
Beverly Mook	Eve Kettle (uncredited)
Rita Moreno	Soubrette (uncredited)
Jay Novello	Andre (uncredited)
Gloria Pall	French Girl (uncredited)
Ronnie Rondell Jr.	Danny Kettle (uncredited)
Elana Schreiner	Nancy Kettle (uncredited)
Robert E. Scott	Teddy Kettle (uncredited)
Ken Terrell	Cab Driver (uncredited)

The Kettles once again leave their familiar surroundings of Cape Flattery, this time heading to Paris to meet up with the Parkers, their once-snobbish in laws. Trusting Pa sits next to a mysterious passenger on the plane, and after striking up a conversation about cigars, agrees to deliver an envelope for his newfound friend. As a result, upon landing in the City of Love, he and the rest of the bunch become involved with a corrupt spy ring.

Some of the funniest moments of the film involve Ma and Pa's enthusiasm for the Parisian lifestyle. Pa makes eyes at the French girls and tries buying himself some raunchy postcards to take home, while Ma's bouncy dance number in the night club is a laugh-out-loud sequence. The car chase at the end is a fitting finale to an enjoyable film.

Trivia: This was also known as *Ma and Pa Kettle Go to Paris* and *Ma and Pa Kettle Hit the Road.*

Marjorie was slated to star alongside Esther Williams in her next underwater feature, *Slippery When Wet* (1953); however, due to a lengthy scene requiring her to be submerged in a pool, Marjorie's doctor strongly advised her against taking the part. Marjorie suffered from a severe sinus condition most of her life, and part of the reason she purchased her house in Palm Springs was to alleviate her symptoms.

77. *Fast Company* (1953)

Director: John Sturges
Producer: Henry Berman
Screenplay: Eustace Cockrell (story), Don Manckiewicz (adaptation) and William Roberts
Cinematographer: Harold Lipstein
Studio: MGM
Running time: 67 minutes
Black and White
Genre: Comedy
Release date: May 12, 1953

Cast

Howard Keel	Rick Grayton
Polly Bergen	Carol Maldon
Marjorie Main	**Ma Parkson**
Nina Foch	Mercedes Bellway
Robert Burton	David Sandring
Carol Nugent	Jigger Parkson
Joaquin Garay	Manuel Morales
Horace McMahon	"Two Pair" Buford
Sig Arno	Hungry
Iron Eyes Cody	Ben Iron Mountain

An inexpensive filler flick between big productions, MGM's *Fast Company* was fairly forgettable, both then and now. Marjorie plays Ma Parkinson, owner of a modest horse stable housing Carol Maldon's (Polly Bergen) newly inherited race horse. Romance blossoms as the handsome man about the track, Rick Grayton (Howard Keel), gives Carol racing advice and somewhat predictably falls in love with her in the process.

78. *The Long, Long Trailer* (1954)

Director: Vincente Minnelli
Producer: Pandro S. Berman
Screenplay: Clinton Twiss (novel), Albert Hackett and Frances Goodrich
Cinematographer: Robert Surtees
Studio: MGM
Filming locations: Alabama Hills, Lone Pine, California; Palos Verdes Estates, California; Red Rock Canyon State Park, Cantil, California; Whitney Portal Road, California; Yosemite National Park, California
Running time: 103 minutes
Color
Genre: Comedy/Romance
Release date: February 18, 1954
Awards and nominations: 1955 Writers Guild of America, Nominated, Best Written American Comedy, Frances Goodrich and Albert Hackett.

Cast

Lucille Ball	Tacy Bolton-Collini
Desi Arnaz	Nicholas "Nicky" Collini
Marjorie Main	**Mrs. Hittaway**
Keenan Wynn	Policeman
Gladys Hurlbut	Mrs. Bolton
Moroni Olsen	Mr. Tewitt
Bert Freed	Foreman
Madge Blake	Aunt Anastacia
Walter Baldwin	Uncle Edgar
Oliver Blake	Mr. Sudloy
Perry Sheehan	Bridesmaid

When Desi Arnaz and Lucille Ball are in a film together, it has to be a barrel of laughs; and *The Long, Long Trailer* is no exception. Made at the height of their *I Love Lucy* television show, and with

Vincente Minnelli directing, the film was a roaring success.

When new bride Tacy (Lucy) coerces her conservative husband Nicky (Desi) into buying a trailer, he has no idea it would be so expensive, so long, or so heavy. In fact, the couple ends up needing to buy a new car to pull it! In debt, but in love, they set off across the country on their honeymoon. The chain of disastrous events that follow truly tests the solidity of their marriage.

For instance, on Nicky's first attempt at backing up the monstrous trailer, he nearly destroys Tacy's Aunt's house, and backs right over her rose garden, sending her into a fit of hysterics. The funniest scenes come when the couple are on the road solo—arguing over directions, praying their brakes hold out as they navigate the winding mountain roads, or watching Tacy attempt to cook her husband a hearty meal in the back of the trailer, while its moving! Their one duet, "Breezin' Along with the Breeze," is a particularly sweet scene early on, but by the end of the film, singing is the last thing on their minds!

The Long, Long Trailer is simplistic '50s fun and the bickering of Lucy and Desi, combined with a dash of Marjorie (as the rowdy Mrs. Hittaway) thrown in for good measure, make it an enjoyable family favorite.

Trivia: Lucy and Desi received a flat salary of $250,000 for their services. The movie was filmed while the couple were on hiatus from their hit television series, *I Love Lucy*.

Martin Leeds, second in command at the Arnazes' Desilu Productions, made the initial deal with MGM for the couple to appear in the film. Despite its ranking as the seventeenth highest grossing film of 1954, Leeds still had to think of a clever way to get the $100,000 promised bonus for his clients. In *Desilu: The Story of Lucile Ball and Desi Arnaz,* he explains: "I managed to get MGM to agree to pay [Lucy and Desi] an extra one hundred thousand dollars if the picture grossed four million. In those days, that was a lot of money. Nobody thought the picture would do that well. At the end of the year, the accounting statement showed three million, nine hundred seventy thousand dollars. We had thirty thousand dollars to go."

With the next statement reflecting the same figures, Leeds had to do something, and fast! "Just three days prior to the next statement, I called Eddie Mannix and asked if I could show the movie at my house, and that I would pay for the projectionist. He said no problem. I then said I would like to pay thirty thousand dollars for the privilege. He started to laugh, saying, 'Okay, I got it, and you will get it.'"

When Leeds received the next statement, it still read three million, nine hundred seventy thousand dollars; however, the difference between this statement and the others was the one-hundred-thousand-dollar check attached. A simple note bearing the initials "E.M." (Eddie Mannix) accompanied it.

Lucy Arnaz, Lucy and Desi's daughter, used the actual "long, long trailer" as a playhouse when she was a child. It was parked at the back of the Desilu ranch and was used as a temporary home for actress June Havoc for a couple of years. When Lucy and Desi sold the ranch to move to Beverly Hills, actress Jane Withers bought the trailer.

The third owner was a woman whom Lucy Arnaz (Lucy and Desi's daughter) eventually tracked down when she was twenty years old. Recently engaged to be married, Lucy thought it would be fun to show her new fiancé a piece of family history that she hadn't seen since she was four years old. After introducing herself to the woman and politely asking if she could quickly give her fiancé a tour of the trailer, the woman said one word: "NO!" The trailer door slammed, and that was that!

Poster taglines: "America's No. 1 Favorites Funnier Than Ever on the Screen!" "M-G-M's Miles of Smiles! And in Color Too!"

79. *Ma and Pa Kettle at Home* (1954)

Director: Charles Lamont
Producer: Richard Wilson
Screenplay: Kay Lenard (story and screenplay)
Cinematographer: Carl Guthrie
Studio: Universal International
Running time: 80 minutes
Black and White
Genre: Comedy
Release date: March 10, 1954

Cast

Marjorie Main	**Ma Kettle**
Percy Kilbride	Pa Kettle
Alan Mowbray	Alphonsus Mannering
Alice Kelley	Sally Maddocks
Brett Halsey	Elwin Kettle
Ross Elliott	Pete Crosby
Mary Wickes	Miss Wetter
Oliver Blake	Geoduck
Stan Ross	Crowbar
Emory Parnell	Billy Reed
Irving Bacon	Mr. Maddocks
Virginia Brissac	Mrs. Maddocks
Richard Eyer	Billy Kettle
Edmund Cobb	Jefferson (uncredited)
Edgar Dearing	Perkins (uncredited)
Tony Epper	Donny Kettle (uncredited)
James Flavin	Motorcycle Cop (uncredited)
Helen Gibson	Ranch Wife (uncredited)
Coral Hammond	Eve Kettle (uncredited)
Whitey Haupt	Henry Kettle (uncredited)
Donald MacDonald	Benjamin Kettle (uncredited)
Betty McDonough	Ranch Wife (uncredited)
Patrick Miller	Teddy Kettle (uncredited)
Pat Morrow	Susie Kettle (uncredited)
Robert Nelson	Motorcycle Cop (uncredited)
Carol Nugent	Nancy Kettle (uncredited)
Judy Nugent	Betty Kettle (uncredited)
Gary Pagett	George Kettle (uncredited)
Ken Terrell	Indian (uncredited)
Rick Vallin	Indian (uncredited)
Guy Wilkerson	Jones (uncredited)
Hank Worden	Indian (uncredited)
Nancy Zane	Sara Kettle (uncredited)

When Ma and Pa's son Elwin (Ross Elliott) becomes a finalist in a competition that will award the winner a fully paid scholarship to agricultural college, everyone is bursting with excitement—that is, until they find out the judges are coming to stay to witness the Kettle farm for themselves.

Since Elwin's report boasted about the state of the art farm he lives on, it's up to the Kettles to perform some long overdue renovations in order to give their son the best chance at winning the scholarship.

When the stuffy judge, Mr. Mannering (Alan Mowbray), turns up, the Kettles turn on all their charm in order to impress him and his more relaxed partner.

Despite their best efforts, mother nature lets them down when a severe rainstorm washes away most of the cosmetic handiwork that Pa, Geoduck (Oliver Blake), Crowbar (Stan Ross) and the kids have done to the place. Elwin is certain he's blown his chances of winning.

The other competitor, Sally (Alice Kelley), lives on the neighboring farm, but her state-of-the-art equipment does little to help her chances of winning, thanks to her crotchety father. In spite of all this, the judges decide that both Sally and Elwin deserve to split first prize, and the twosome are each awarded a fully paid two-year scholarship to agricultural school.

Poster tagline: "They've Got the Whole County in Hysterics!"

80. *Rose Marie* (1954)

Director: Mervyn LeRoy
Producer: Mervyn LeRoy
Screenplay: George Froeschel, Oscar Hammerstein II (story), Otto A. Harbach (story) and Ronald Millar
Cinematographer: Paul Vogel
Studio: MGM
Filming locations: Mammoth Lakes, California; Jasper National Park, Alberta, Canada
Running time: 104 minutes
Color and Cinemascope
Genre: Musical
Release date: April 1, 1954

Cast

Ann Blyth	Rose Marie Lemaitre
Howard Keel	Capt. Mike Malone
Fernando Lamas	James Severn Duval
Bert Lahr	Barney McCorkle
Marjorie Main	**Lady Jane Dunstock**
Joan Taylor	Wanda
Ray Collins	Inspector Appleby
Chief Yowlachie	Black Eagle

Rose Marie (Ann Blyth) and Captain Mike Malone (Howard Keel) are smitten songbirds in this overly drawn-out MGM musical.

Marjorie plays Lady Jane Dunstock. The brief romantic subplot between Marjorie and Bert Lahr is the highlight of the film. Their perfect comedic timing only makes one wish they'd been cast as an onscreen couple more often; however, Bert Lahr was glad to see the back of Marjorie when filming was over (see "Trivia" for his memories).

This was Marjorie's last film for MGM, rounding out her fourteen-year contract with the studio. Surprisingly, most of her scenes were cut from the final print. Ironically, it was her brief appearance that received most of the film's praise from critics.

Trivia: This same story was filmed twice before—*Rose Marie* (1928) and *Rose Marie* (1936).

Despite their apparent onscreen chemistry, Bert Lahr was less than enthused about his scenes with Marjorie. They were not only choreographically difficult, they were painful! Their song and dance number called for Lahr to avoid Marjorie's hearty advances; however, Marjorie was not always on her marks, which in turn threw Lahr off *his* marks. In John Lahr's book *Notes on a Cowardly Lion*, Bert explained the scene in detail:

"In motion pictures, you've got to be on

your mark to be photographed because of the lighting. There were certain places in this number where we had to hold and sing the lyrics. Marjorie was not adept at it, and, of course, song and dance is my business. When we were rehearsing I was always on my marks, but when the cameras rolled she'd always get me off it. There was a big oak mantelpiece, and I was supposed to fall back against it. They had to cut out a large chunk of the mantelpiece and insert rubber, painted to look like wood. I kept getting off my mark every-time. Finally, Mervyn [the director] said, 'Don't worry, Bert. I'll come around and get you in close-up.' We started shooting; I did the song, and then fell back against the mantelpiece. I missed the rubber and cracked my head against the oak. I finished the song with a gash in my head. When I looked out at the camera, I saw Georgie Stoll, the musical director, rolling on the floor with laughter. It wasn't funny."

Poster tagline: "M-G-M presents the first great musical in Cinemascope! In Color Glory!"

81. *Ricochet Romance* (1954)

Director: Charles Lamont
Producers: Robert Arthur and Richard Wilson
Screenplay: Kay Lenard
Cinematographer: George Robinson
Studio: Universal International
Running time: 80 minutes
Black and White
Genre: Comedy/Western
Release date: November 1, 1954

Cast

Marjorie Main	**Pansy Jones**
Chill Wills	Tom Williams
Pedro Gonzales-Gonzales	Manuel Gonzales
Alfonso Bedoya	Alfredo Gonzales
Rudy Vallee	Worthington Higgenmacher
Ruth Hampton	Angela Mansfield
Benay Venuta	Claire Renard
Rachel Ames	Betsy Williams (as Judith Ames)
Darryl Hickman	Dave King
Lee Aaker	Timmy Williams
Irene Ryan	Miss Clay
Philip Tonge	Mr. Webster
Phil Chambers	Mr. Daniels
Charles Watts	Mr. Harvey
Marjorie Bennett	Mrs. Harvey

Marjorie plays Pansy Jones, the nosy cook at the Flying W. Guest Ranch who sticks her nose into her boss Tom Williams' (Chill Wills) business whenever she sees fit. The story development and character personalities are similar to the simplistic plots and relationships that Marjorie had shared with Wallace Beery in previous outings, but lightning wasn't about to strike twice; this time, the spark just wasn't there.

Trivia: Not content with having Marjorie involved in the highly successful Kettle series, Universal decided to try and recapture the "couples" spark that she and Wallace Beery once shared by pairing her with the equally crusty Chill Wills. Despite their enthusiasm, the planned series of films for the duo was swiftly shelved after box office receipts showed less than impressive numbers on their debut effort. One of the main reasons that Universal tried launching this new "couple" was the very real threat from Percy Kilbride that the next Kettle film would be his last. Suddenly, the money train was about to run out of coal, and in a desperate bid to keep it running, they had every writer in the studio working overtime with the hope that one of them would come up with the next box-office gold mine.

82. *Ma and Pa Kettle at Waikiki* (1955)

Director: Lee Sholem
Producer: Leonard Goldstein
Screenplay: Connie Lee Bennett (story), Harry Clork, Jack Henley and Elwood Ullman
Cinematographer: Clifford Stine
Studio: Universal International
Running time: 79 minutes
Black and White
Genre: Comedy
Release date: April 1955

Cast

Marjorie Main	**Ma Kettle**
Percy Kilbride	Pa Kettle
Lori Nelson	Rosie Kettle
Byron Palmer	Bob Baxter
Russell Johnson	Eddie Nelson
Hilo Hattie	Mama Lotus
Loring Smith	Rodney Kettle
Lowell Gilmore	Robert Coates
Mabel Albertson	Mrs. Andrews
Fay Roope	Fulton Andrews
Oliver Blake	Geoduck
Teddy Hart	Crowbar
Esther Dale	Birdie Hicks
George Arglen	Willie Kettle (uncredited)
Margaret Brown	Ruthie Kettle (uncredited)
Ben Chapman	Extra (uncredited)
Billy Clark	George Kettle (uncredited)
Bonnie Kay Eddy	Susie Kettle (uncredited)
Norman Field	Dr. Fabian (uncredited)
Jon Gardner	Benjamin Kettle (uncredited)
Cindy Garner	Secretary (uncredited)
Harold Goodwin	Dr. Barnes (uncredited)
Timmy Hawkins	Teddy Kettle (uncredited)
Myron Healey	Marty (uncredited)
Jackie Jackson	Henry Kettle (uncredited)
Byron Kane	Prof. Gilfallen (uncredited)
Donna Leary	Sally Kettle (uncredited)
Jenny Linder	Sara Kettle (uncredited)
Charles Lung	Papa Lotus (uncredited)
Luukiuluana	Masseuse (uncredited)
Beverly Mook	Eve Kettle (uncredited)
Ida Moore	Miss Pennyfeather (uncredited)
Richard Reeves	Lefty Conway (uncredited)
Ric Roman	Chuck Collins (uncredited)
Ronnie Rondell Jr.	Donnie Kettle (uncredited)
Elana Schreiner	Nancy Kettle (uncredited)
Sandra Spence	Pa's Secretary (uncredited)
Ben Welden	Shorty Bates (uncredited)

Ma and Pa Kettle at Waikiki marked a solid end to Percy Kilbride's career and, more importantly, his portrayal of Pa Kettle, so it's fitting that he's the featured player in this installment.

Pa takes on the daunting task of running his cousin Rodney's (Loring Smith) thriving Hawaiian pineapple plant while Rodney takes a few days off due to stress. Well, if Rodney thought he was stressed before, just wait until cousin Pa hits the tropical island! Poor ol' Rodney has been getting letters from his lazy cousin about what a sharp, savvy businessman he is in Cape Flattery. With no reason to doubt him, Rodney decides that Pa would be the ideal man for the job of pineapple plantation manager in his absence. Well, in the days that follow, Pa blows up the plant, is lured to another island by rival pineapple growers, and even bumps into the Hawaiian equivalent of the Kettles while there. When Pa is kidnapped by the bad guys, it's up to Ma to get to the other island and save him as only she can. The last frame fades out as Pa gives Ma a kiss on the cheek.

Trivia: In *Ma and Pa Kettle at Waikiki* we hear Ma's given name for the very first time. Pa's real name was Franklin, a fact that was mentioned earlier in the series. However, Ma's real name had remained a mystery — that is, until Pa's cousin Rodney (Loring Smith) warmly greets her as "Phoebe"!

Ma and Pa Kettle at Waikiki was Marjorie's only film for the year, a sign that she was slowing down.

Poster tagline: "Ma and Pa go native... and Waikiki goes wacky!"

83. *The Kettles in the Ozarks* (1956)

Director: Charles Lamont
Producer: Richard Wilson
Screenplay: Kay Lenard
Cinematographer: George Robinson
Studio: Universal International
Running time: 81 minutes
Black and White
Genre: Comedy
Release date: April 1956

Cast

Marjorie Main	**Ma Kettle**
Arthur Hunnicutt	Sedgewick Kettle
Ted de Corsia	Professor
Una Merkel	Miss Bedelia Baines
Richard Eyer	Billy Kettle
Dave O'Brien	Conductor
Joe Sawyer	Bancroft Baines
Richard Deacon	Big Trout
Sid Tomack	Benny
Pat Goldin	Small Fry
Harry Hines	Joe
Jim Hayward	Jack Dexter (as James Hayward)
Olive Sturgess	Nancy Kettle
George Arglen	Freddie
Eddie Pagett	Sammy
Cheryl Callaway	Susie
Pat Morrow	Sally
Bonnie Franklin	Betty
Louis Da Pron	Mountaineer
Sarah Padden	Miz Tinware
Roscoe Ates	Man
Kathryn Sheldon	Old Woman
Stuart Holmes	Bald Man
Elvia Allman	Meek Man's Wife
Paul Wexler	Reverend Martin
Robert Easton	Lafe

Despite Percy Kilbride's departure from the series, the studio made the somewhat brave decision to continue making the Kettle films without him. This time, Ma carries most of the burden herself; however, the male influence is introduced in the form of Sedge Kettle (Arthur Hunnicutt), Pa's equally lazy brother. Ma travels to the Ozarks with her brood of wild kids in tow. Once there she plays matchmaker for Sedge and his longtime love of twenty years, Miss Bedelia Baines (Una Merkel). This is a poor entry in the Kettle series; with its weak story line and Percy Kilbride's absence, one can only wish that Universal had retired the series at the same time *he* did.

Trivia: With Marjorie's MGM contract finished, she now exclusively signed with Universal International for a picture-to-picture deal. Unfortunately, what would have been a lucrative career move years before was now too little, too late for Marjorie. The Kettle series was on its way out, so she was no longer in the powerful position to ask for healthy remuneration for her services. Her new picture-to-picture contract with the studio that churned out the Kettle features gave her little more than she earned while on loan-out from MGM years before.

84. *Friendly Persuasion* (1956)

Director: William Wyler
Producer: William Wyler
Screenplay: Jessamyn West (novel) and Michael Wilson (screenplay)
Cinematographer: Ellsworth Fredericks
Studio: Allied Artists Pictures Corporation
Filming locations: Bidwell Park, Chico, California; Rowland V. Lee Ranch, Canoga Park, Los Angeles, California
Running time: 137 minutes
Color
Genre: Drama
Release date: November 25, 1956
Awards and nominations: 1957 Academy Awards: Nominated, Best Actor in a Supporting Role, Anthony Perkins; Nominated, Best Director, William Wyler; Nominated, Best Music, Original Song, Dimitri Tiomkin (music) and Paul Francis Webster (lyrics) for the song "Friendly Persuasion"; Nominated, Best Picture, William Wyler; Nominated, Best Sound Recording, Gordon R. Glennan and Gordon Sawyer; Nominated, Best Writing, Best Adapted Screenplay, Michael Wilson. 1957 Cannes Film Festival, Won, Golden Palm Award, William Wyler. 1957 Director's Guild of America, Nominated, Best Director, William Wyler. 1957 Golden Globe Awards: Nominated, Best Actor, Gary Cooper; Nominated, Best Supporting Actress, Marjorie Main. 1957 National Board of Review, Won, Best Actress, Dorothy McGuire. 1957 Writers Guild of America, Won, Best Written American Drama, Michael Wilson.

Cast

Gary Cooper	Jess Birdwell
Dorothy McGuire	Eliza Birdwell
Anthony Perkins	Josh Birdwell
Richard Eyer	Little Jess
Robert Middleton	Sam Jordan
Phyllis Love	Martha "Mattie" True Birdwell
Peter Mark Richman	Gardner "Gard" Jordan
Walter Catlett	Prof. Waldo Quigley
Richard Hale	Purdy (violent Quaker)

Joel Fluellen	Enoch
Theodore Newton	Maj. Harvey (recruiter in meeting)
John Smith	Caleb Cope (wrestling Quaker)
Edna Skinner	Opal Hudspeth
Marjorie Durant	Pearl Hudspeth (pipe-smoking woodcutter in braids)
Frances Farwell	Ruby Hudspeth
Marjorie Main	**Widow Hudspeth**

In this heavily-nominated production, Marjorie plays the overbearing matriarch Widow Hudspeth, whose sole purpose in life is to marry off her-less-than desirable spinster daughters to any man on a horse. When Gary Cooper rides into town with his handsome bachelor son Anthony Perkins, Widow Hudspeth sets her sights on him as a potential son-in-law for any one of her girls—just so long as he takes one of them!

Trivia: A television remake of the film, under the same name of *Friendly Persuasion*, aired in 1975.

Due to the 1950s blacklisting of screenwriter Michael Wilson, his name was initially excluded from the credits of the film. Thanks to modern thoughts on the subject of blacklisting, his name was restored to film prints in 1996. Unfortunately, his death in 1978 prevented him from seeing his work re-credited and recognized. In 1995 his recognition as a screenwriter was amended to the credits of another major film, *Lawrence of Arabia* (1962). He eventually received credit, and his family accepted a posthumous Oscar, for his work on the war classic *The Bridge on the River Kwai* (1957).

Poster taglines: "Try FRIENDLY PERSUASION: It's Powerful!" "When You Looked at Jess Birdwell YOU LOOKED UP." "Anthony Perkins, the most exciting screen discovery since James Dean!" "Pat Boone, the sensational Dot Recording artist, can be heard singing the big hit title-song, 'Friendly Persuasion.'"

85. *The Kettles on Old MacDonald's Farm* (1957)

Director: Virgil W. Vogel
Producer: Howard Christie
Screenplay: Herbert H. Margolis and William Raynor
Cinematographer: Arthur E. Arling
Studio: Universal International
Running time: 81 minutes
Black and White
Genre: Comedy
Release date: May 10, 1957

Cast

Marjorie Main	**Ma Kettle**
Parker Fennelly	Pa Kettle
Gloria Talbott	Sally Flemming
John Smith	Brad Johnson
George Dunn	George
Roy Barcroft	J.P. Flemming
Claude Akins	Pete Logan
Pat Morrow	Bertha
George Arglen	Henry
Ricky Kelman	Elmer
Donald Baker	Abner
Polly Burson	Agnes Logan
Hallene Hill	Granny
Sara Taft	Clarabelle
Harvey B. Dunn	Judge

Don Clark	Shivaree Man
Boyd Morgan	Shivaree Man
Glenn Thompson	Shivaree Man
Edna Smith	Shivaree Woman
Verna Kornman	Shivaree Woman
Roger Creed	Townsman
Frank Hagney	Townsman
Clem Fuller	Townsman
Carl Saxe	Hunter
George Barrows	Hunter
Eva Novak	Woman
Chuck Hamilton	Man
George Hickman	Man
Henry Wills	Townsman

It's fitting that Marjorie's final film foray came as Ma Kettle. This was the last entry of the Kettle series and the last film of her prolific career. Ma (Marjorie) and Pa (Parker Fennelly) purchase a new house and farm just a hop, skip and a jump from their old place. The new owners of their previous property are a young, soon-to-be-married couple, and Ma and Pa make it their business to teach them the way of the land and the secret to a happy marriage, Kettle style! In some ways, the Kettles have come full circle with this film, since in certain places the story mirrors *The Egg and I* (1947), the film that started the Kettle phenomenon a decade earlier.

All popular film or television series have to end at some point, it's inevitable. However, the sad element to most of those endings is the poor quality of the last installments. *The Kettles on Old MacDonald's Farm* is no exception to this rule; it's without a doubt the weakest effort in the nine-film series.

Despite Parker Fennelly doing a fine job as Pa Kettle, he wasn't Percy Kilbride, and the chemistry that Marjorie shared with Percy just didn't transfer over when Parker took his place. The major factor in this film being so lackluster was this crucial lack of onscreen chemistry. Although sad that the Kettles were leaving the big screen for good, by the end of this film, audiences knew it was time to say goodbye. It was sadder to watch them in a poor quality effort than to say a final farewell altogether.

As television began to sweep the country, similar hillbilly families moved onto the small screen, all riding on the coattails of the Kettle phenomena. *The Real McCoys, Green Acres, The Beverly Hillbillies and Petticoat Junction* emulated the Kettles on television (successfully, too) for many years. Still, there is nothing like the original — of anything — and the Kettles were most certainly original.

More importantly, the Kettles were unforgettably vital to a country who desperately needed to laugh, and to a studio who desperately needed to survive. Ma and Pa Kettle represented the American ideal in the most outlandish way possible. They were the most functional, most together, most close-knit family on the face of the earth, and that's why audiences loved them. They were real.

Trivia: Parker Fennelly died on January 22, 1988, age 96. His beloved wife Catherine had passed away just 12 days before; she was 95 years of age.

Poster tagline: "America's Fun Famed Family in a Rural Riot of LAUGHS!"

Broadway Performances

Before Marjorie Main's noted film career, like all quality performers, Marjorie worked on the stage. Unfortunately, the countless small-town productions that she appeared in are now untraceable. Her Broadway performances are listed here.

1. *The Wicked Age* (1927)

Daly's 63rd Street Theater: November 4, 1927; unknown closing date
Total performances: 19; Original Broadway Play
Producer: Anton Scibilia
Writing credits: Anton Scibilia

Opening Night Cast

Robert Bentley, Hassell Brooks, Hal Clarendon, Carroll Daly, Peggy Doran, Emily Francis, Doris Haslett, Ruth Hunter, Raymond Jarno, Louise Kirtland, William Langdon, David Newell, Augusta Perry, Francis Reynolds, Mae West, Hub White, Harry W. Williams, **Marjorie Main.**

This play not only starred Mae West, it was also written by her. Most of her productions dealt with controversial subjects and graphic sexual content. If her risqué plays weren't shut down for indecency, it was because of poor box office sales. *The Wicked Age* lasted all of three weeks.

Mae West truly suffered for her art. Her first Broadway production, titled *Sex,* was raided, and West and the rest of the cast were arrested for public indecency. On April 27, 1927, she was sentenced to ten days in jail. She served eight days, two less than her original sentence, as a reward for good behavior.

2. *Salvation* (1928)

Empire Theater: January 31, 1928; unknown closing date
Total performances: 31; Original Broadway Play
Producer: Arthur Hopkins
Writing credits: Sidney Howard and Charles MacArthur

Opening Night Cast

Emily Boileau, Edward Broadley, George Colan, Elmer Cornell, Donald Gallaher, Mary Hubbard, Stephen Irving, Pauline Lord, George MacFarlane, **Marjorie Main**, Thomas Meegan, James Mulady, Osgood Perkins, Bernice Richmond, Maud Sinclair, Helen Ware, Emma Wise.

A synopsis for this play is unavailable.

3. *Scarlett Sister Mary* (1930)

Ethel Barrymore Theater: November 25, 1930; unknown closing date
Total performances: 34; Original Broadway Play
Setting: The dooryard at Maum Hannah's, twenty years ago. July and Mary's home, one year later. The crossroads at Heaven Gate Church, present.
Producer: Lee Shubert
Writing credits: Daniel Reed, from the novel by Julia Peterkin
Director: E. M. Blyth

Opening Night Cast

Ethel Barrymore	Sister Mary *(Si May-e)*
Sylvia Allen	The Heaven Gate Singers
Daniel Bagnell	Brer Dee *(an old churchman)*
Horace Braham	Budda Ben *(Hannah's son)*
Alan Campbell	Brunton
Alice Cannon	The Heaven Gate Singers
Joseph Christian	The Heaven Gate Singers
Burke Clarke	Luke
Blanche Collins	Tussie
Ethel Barrymore	Seraphine
Wilbur Cox	Gadsen
Theodore De Corsia	Big Boy at age 30
Marcel Dill	Reverend Duncan Thatcher
Helen Dowdy	The Heaven Gate Singers
Toussaint Duers	The Heaven Gate Singers
Herbert Gentry	Big Boy *(Andrew's son)*
Walter Gilbert	July *(twin brother)*
Sam Gray	The Heaven Gate Singers
Corrine Harris	Flower Girl
Frank Jackson	The Heaven Gate Singers
Leo Kennedy	Cousin Andrew *(a deacon)*
Marjorie Main	**Gracey**

The play was described as a "Gullah Island Drama." Ethel Barrymore and the entire white company (yes, even Marjorie) appeared in blackface.

In Margot Peters' book *The House of Barrymore,* she describes opening night at the Ethel Barrymore Theater: "A glittering and curious first night audience packed the theater on November 25, crowds jostling on the sidewalk, photographers going up and down the aisles flashing bulbs at celebrities. Everyone wanted to see how Queen Ethel would pull off black face. By the end of the evening the verdict was in: Ethel was 'amazingly unsuited' to the role. *Scarlett Sister Mary* lasted thirty-four performances into 1931; on tour the reaction was the same, 'Why did Miss Barrymore do it?'"

By Chicago Ethel was wondering the same thing. She was infuriated that her entrances were never applauded because audiences didn't recognize her. As the weeks went by she modified her make-up to a high brown; she also modified the muddy Gullah dialect. But nothing could make *Scarlett Sister Mary* less than a disaster.

4. *Ebb Tide* (1931)

New Yorker Theater: June 8, 1931; unknown closing date
Total performances: 16; Original Broadway Play
Produced by: Artmart Production, Inc.
Writing credits: Harry Chapman Ford

Opening Night Cast

Charles Aitken, Eleanora Barrie, Adele Carpell, William Castle, Janice Dawe, Sidney Eliot, Samuel Flint, **Marjorie Main**, Saul Z. Martell, Sydney Mason.

Despite four film productions of *Ebb Tide* (1915, 1922, 1932 and 1937), little is known about the plot. Few, if any, prints of the above mentioned film versions exist today. The 1937 adaptation is broodish and hard to follow because of severe editing. Dubbed as a "South Seas Drama," the 1937 film starred Frances Farmer in the only color role of her career. The story surrounds three tortured souls onboard a quarantined ship heading toward the island of Tehua.

Ebb Tide lasted sixteen performances before closing for good. The watery theme was not popular with the Broadway audiences of 1931.

5. *Music in the Air* (1932–1933)

Alvin Theater: 11/8/1932–3/13/1933; 44th Street Theater: 3/31/1933–9/16/1933
Total performances: 342
Setting: Switzerland, present day
Genre: Musical/Comedy (Original Play)
Producer: Peggy Fears
Directors: Jerome Kern and Oscar Hammerstein II

Opening Night Cast

Ivan Arbuckle	Town Crier
Edward Austen	Tenor/Choral Society and Man/Walking Club
Ann Barrie	Sieglinde Lessing and Tessie
Joe Barrie	Basso/Choral Society
Thea Bayles	Soprano/Walking Club
Charles Belin	Herman
Nomy Bencid	Mezzo/Walking Club
Beatrice Berenson	Soprano/Walking Club
Eric Berlenbach	Waiter
Carrie Bridewell	Mrs. Pflugfelder
Peggy Burgess	Mezzo/Walking Club
Betty Cardozo	Edendorf Child
Tullio Carminati	Bruno Mahler
Katherine Carrington	Sieglinde Lessing
Marie Cartwright	Soprano/Walking Club
Claire Cole	Frau Lena Baum
Mlle. Desha	Hulde
George Dieter	Son
Georgina Dieter	Contralto/Walking Club
Paul Donah	Assistant Stage Manager and Father Joch

Evelyn Eaton	Edendorf Child
Carl Edem	Stout Father
Kathleen Edwards	Sophie
Georg Gerhardi	The Tobacconist
Gloria Gilbert	Edendorf Girl
Gabrielle Guelpli	Mrs. Pflugfelder
Sally Hadley	Mezzo/Choral Society
Edna Hagan	Tila
Natalie Hall	Frieda Hatzfeld
Beatrice Hannen	Contralto/Walking Club
Edward Hayes	Hans
Clifford Heckinger	Heinrich
George Herman	Son
Gertrude Houk	Mezzo/Choral Society
Betty Howson	Contralto/Walking Club
Paul Janert	The Doctor
Dorothy Johnson	Marthe
Ruth Johnson	Soprano/Choral Society and Edendorf Girl
Nicholas Joy	Ernst Weber
Elise Joyce	Contralto/Walking Club
Eugene King	Tenor/Choral Society
Mary Lange	Soprano/Choral Society
Laura	The Bear
Anton Lieb	The Apothecary
George Ludwig	Waiter
Marjorie Main	**Anna**

An eccentric cast of characters star in this comedic operetta set in the picturesque German countryside. A bickering couple use a young innocent couple to their advantage in order to make each other jealous. The tune "We Belong Together" was the most popular song of the play.

Marjorie Main revived her role of Anna in the 1934 film of the same name.

6. *Jackson White* (1935)

Provincetown Playhouse: April 20, 1935; unknown closing date
Total performances: 17
Setting: Bark's Cabin in the Ramapo Mountains
Genre: Drama (Original Play)
Producer: A. Lawton McElhone
Writing credits: David Arnold Balch

Opening Night Cast

William Balfour	Emanuel Sisko
Ruth Conley	Birdie
Ross Forrester	Kelsey
John Galedon	Rance
Katherine Hirsch	Ella
Kirke Lucas	Martin Carey
Marjorie Main	**Mrs. Bark**
Frank McCormack	Elijah Bark
William Phillips	Bert Rink
Mary Talbot	Ruth Davison

A synopsis for this play is unavailable.

7. *Dead End* (1935–1937)

Belasco Theater: October 28, 1935; closing night, June 12, 1937
Total performances: 687
Setting: East River Terrace, New York City
Genre: Drama
Producer: Norman Bel Geddes

Writing credits: Sidney Kingsley
Director: Sidney Kingsley

Opening Night Cast

Carroll Ashburn	Mr. Griswald
Charles Bellin	Philip Griswald
Charles Benjamin	1st Chauffeur
Philip Bourneuf	Interne
Marie R. Burke	Old Lady
Richard Clark	2nd Chauffeur
Francis G. Cleveland	Policeman
George Cotton	Doorman
Marc Daniels	Ensemble
Francis De Sales	G-Man
Ethel Dell	Ensemble
Gabriel Dell	T B
Joseph Downing	"Babyface" Martin
Charles R. Duncan	Spit
Willis Duncan	Policeman
Dan Duryea	G-Man
Elspeth Eric	Drina
Sidonie Espero	Governess
Martin Gabel	Hunk
Edward P. Goodnow	G-Man
David Gorcey	Second Avenue Boy
Leo Gorcey	Second Avenue Boy
Huntz Hall	Dippy
Billy Halop as Tommy	(*Broadway debut*)
Drina Hill	Ensemble
Bobby Jordan	Angel
Margaret Linden	Lady with Dog
Sidney Lumet	Small Boy
Blossom MacDonald	Ensemble
Marjorie Main	**Mrs. Martin**
Margaret Mullen	Kay
Robert J. Mulligan	Patrolman Mulligan
Theodore Newton	Gimpty
George N. Price	Old Gentleman
Bernard Punsly	Milty
Lewis L. Russell	Medical Examiner
Harry Selby	Plainclothesman
Joseph Taibi	Small Boy
William Toubin	Ensemble
Sheila Trent	Francey
Cyril Gordon Weld	Jack Hilton
Billy Winston	Small Boy
Louis Woods	Mr. Jones
Elizabeth Wragge	Ensemble
Bernard Zanville	Sailor

Dead End, the play, starred the same ensemble cast as the 1937 film of the same name. Based on the struggles of a group of wayward teens in the East Side slums of New York City, *Dead End* is a gloomy tale of harsh consequences—the direct result of poor choices and poor living.

The stage production of *Dead End* was the debut performance of the popular Dead End Kids gang. Leo Gorcey, David Gorcey, Billy Halop and Huntz Hall went on to become the most lovable hoodlums on Broadway. They revived their gangster characters in dozens of low-budget films over a period of two decades.

8. *The Women* (1936)

Ethel Barrymore Theater: December 26, 1936; unknown closing date
Total performances: 657
Setting: New York and Reno
Genre: Comedy (Original Play)
Producer: Max Gordon
Writing credits: Clare Boothe

Opening Night Cast

Charita Bauer	Little Mary
Eloise Bennett	Euphie
Eileen Burns	Miss Fordyce
Jessie Busley	Mrs. Morehead
Mary Cecil	Maggie

Ilka Chase	Sylvia *aka Mrs. Howard Fowler*
Virgilia Chew	Miss Watts
Audrey Christie	Miriam Aarons
Beatrice Cole	Second Model
Doris Day	First Saleswoman
Margaret Douglass	Countess de Lage
Lucille Fenton	Head Saleswoman and a Nurse
Arlene Francis	Princess Tamara and Helene
Margalo Gillmore	Mary *aka Mrs. Stephen Haines*
Ruth Hammond	Olga
Joy Hathaway	A Fitter
Anne Hunter	Exercise Instructress
Ethel Jackson	Mrs. Wagstaff
Betty Lawford	Crystal Allen
Marjorie Main	**Lucy**
Adrienne Marden	Peggy *aka Mrs. John Day*
Jane Moore	Second Hairdresser
Mary Murray	Miss Trimmerback
Lillian Norton	Cigarette Girl
Phyllis Povah	Edith *aka Mrs. Phelps Potter*
Jean Rodney	Second Saleswoman
Jane Seymour	Nancy Blake
Mary Stuart	First Hairdresser
Ann Teeman	Jane
Martina Thomas	Third Saleswoman
Beryl Wallace	First Model
Ann Watson	Pedicurist
Marjorie Wood	Sadie

Adapted into one of the most successful films ever, *The Women*, a play written by Clare Booth Luce, opened at the Ethel Barrymore Theater in 1936. The 1939 film followed the play's tradition of an all-female cast. Despite males being the topic of most of the dialogue, the cast, both in the play and on film, are all female. Attention to the theme was so precise that only female animals and feminine artwork was used throughout.

The play follows the lives of a group of rich, catty women all wanting to obtain quickie divorces from their cheating husbands. They travel to Reno to reverse their marital bond and are subsequently forced to live together until their divorces become final. Despite the common bond of an impending single life, it is in Reno where the power struggles between *The Women* really begin.

The play was revived on Broadway in 1973. Dorothy Loudon, Myrna Loy, Jan Miner and Alexis Smith starred. A 2001 revival starred Kristen Johnson, Rue McClanahan, Cynthia Nixon and Jennifer Tilly.

A remake of the 1939 film version is now in the works. Such noted stars as Annette Benning, Meg Ryan, Ashley Judd and Sandra Bullock are negotiating to star in a 2006 revamp of *The Women.* Diane English will be writer-director, and legendary *Rolling Stones* front man Mick Jagger will produce the movie for New Line Cinema.

Bibliography

Berg, Scott A. *Goldwyn: A Biography.* New York: Riverhead Books, 1989.

Bowers, Ronald. *The Selznick Players.* New Jersey: Barnes, 1976.

Burk, Margaret, and Gary Hudson. *Final Curtain.* California: Seven Locks Press, 1996.

Cagney, James. *Cagney by Cagney.* New York: Doubleday, 1976.

Dick, Bernard F. *City of Dreams: The Making and Remaking of Universal Pictures.* Lexington: University Press of Kentucky, 1997.

Ellenberger, Allan R. *Margaret O'Brien: A Career Chronicle and Biography.* Jefferson, N.C.: McFarland, 2004.

Finler, Joel W. *The Hollywood Story.* New York: Crown Publishers, 1988.

French, Philip. *The Hollywood Moguls: An Informal History of the Hollywood Tycoons.* Chicago: Henry Regnery, 1969.

Hadleigh, Boze. *Hollywood Lesbians.* New York: Barricade Books, 1994.

Hirschhorn, Clive. *Gene Kelly: A Biography.* New York: Regency, 1975.

Kanin, Garson. *Hollywood.* New York: The Viking Press, 1974.

Kremer, John. *1001 Ways to Market Your Books, Fifth Edition.* Fairfield, Iowa: Open Horizon, 1998.

Lahr, John. *Notes on a Cowardly Lion.* New York: Alfred A. Knopf, 1969.

Lamparski, Richard. *Whatever Became of...?: Second Series.* New York: Crown Publishers, 1968.

MacDonald, Betty. *The Egg and I.* Philadelphia, New York: J.P. Lippincott, 1945.

Madsen, Axel. *The Sewing Circle.* New York: Birch Lane Press, 1995.

Maltin, Leonard, ed. *The Real Stars.* New York: Curtis, 1973.

Marx, Arthur. *Goldwyn: A Biography of the Man Behind the Myth.* New York: W. W. Norton, 1976.

McClelland, Doug. *Forties Film Talk: Oral Histories of Hollywood.* Jefferson, N.C.: McFarland, 1992.

Parish, James Robert, and William T. Leonard. *The Funsters.* New York: Arlington House, 1979.

Pasternak, Joe. *Easy the Hard Way.* New York: G.P Putnam's Sons, 1956.

Peters, Margot. *The House of Barrymore.* New York: Alfred A. Knopf, 1990.

Reynolds, Debbie, and David Patrick Columbia. *Debbie: My Life.* New York: William Morrow, 1988.

Sanders, Coyne Steven, and Tom Gilbert. *Desilu: The Story of Lucille Ball and Desi Arnaz.* New York: William Morrow, 1993.

Sherman, John. *Marjorie Main: Rural Documentary Poetry.* Indianapolis: Mesa Verde Press, 1999.

Shipman, David. *Judy Garland: The Secret Life of an American Legend.* New York: Hyperion, 1992.

Smith, Ella. *Starring Miss Barbara Stanwyck.* New York: Random House, 1988.

Stanley, Robert. *The Celluloid Empire: A History of the American Motion Picture Industry.* New York: Hastings House, 1978.

Steen, Mike. *Hollywood Speaks.* New York: Putnam, 1974.

Tierney, Gene, with Mickey Herskowitz. *Gene Tierney: Self Portrait.* New York: Peter Wyden, 1979.
Troyan, Michael. *A Rose for Mrs. Miniver: The Life of Greer Garson.* Lexington: University Press of Kentucky, 1998.
Vogel, Michelle. *Gene Tierney: A Biography.* Jefferson, N.C.: McFarland, 2004.
Williamson, J.W. *Hillbillyland.* Chapel Hill & London: The University of North Carolina Press, 1995.

Magazines and Newspapers

Adams, Joe. "Century-Old Acton." *Indianapolis Star,* August 17, 1958, p. 28.
"Deanna Durbin." *Fortune,* October 1939, p. 66.
Farmer, James E. "That Reminds Me!" *Indianapolis Star,* September 6, 1952, p. 17.
"From the Inside: The Business of Motion Pictures." *Saturday Evening Post,* September 3, 1927, p. 86.
"Golden Key Opens Universal City to the World." *Motion Picture News,* March 27, 1915, pp. 33–34, 51.
Graham, Sheilah. "Hoosier Marjorie Main Is a Character Even When She's Not Acting." *Indianapolis Star,* September 18, 1949, p. 17.
Heffernan, Harold. "That Is Known as Movie Jackpot; Marjorie Main Hit in Egg." *Indianapolis Star,* April 20, 1947, p. 20.
Heyn, Howard C. "Ex-Hoosier Star Is Wholly Unpredictable." *Indianapolis Star,* November 7, 1948, p. 3.
Hopper, Hedda. "Sad Marjorie Main's Really Jovial Off Screen." *Los Angeles Times,* January 27, 1947.
"Laemmle, The Art of Producing a Film." *Universal Filmlexikon,* 1932, p. 30.
Lewis, Carl. "Marjorie's Hoosier Twang Still Main Line." *Indianapolis Star,* March 31, 1947, pp. 1, 2.
"Ma Kettle Dies at 85." *The Indianapolis News,* April 11, 1975, p. 21.
"Marjorie Main Hoosier Film Actress Dies." *Indianapolis Star,* April 11, 1975, p. 1.
"Marjorie Main Takes Hollywood Success in Stride." *The Indianapolis News,* April 3, 1947, p. 20.
McHattan, Martha. "Marjorie Main Here on Visit; Will See Picture Premiere." *The Indianapolis News,* March 31, 1947, p. 1.
McMurphy, Jean. "Miss Main Riding TV Range." *Los Angeles Times,* June 1, 1958.
"'Pa Kettle' of Movies, Percy Kilbride Dies." *Los Angeles Times,* December 12, 1964.
Patrick, Corbin. "Marjorie Main to Join Other Celebrities Here at Fair Exhibit." *Indianapolis Star,* August 24, 1952, p. 11.
Ross, Paul M. "Marjorie Main Here to Sell War Bonds, Is Kept Busy by Autograph Hunters." *Indianapolis Star,* December 11, 1942, p. 9.
Scott, Vernon. "Retiree Marjorie Main Enjoys Life of Leisure." *Indianapolis Star,* March 2, 1969, p. 1.
"Sell Out Is Seen for Miss Main's Appearance Here." *Indianapolis Star,* December 12, 1942, p. 1.
"Series Is Wonderful for Kettle." *Valley Times,* March 5, 1956, p. 8.
Smith, David. "The Marj Who Was Ma (as in Hoosier) Kettle." *Indianapolis Star,* March 12, 1978, pp. 26–29.
"Untitled Barbara Stanwyck Interview." *Movie Digest,* no date, 1972.

Internet Resources

Academy Awards and Oscar Winners. www.filmsite.org/oscars.html
Astounding B Monster Archive. *Lori Nelson: Confessions of a Hot Rod Girl.* www.bmonster.com
Henricks, Sylvia. *Marjorie Main: Good for a Lot of Laughs.* www.indianahistory.org/pub/traces/mjmain.html
Hicks, Jim. *Marjorie Main.* www.geocities.com/gimcrack.geo/MarjorieMain.html
The Internet Broadway Database. www.IBDB.com
The Internet Movie Database. www.IMDB.com
Ma and Pa Kettle Fan Club. http://movies.groups.yahoo.com/group/maandpakettlefanclub
Oliver, Phillip. "Glorious Gloria." http://home.hiwaay.net/~oliver/swanson.htm
Turner Classic Movies Online. www.tcm.com
Wilson, Liza, and David McClure. *Ma and Pa Kettle: Hollywood Gold Mine.* www.geocities.com/gimcrack.geo/goldmine.html

Periodicals

Many untitled articles relating to Marjorie Main (snippets would be a better way of describing them) originally came from the following periodicals. The unfortunate side to purchasing fan scrapbooks that are well over fifty years old is that most of these articles are unidentified as to what publication they originally appeared in. Dates are often missing, too.

I am eternally grateful to the University of Southern California for allowing me full access to Universal International Studio's production reports, notes, promotional material and audience preview cards for most of the Kettle films. Access to the Margaret Herrick Library's Special Collections/Marjorie Main folders 17 and 18: Correspondence from Dr. Stanley L. Krebs, June 1, 1923, to June 17, 1935, was equally helpful in making this book a reality.

American Classic Screen
American Film
American Movie Classics
The Chicago Tribune
Cinefantastique
Cinema
Classic Images
Film Facts
Film Fan Monthly
Film History
Films in Review
Franklin College Reporter
Good Old Days
The Hollywood Reporter
Hollywood Then & Now
The Indianapolis News
Indianapolis Star
Modern Screen
Motion Picture
Movie Collector's World
Movie Digest
Movie Show
Movie Stars Parade
Movieland
National Enquirer
New York Herald Tribune
New York Post
The New York Times
On Film
Parade
People
Photoplay
Screen Facts
Screen Stars
Screen Stories
Screenland
Silver Screen
Star Magazine
Time Magazine
TV Guide

Universal International (UI) Production Reports

January 14, 1946
January 15, 1946
January 16, 1946
January 18, 1946
January 22, 1946
February 2, 1949
August 29, 1949
October 8, 1949
March 16, 1950
May 17, 1950
July 12, 1950
January 7, 1951
January 18, 1951
July 12, 1951
February 28, 1952
March 3, 1952
September 21, 1952
March 11, 1953
April 6, 1953
April 22, 1953
April 23, 1953
May 12, 1953
November 12, 1953
September 20, 1954
September 27, 1954
October 13, 1954
October 19, 1954
February 25, 1955
February 26, 1955
November 12, 1955
April 18, 1956
June 25, 1956
August 18, 1956
August 27, 1956
April 8, 1957

Index